"By detailing her own political battles, Cecile Richards has crafted a blueprint for budding activists. . . . Genial, engaging, and humorous. . . . If you're looking for books to fill you with energy for the long haul that lies before us, this one is a great place to start."

—THE NEW YORK TIMES BOOK REVIEW

"Documenting an inspiring life and offering a call to action, this timely volume is for all readers."

—LIBRARY JOURNAL

D1016544

"Cecile Richards is whip-smart, clear-eyed, quick-witted, levelheaded, and lionhearted. She employs all of these virtues in her fight for women's health and women's rights. . . . The book, like its author, is a powerhouse."

—ANN PATCHETT

"By inviting us beyond her frontline fight for justice and into her heart, Richards shows us that a life of activism isn't reserved for the perfect—it's for the passionate—and that it's never too early or too late for women to show up for themselves and each other. In these difficult times in which equality-minded folks are desperate to find purpose and connection, *Make Trouble* is a road map to both."

—GLENNON DOYLE

"A blueprint for budding activists." —*The New York Times Book Review*

PRAISE FOR **MAKE TROUBLE**

"By detailing her own political battles, Cecile Richards has crafted a blueprint for budding activists. . . . Genial, engaging, and humorous. . . . If you're looking for books to fill you with energy for the long haul that lies before us, this one is a great place to start."

—New York Times Book Review

"For more than a decade, America has known Cecile Richards as the fierce and fearless president of Planned Parenthood. *Make Trouble* offers a window into her life: the early organizing effort that landed her in the principal's office; the historic campaign of her mother, Ann Richards, for governor of Texas; her courageous leadership on behalf of women; her travels during the 2016 presidential election; and the lessons she's learned from the outpouring of activism America has seen since. With humor, heart, and hope, Cecile Richards offers practical advice and inspiration for aspiring leaders everywhere."

—Hillary Rodham Clinton

"Cecile Richards's story is powerful and infinitely readable. Whether you are newly 'woke,' a longtime activist, or just a caring citizen wondering how to advance democracy in hard times, *Make Trouble* has the answers. Cecile takes the mystery out of activism, gives you practical examples of how it's done, and tells stories that melt the distance from your front porch to Washington. She is the best teacher on earth—someone you trust."

—Gloria Steinem

"Part autobiography, part handbook for the resistance, this inspiring tale of advocacy is a must-read."

—Bustle

"This memoir/feminist manifesto from Planned Parenthood president Cecile Richards will inspire you to make waves and be brave."

—Glamour

"*Make Trouble* is a timely reminder that each of us has the power to fight for justice and create the change we want to see. With insight and humor, Cecile Richards offers a call to action for aspiring organizers and leaders. A must-read for anyone hoping to make a difference and trying to figure out where to start."

—Senator Kamala Harris

"Cecile Richards is whip-smart, clear-eyed, quick-witted, levelheaded and lionhearted. She employs all of these virtues in her fight for women's health and women's rights. She's also employed them in the writing of this wonderful memoir, *Make Trouble*. The book, like its author, is a powerhouse."

—Ann Patchett

"Cecile Richards has always been willing to act up, if need be, to make a difference. *Make Trouble* is more than a memoir, it's a how-to manual for effecting change."

—Dr. Willie Parker

"With *Make Trouble*, Cecile Richards—the fiery feminist icon to whom we are indebted—is now also the relatable warrior we adore. By inviting us beyond her frontline fight for justice and into her heart, Richards shows us that a life of activism isn't reserved for the perfect—it's for the passionate—and that it's never too early or too late for women to show up for themselves and each other. In these difficult times in which equality-minded folks are desperate to find purpose and connection, *Make Trouble* is a road map to both."

—Glennon Doyle

"An intimate yet wide-ranging chronicle of a life in the trenches and at the pinnacle of her profession, Richards' enthralling memoir will provide rousing motivation for anyone passionate about social and political causes."

—*Booklist* (starred review)

"[T]he guidelines for starting any organization are spot-on: direct, down-to-earth, and highly practical. . . . A memoir that makes palpable the immense influence of an organization that has improved so many women's lives."

—*Kirkus Reviews*

"In this passionate self-portrait, activist Richards maps her road to success from union organizer to her tenure as president of Planned Parenthood, recalling the experiences that shaped her career. . . . It serves as a call to action for women who are mobilizing to make a difference in government and healthcare policies."

—Publishers Weekly

"Truly inspiring."

—Redbook

"Documenting an inspiring life and offering a call to action, this timely volume is for all readers."

—Library Journal

MAKE TROUBLE

Stand Up, Speak Out, and Find the Courage to Lead

CECILE RICHARDS

with **LAUREN PETERSON**

G

GALLERY BOOKS

New York   London   Toronto   Sydney   New Delhi

Gallery Books
An Imprint of Simon & Schuster, Inc.
1230 Avenue of the Americas
New York, NY 10020

First Gallery Books trade paperback edition March 2019

GALLERY BOOKS and colophon are registered trademarks of Simon & Schuster, Inc.

For information about special discounts for bulk purchases,
please contact Simon & Schuster Special Sales at 1-866-506-1949
or business@simonandschuster.com.

The Simon & Schuster Speakers Bureau can bring authors to your live event.
For more information or to book an event, contact the Simon & Schuster Speakers Bureau
at 1-866-248-3049 or visit our website at www.simonspeakers.com.

Interior design by Erich Hobbing
Photograph on page 10 by Mark Wilson/Getty Image News Collection/Getty Images.
Photograph on page 71 by Alan Pogue.
Photograph on page 76 by Iris Schneider.
Photographs on pages 85 and 94 by Ave Bonar.
Photograph on page 204 by Callie Richmond.
Photograph on page 217 by Barbara Kinney/Hillary for America.
All other photographs courtesy of the author.

Manufactured in the United States of America

1   3   5   7   9   10   8   6   4   2

The Library of Congress has cataloged the hardcover edition as follows:

Names: Richards, Cecile, author. | Peterson, Lauren, author.
Title: Make trouble : standing up, speaking out, and finding the courage to
lead—my life story / Cecile Richards with Lauren Peterson.
Description: New York, NY : Touchstone, 2018.
Identifiers: LCCN 2017061243| ISBN 9781501187599 (hardback) |
ISBN 9781501187605 (trade paperback) | ISBN 9781508250784 (audio cd) |
ISBN 9781501187612 (ebook) | ISBN 9781508250791 (eaudio)
Subjects: LCSH: Richards, Cecile. | Women political activists–Biography. |
Leadership in women—United States—History. | Women's rights—
United States—History. | Social justice—United States—History. |
BISAC: BIOGRAPHY & AUTOBIOGRAPHY / Personal Memoirs. |
BIOGRAPHY & AUTOBIOGRAPHY / Women.
Classification: LCC HQ1236.5.U6 R53 2018 | DDC 305.420973 [B]—
dc23 LC record available at https://lccn.loc.gov/2017061243

ISBN 978-1-5011-8759-9
ISBN 978-1-5011-8760-5 (pbk)
ISBN 978-1-5011-8761-2 (ebook)

To Kirk, Hannah, Daniel, and Lily.
And to Mom and Dad for getting this whole party started.

Contents

Introduction

"Little lady, you are just trying to make trouble."

That was my sixth grade teacher, Mrs. Powers, at University Park Elementary School in Dallas. She had spent the past fifteen minutes conducting an interrogation: Why was I refusing to recite the Lord's Prayer with the rest of the class?

Mrs. Powers was a lifer at UPS, with permed helmet hair that was the fashion back then. She was a good old gal who probably smoked with the other teachers in the teachers' lounge. Looking back, I'm not even sure I knew that it was unconstitutional to have us start each day with the Lord's Prayer—but by God, we did, right after the Pledge of Allegiance. That morning, though, I just wasn't having it. When Mrs. Powers asked me why I wasn't participating, I said calmly, "We don't read the Bible in my house." Mrs. Powers's eyes flew open. I could see from her stricken look that she had taken my candor for cheekiness. I suppose in a way it was.

We weren't a religious family, not in a traditional sense, but we did go to the Unitarian church, which was sort of a home away from home for progressive families like ours in Dallas—our own little bunker in the middle of the crazy culture war of the '60s, and the heart of the local anti–Vietnam War movement. Folks in our congregation were involved in everything from the United Farmworkers organizing to *Notes from the Underground*, Dallas's radical newspaper, which my dad happened to be defending in court. Religion was cool with me; it just didn't include the Lord's Prayer. It was pretty obvious from Mrs. Powers's reaction what she thought about that. There was no hope for me; clearly, I was headed for a life of crime.

Up until then I was the classic all-A's first child. I lived to make my parents proud of me, which, given their relative youth and inexperience in child-rearing, meant adhering to certain rules. I was the kid who never got in trouble—a trait that annoyed my younger brother, Dan, to no end. I never forgot the shame and humiliation of being called out in front of my class at age eleven. But in that moment I realized something about myself: my parents weren't the only ones who didn't fit into the right-wing Dallas establishment. I too was an outlier.

It was the first time I remember having to decide: Do I accept things the way they are, or question authority? I chose the latter, and from that point forward I was branded a troublemaker. Once the initial shock wore off, it became a badge of honor. I've been making trouble ever since—which, to me, means taking on the powers that be, being a thorn in someone's side, standing up to injustice, or just plain raising hell.

Sometimes being a troublemaker can be pretty damn awesome. After all, it was one of the great troublemakers of all time, Emma Goldman, who said, "If I can't dance, I don't want to be part of your revolution." Other times, it's scary and carries big risks—the risk of losing your job, your friends, your reputation, or all of the above. Over the years I've had the good fortune to meet troublemakers from all walks of life: nursing home workers in East Texas, janitors in Los Angeles, members of Congress, organizers and activists of every age on the front lines of the struggle for justice. I've watched in awe as my mother, Ann Richards, went from frustrated housewife to governor of Texas, defying convention and the political establishment. That was one of the things that drew me to Planned Parenthood: its history is the history of brave, troublemaking women (and a few good men) who risked their reputations and even their lives to change things. We fellow travelers have a way of finding each other, whether we set out to or not.

This book is the story of the people who have taught me about courage and defiance and making change. It's also my story, which has been somewhat daunting to write. Like a lot of rabble-rousers (particularly rabble-rousing women), I'm a lot more comfortable talking about my work than myself. But now almost every day people come up to me, usually with a look of distress, to ask, "How are you doing?" They seem to think working for progressive causes is unpleasant or burdensome. The truth is, anything worth doing has its challenges. And, yes, fighting for what you believe in can be discouraging, defeating, and sometimes downright depressing. But it can also be powerful, inspiring, fun, and funny—and it can introduce you to people who will change your life. That's the message I want to spread far and wide. That's why I wrote this book.

I started my career organizing women who were working for the minimum wage. There were women in New Orleans who cleaned hotel rooms or did the laundry because only white women got to work the front desk. Women in small-town Texas who used to joke that they'd stick around their job at the local nursing home until a Walmart opened nearby and they could move on to a better—or at least easier—job. Women who were earning a living and didn't have much choice about the kind of work they did.

As for me, I know full well what a privilege it is to work for social justice. I've had the chance to work on historic political campaigns, go toe-to-toe with the Far Right in Texas, and come back years later to occupy the capitol in Austin as part of the fight for abortion rights. I've served the first woman to lead her party in the US House of Representatives and the 2.4 million people who count on Planned Parenthood for health care each year. I've seen generational progress through the eyes of my three incredible kids. Sure, there have been some brutal moments along the way—appearing before a certain belligerent congressional committee comes to mind, not to mention a couple of awful election nights—but I wouldn't trade it for anything.

Maybe activism is your avocation, not your vocation. You might even be wondering if it's worth it—especially now, when nothing seems certain. For the first time in my life, I'm wondering whether my own daughters will have fewer rights than I've had. That alone is enough motivation for me to keep making trouble. Maybe you're thinking that any job that might involve sitting in front of a hostile congressional committee for the better part of a day just isn't your thing. Well, this book is for you too. You don't have to be a professional troublemaker to take a stand (though it's a terrific career path I highly recommend).

This is a once-in-a-lifetime moment to decide who we are—as individuals and as a country. Unless we want to be defined by a stream of divisive late-night tweets (not to name any names), we're all going to have to be brave. Everywhere I look I see people who are stepping up to do things they never could have imagined. Showing up in a town hall meeting with a US senator, wearing a pink pussy hat. Publicly sharing a personal, intimate story about how Planned Parenthood made a difference in their life. Marching with their kids, grandkids, mothers, sisters, and brothers. Risking arrest to stand up for the rights of immigrants and refugees. Or turning their life upside down to run for office or become a grassroots organizer. If you're not scaring yourself, you're probably not doing enough.

Maybe there's some injustice that's bothering you; maybe you see something in your community or at work that you want to change; maybe you're trying to get up the courage to share your beliefs with friends or family who see things differently; maybe you're worried about the world your kids will inherit. I hope this book will inspire you to get out there and do something about it. Just don't forget: to make a difference, you have to make a little trouble.

CHAPTER 1

Don't Let the Bastards
Get You Down

The congressional hearing room on Capitol Hill was packed with Planned Parenthood staff and supporters and with anti-abortion activists. Some of the activists had black tape over their mouths or huge buttons that said simply, "Life." They looked like the same people who stood outside our health centers on Saturday mornings, trying to intimidate patients with graphic pictures on huge poster boards and signs with gruesome, threatening slogans. The kinds of people who wrote me letters that said, "I wish your mother had aborted you." Taking my seat at a large table at the front of the hearing room, I could feel them behind me in the gallery, their hostility radiating through the room.

On the other side of the table were dozens of members of the press corps, nearly all men, with blank expressions and their cameras pointing at me. I was used to the crazy opposition; the rest, not so much.

I poured myself a glass of water and looked around the room, trying to focus on the people and not the bright TV lights or the constant click of cameras. It helped to know that my team was there, along with throngs of supporters in pink T-shirts in the hearing room and lining the hallways outside. Congresswoman Carolyn Maloney had waved to me as I sat down, and Sheila Jackson Lee, a congresswoman from my home state of Texas who wasn't even on the committee, was sitting there in solidarity. I reminded myself that across the country, hundreds of "Stand with

Planned Parenthood" rallies were happening. I was by myself at the table, but I definitely wasn't alone in the fight.

Besides, I had a mission to accomplish that was bigger than me.

The purpose of the hearing was, at least in theory, to examine whether Planned Parenthood had committed any wrongdoing. That question was being hotly debated across America since anti-abortion activists released a series of misleadingly and sensationally edited videos claiming that our organization sold fetal tissue—which, of course, was not true. Congressional Republicans were leveraging the attack to launch their latest assault on Planned Parenthood. Some had even threatened to shut down the government unless our funding was cut. I was keenly aware that Committee Chairman Jason Chaffetz and his House Republican allies were spoiling for a fight.

I had prepared well—the stakes were too high not to. My secret weapon? Taped on the inside flap of my massive binder was a photograph of my three kids taken years ago, when they were toddlers. If the hearing got heated—as I assumed it would—I could sneak a peek and remember my support system. I hoped they would help get me through anything headed my way, as they had more than once before.

At 10:00 a.m. Congressman Chaffetz rapped his gavel on the table in front of him and called the committee to order. He warned the audience that anyone being disruptive would be asked to leave and added with a smirk, "We hope to have a good, lively debate. This is what Congress is intended to do, and we need everybody's participation along the way."

Chaffetz launched into an emotional opening statement, talking about women in his life and their experiences with cancer, and the fact that his wife was working for a plastic surgeon whose patients were breast cancer survivors. Then the mudslinging began.

He didn't mention the 320,000 breast exams Planned Parenthood provides to women each year, or the fact that if Planned Parenthood were defunded, many of those women would have nowhere else to go. He did talk about supposedly "massive" staff salaries, "first-class" plane tickets (Who was he kidding?), and political contributions. It was clear from the get-go that this "hearing" was all for the television cameras and the constituents watching on Fox News. There wasn't going to be any fact-finding; he already had the "facts" he wanted.

The reams of documentation we provided to Congress ahead of the hearing had already made it clear that Planned Parenthood had not done anything wrong. So if I was going to go through this exercise, I was going to use my time in front of the committee to talk about the incredible health care women get at Planned Parenthood centers across the country every day and to be a voice for our doctors, staff, and patients. I was not about to let them down.

• • •

Two months earlier, on July 14, 2015, I woke up to an email from Planned Parenthood's vice president of communications, Eric Ferrero. Whenever a story in the news had the potential to become a problem, Eric made sure I found out about it first thing. In my nearly ten years as president of the organization, I had learned that an early-morning email from the communications director usually wasn't a good sign.

Sure enough, he wanted to let me know about a new "undercover" video that had been released by a group calling itself the Center for Medical Progress and showed Planned Parenthood doctors and staff purportedly talking callously about selling fetal tissue. Despite the name of the group, they were not a center, and they definitely weren't for medical progress; they were just another offshoot of the same anti-abortion leaders who had been trying to tear down the organization for years. The heavily edited video showed physicians and staff in conversations about fetal tissue donation, implying that they were cavalier when talking about the topic and had broken the law or at least acted unethically (which they had not).

This wasn't our first rodeo with video scams, but this was much more elaborate than anything we'd seen before. It would later become clear— after the damage had already been done—that these videos had come from the same people responsible for ten separate video smear campaigns over the last eight years. This time around, they had spent tens of thousands of dollars creating a fake website and building a fake organization. Posing as representatives of a biotechnology company, they infiltrated medical conferences with sophisticated spy cameras and asked leading questions of Planned Parenthood doctors and staff while they secretly recorded them. We had become the victims of fake news before anyone had ever coined the phrase. We just didn't know it yet.

The videos were on every news channel. The next day's headline in the *New York Times* read, "Video Accuses Planned Parenthood of Crime." Politicians seized the opportunity to pile on. Louisiana's governor Bobby Jindal, who was seeking the Republican presidential nomination, called for an investigation into "this alleged evil and illegal activity." One of his primary opponents, Governor Rick Perry of Texas, called the videos "a disturbing reminder of the organization's penchant for profiting off the tragedy of a destroyed human life." We were under siege.

My first concern was for our patients and for our staff on the front lines who had been the unknowing victims of the video campaign. If what was happening was awful for the rest of us, it was even more excruciating for them.

I will never forget the people who called me in solidarity—and there were many. To balance out the calls from reporters and the anger I felt about what had happened, I tore off a sheet from a gigantic roll of paper and taped it to the wall of my office in Washington. Every time someone called to offer help, I wrote down their name. The early calls came from across the board. My friend Will Robinson in Maine sent a donation right away, writing, "I am 100 percent behind you and Planned Parenthood!" I heard from Senator Cory Booker in New Jersey, who had been a champion of our work since his first day in office. Author and Planned Parenthood board member Anna Quindlen called. By the end of the first week, there were so many names on the list I had to add more sheets, until the wall was completely covered. It was an important way to remind my staff and myself of the outpouring of love and support for Planned Parenthood at such a terrifying time.

Of course not all the calls were helpful. Plenty of folks offered unsolicited advice about how to make it all go away. *If you'd just do this or that*, they suggested, *everything would be okay again*. It was hard to make it clear even to some of our strongest supporters that we had been the victim of a scam. Several of our progressive allies called asking what they could do to protect themselves and their work from similar attacks. We were all on high alert. We would get to the other side of this, but it would be painful and take time.

For the rest of the summer and into the fall we were living in a state of fear and uncertainty; it was almost like dealing with kidnappers. I'd wake up every morning not knowing what was coming, while the group continued releasing more doctored footage. Each video unleashed a new frenzy of harassment and threats that were worse than anything we'd ever seen. Our clinicians, doctors, volunteers, and patients were facing an even more insidious kind of assault: the outrageous rhetoric from politicians and others who painted them as coldhearted conspirators in an illicit business, rather than the caring, compassionate, and deeply committed people I knew them to be.

Everyone at Planned Parenthood felt incredibly vulnerable, knowing our opponents were trying to infiltrate the organization. There were people out there with hidden cameras, trying to entrap our staff, "befriend" them, or even get a job at Planned Parenthood—all for the purpose of shutting us down. Still, we banded together and didn't lose a single national staff member during that time. I'm really proud of that.

Folks dug deep to find ways to stay focused and sane, and I was no exception. I had a hard time sleeping, and felt even worse knowing how worried my kids were about me. I could understand; I had felt the same way years earlier watching my own mother, Ann Richards, endure withering political attacks as governor of Texas. My friend Laurie Rubiner, who was working as a chief of staff on Capitol Hill and was one of our staunchest allies, had been through plenty of tough battles before. One night over dinner she asked, "Have you ever tried meditation?" She had downloaded Headspace on her phone and said it was a lifesaver. So I tried it. It was a bewildering sight for my husband: me, the frenetic organizer, sitting quietly every morning, listening to meditation exercises. Thank goodness for friends with practical advice.

It quickly became clear to us that the creators of these videos had been coordinating with other anti-abortion activists and were colluding with members of Congress who were trying to defund Planned Parenthood. Many Republicans in Congress were licking their chops. They thought they finally had their chance to get rid of us. As we dealt with the constant attacks, they held vote after vote to try to block Medicaid patients from being able to come to Planned Parenthood for preventive care.

Their actions prompted many impassioned speeches on the Senate floor. One night I was sitting in Senate Majority Leader Harry Reid's office, watching the television monitor as one senator after another stood up and voiced support for Planned Parenthood. Senator Elizabeth Warren, the Democrat from Massachusetts, began: "I come to the Senate floor today to ask my Republican colleagues a question: Do you have any idea what year it is? Did you fall down, hit your head, and think you woke up in the 1950s or the 1890s? Should we call for a doctor? Because I simply cannot believe that in the year 2015, the United States would be spending its time trying to defund women's health care centers." Despite the heroic efforts of allies like Senator Warren, congressional Republican leadership managed to pass a bill defunding Planned Parenthood. If not for President Obama's veto pen, it would have become law.

At that point four congressional committees were investigating Planned Parenthood. To put that in perspective, that's more congressional committees than were assigned to investigate Enron or the 2008 global financial crisis. We were asked to provide thousands of pages of confidential documents to Congress, which we knew full well could show up in the newspaper the next day. We knew that our attackers had direct communication with our opponents in Congress—some members even acknowledged that they had seen the videos before they became public. We felt like we were dealing with a well-financed, well-organized conspiracy. The intent of our opponents on Capitol Hill was to destroy Planned Parenthood. And leading the opposition was the House Oversight and Government Reform Committee and its politically ambitious leader, Jason Chaffetz. This was the same highly partisan committee that spent months hounding Secretary of State Hillary Clinton over events related to the attack on US personnel in Benghazi, Libya, in 2012. They were taking the lead, and they were determined to have my head.

Dana Singiser, Planned Parenthood's director of government relations, who was doing daily combat, warned us that we should be prepared for a no-holds-barred public hearing on Planned Parenthood. The committee was going to use the videos as a chance to hold a fishing expedition, going after us for anything they could get. I had two choices: I could either appear voluntarily or have them subpoena me to testify. I knew there was nothing to hide and I believed it would be better to participate and tell our own story.

Along with members of our senior staff, I spent the weeks leading up to the September 29 hearing delving into any topic the committee might raise. In addition to Eric and Dana, our team consisted of Dawn Laguens, Planned Parenthood's executive vice president, and my strategic partner through several years of improbable victories; Roger Evans, our director of litigation; chief medical officer Dr. Raegan McDonald-Mosley; and Amanda Harrington, an eagle-eyed member of the communications team and a veteran of past video smear campaigns. And of course there was our legal firm, O'Melveny and Myers, along with two advisers who were absolutely invaluable, Phil Schiliro and Phil Barnett.

Though my home was in New York, I had pretty much moved to Washington while we prepared for the hearing, staying in a temporary apartment. The days and nights were long, and my husband, Kirk, stayed with me. A big night for us was watching *Law & Order* reruns and eating take-out Thai food or frozen enchiladas. Kirk is a rock, and I could never have gotten through this without him. He has seen me through many nerve-racking moments: union campaigns, political elections, births, deaths, victories, and defeats. As I prepared for the hearing, he would remind me that I'm the quintessential "grace under pressure" performer: nervous and full of doubt beforehand, but when the bell rings, I somehow manage to pull it off.

Day after day our team pored over the thousands of documents we'd already submitted to Congress because I insisted on being up to speed on everything they requested. I knew that in a congressional hearing the members of the committee could call me on any obscure thing. Judging from the scope of the documents they'd asked for, the questions were certain to center on issues of character and morality, as well as every dollar we'd ever spent—for every hire, every trip, every one of our more than six hundred health centers, and the programs we worked with around the world. Every piece of information in every public document was fair game. As was I. I suspected that some of the committee members, rather than ask questions, would use their time to make statements intended to put me on edge. *How can we make this woman squirm? How can we embarrass her, or trick her, and make her and Planned Parenthood look bad?*

Tensions ran high as we got ready for the big day. I drove the team crazy, trying to memorize every relevant piece of paper and every fact. In my spare time I was researching everything from which forms of birth control a patient could get at a clinic in Oregon to how many young people use Planned Parenthood's text/chat helpline each month. By the time I was finished, I had a gigantic binder of background information, easily six inches thick.

Throughout the preparation process, I asked the team over and over, *Where are our patients in this? Where are their stories?* I called Dayna Farris-Fisher, a woman from Texas whose experience with Planned Parenthood had stuck in my mind, and asked her, "Is it okay if I talk about you?" She bravely agreed and wished me luck.

A couple of days before the hearing, we did a run-through so our team could explain how the room would be set up and demonstrate how things would work. There was a row of chairs, raised on a platform, like a judge's bench, and then a place for me in the front of the room.

"Who sits with me at the table during the hearing, so I can ask questions or get help?" I asked.

Lee Blalack, one of our lawyers whom I grew to admire greatly, said, "I think it's better if you are up there by yourself. You don't need anyone."

I had a brief moment of panic. "Wait a minute," I said. "I've seen these hearings on TV. Everyone always has a lawyer!" I was madly racking my brain, recalling every TV courtroom drama I'd ever seen, from *Perry Mason* to *Matlock*. People on trial were always represented by lawyers sitting at their side.

"You can do it. You'll be ready," Lee replied. Though I wanted to strangle him at the time, his confidence in me went a long way.

For our last run-through, the lawyers said I had to come in the clothes I would wear on the day of the hearing. A kind of dress rehearsal, I guess. I picked out a basic blue suit and a pin of my mom's that had always reminded me of a sheriff's badge. Whenever I'm up against something really tough, I bring Ann Richards with me.

One of the young women associates looked me up and down. "If that's what you're going to wear, you should change your shoes," she said.

"My shoes?"

She pointed out that the pair I had chosen had a designer decal on the sole: ammunition for the opposition.

I hadn't even noticed. I don't think I actually bought the shoes. I'm pretty sure I got them from Mom, who was much more fashion conscious than I. It was hard to imagine having such a serious conversation with a male witness about what he was wearing.

The mention of my shoes was when I understood that I was going to be scrutinized from head to toe. That realization was later confirmed when the right-wing blogs went into a frenzy over the fact that I had not worn panty hose to the hearing. You have to look pretty close to see a detail like that.

At day's end there wasn't much more to do. I'd reread the facts and packed my binder. I'd steamed my suit again and set out a different pair of shoes. Kirk made us dinner. "Just remember," he said, "you know more about Planned Parenthood than anyone in that hearing room." I stopped to consider that, but was loath to admit that he just might be right.

I called the kids. Lily was in Iowa, where she had moved for the Clinton campaign; Hannah was in Indiana, working on a campaign of her own; and Daniel was in school in Maryland. They each wished me luck, and I went to bed early.

When I woke up the next morning I tried to meditate. It didn't work. The team packed into a car and we headed to Capitol Hill. There were protesters standing outside the hearing, which was nothing new. It reminded me of a Planned Parenthood luncheon we'd had years earlier on rural Long Island. The place was difficult to find, and at the turnoff we'd had to drive past a group of protesters with ugly signs. Once we made it inside, one of our elderly donors, neatly dressed in her "ladies who lunch" suit and pearls, approached me. "I saw those protesters outside," she said, and before I could say anything, she went on: "I was so glad they were there—otherwise I never would have known where to turn!" Remembering her made me smile.

Walking into the hearing room, I checked my phone one last time. I had an incoming text from my friend Terry McGovern, who works in global and maternal health. Her message read, "Just remember to carry the rage of women through the centuries with you this morning!"

• • •

During their prepared remarks, I had quietly listened to the chairman and his committee members describe their version of women's health, the videos, and Planned Parenthood. Now it was my turn.

Chaffetz looked at me. "We will now recognize our witness. Please welcome Ms. Cecile Richards, president of Planned Parenthood Federation of America. Ms. Richards, pursuant to committee rules, all witnesses will be sworn in before they testify. If you will, please rise and raise your right hand."

I pushed back the chair, stood up, and smoothed my skirt. The room was silent except for the clicking of shutters. The photographers in front of me leaned in closer, so close they could rest their elbows on the edge of the desk. Surreal as the experience was, they were a comforting reminder that somewhere out in the ether, people across the country, including my family and thousands of Planned Parenthood patients and staff, were watching on C-SPAN and were with me. I raised my hand.

"Do you solemnly swear or affirm that the testimony you're about to give will be the truth, the whole truth, and nothing but the truth?"

"I do," I said, smiling.

"Thank you," said Chaffetz, looking at me the way Sylvester the cat looks at Tweety Bird in the cartoons. It was a look that said *I've got you now!* I could feel how desperately he wanted to trap me. But I wasn't about to let that happen. Sitting there in front of the committee, composed on the Republican side almost exclusively of white men, I didn't feel nervous, upset, or intimidated. I felt ready. I was overcome with a surprising sense of calm.

I took a deep breath and started my remarks. I talked about the long history of discredited attacks against Planned Parenthood and covered some basics about our patients. I ended with the experience of my friend Dayna: "Two weeks ago, I was in Plano, Texas, with one of these patients, Dayna Farris-Fisher. Dayna can't be here today because she has a new job and she's supporting her family, but if Dayna were here, she would tell you what she told me: that Planned Parenthood saved her life.

"In 2013 her husband lost his job, and therefore their health insurance. And not long after, Dayna found a lump in her breast. And the only two clinics that would take a patient without health insurance couldn't see her for at least two months. So Dayna came to Planned Parenthood for a breast exam. And there, our clinician of twenty-two years, Vivian, guided her through the process of follow-ups and referrals and helped make sure her treatment was covered. She called Dayna repeatedly to check on her treatment. And I am really happy to say today that Dayna is now cancer-free.

"Mr. Chairman, I wish this Congress would spend more time hearing from women like Dayna. All women in this country deserve to have the same opportunities as members of Congress and their families, for high-quality and timely health care."

For all of Congressman Chaffetz's earlier emotion when he was talking about family members and cancer and his wife's job, he didn't even acknowledge Dayna's story. Instead, without a break, he launched into his first question, asking why Planned Parenthood funded work around the globe instead of focusing solely on the United States.

I started to answer: "Congressman, let me tell you—"

He immediately cut me off, shaking his head. "Oh no, no, no, we don't have time for a big narrative."

So that was how it was going to be.

After more rapid-fire questions and more interruptions, Chaffetz ended his remarks in time for a theatrical flourish, unveiling a slide.

The chart was labeled "Planned Parenthood Federation of America: Abortions up—life-saving procedures down." It had two arrows, in pink and red, neither of which related to the other. It was completely unintelligible.

He asked me to explain the slide, and I told him I'd never seen it before. "I pulled those numbers directly out of your corporate reports," he said without hesitation.

At that moment Lee Blalack, seated behind me, leaned over and pointed out that a well-known anti-abortion group had actually produced the chart. Its name was printed right on the slide.

"My lawyer's informing me that the source of this is actually Americans United for Life, which is an anti-abortion group. So I would check your source," I told him.

Chaffetz was flustered. He ruffled some papers in front of him and his hands shook. "Then we will get to the bottom of the truth of that," he exclaimed, and moved to recognize the next member of Congress.

His blunder helped me to realize, for the first time, how right Kirk had been the night before. This was my chance not only to defend Planned Parenthood but also to shine a light on the fact that many of the members of Congress who are the most obsessed with restricting women's health care know the least about it.

What followed was a barrage of ridiculous questions, like "How does Planned Parenthood make a profit?" Anyone who had glanced at the thousands of pages we'd sent over would have known that the organization is a nonprofit. But the minute I opened my mouth to reply to their questions, the committee members would quickly shut me down, as if to say, "We are in charge here!" Congressman Jim Jordan of Ohio kept raising his voice louder and louder until I finally said, "I think we're just going to have to agree to disagree." All the members were quick to point out why they were actually one of the good guys; one congressman even made sure to note that he was wearing a pink tie "in solidarity with women's health issues" before launching into a rant against Planned Parenthood. Another member of Congress intoned about the "killing of children" and "acts of barbarity," his voice growing more and more dramatic until his final declaration: "We cannot escape our accountability before the creator of life!" With that, he turned and walked out of the chamber without giving me the chance to respond.

The entire hearing was a painful display of the lack of interest in understanding the lives of the millions of women who turn to Planned Parenthood. Most of the committee members weren't there to get answers; they were using the opportunity to grandstand. I was constantly cut off, questioned about my salary, my attitude, and my qualifications.

There were many choice moments. One of my favorites was from Congressman John Duncan from Tennessee, who clearly knew he and his colleagues were acting like fools. To try to rattle me he said, "I'm sure I have seen many male witnesses treated much tougher than you have today. And surely you don't expect us to be easier on you because you're a woman?"

"Absolutely not," I replied. "That's not how my mama raised me."

Silence.

Coming to his final question, Duncan tried again. "I'm not clear on this: do you defend the sale of baby body parts?" he asked.

Seriously? "No," I said definitively.

In the middle of the hearing we took a short break. I checked my phone and was glad that I did; because as usual, my son, Daniel, came to the rescue with a text message of support. He had been watching on

C-SPAN and sent a note that only Daniel could write: "Mom, you are really doing a good job. I think raising me all those years helped prepare you for dealing with these guys."

Then it was back into the lion's den.

Since there were so many more Republicans than Democrats on the committee, eventually the Democrats ran out of opportunities to question me. After that, it was one Republican after another. I thought, *Will this ever end?*

Near the conclusion of the hearing, Congressman Trey Gowdy asked me if I understood the pro-life narrative. I replied, "I understand how people can disagree based on their religious beliefs, their background, their own personal experiences. And I also understand that people sometimes change over time and that's the human condition."

Gowdy looked at me with scorn and said, "I appreciate the way you try to frame these issues, that you're the reasonable one, and those of us who have a contrary position are not reasonable."

"I didn't say that," I said matter-of-factly. I knew he wanted me to take him up on his dare, and it made him absolutely crazy that I wouldn't. I clarified that I had never called him unreasonable.

"No, that's exactly the answer you gave," he said.

I reiterated that he'd gotten it wrong and restated my case, to which he finally replied, "It's not always what you say. It's sometimes just what you mean." As I looked him in the eye, there was something familiar about him. Then I realized what it was: with his face all scrunched up and twisted with anger, he looked just like Draco Malfoy in *Harry Potter.*

Sometimes, when someone is making an idiot of themselves, especially on live television, it's just better to let them go ahead. I couldn't help but think to myself, *This is how Mom must have felt dealing with the old boys' club in Texas.* Listening to their blustering and bullying, I realized that I had given them the opportunity to show their ignorance and contempt for women's health. That was almost more important than anything I could say.

Nearly five hours after we began, the inquisition finally ended.

I couldn't believe I lived through it. The experience was utterly exhausting. I saw Congressman Elijah Cummings as I walked through the committee staff room. The panel's top-ranking Democrat, Cummings had made an impassioned speech in support of Planned Parenthood during the hearing. He had recently lost his mother-in-law to breast cancer, and now he stopped and looked me in the eye.

"I just think of all the women who without Planned Parenthood wouldn't get the care they need. Having just gone through this with my mother-in-law, I can't tell you how important it is to me."

I broke down in tears. His words had brought home exactly why we were there and why we had to keep fighting. I felt a combination of relief, exhaustion, and gratitude.

Afterward I went back to the office and had a group hug with the Planned Parenthood staff. At the first opportunity I changed out of my business suit and put on a Planned Parenthood pink dress. What I really wanted to do was go home and crawl into bed, but I was scheduled to go on *The Rachel Maddow Show*. As I was walking into the NBC studio, my phone rang.

"Cecile, it's Hillary Clinton. I saw the hearing. You were wonderful. I'm going to be up there myself soon. Good for you for standing up to them." She would be facing the same committee in just a few weeks and spend twice as long, with much the same results.

• • •

After the hearing, the floodgates opened. I could barely walk down the street without someone—women and men of all ages and backgrounds—sharing their exasperation at the rampant sexism on display that day. Women my mother's age came up to me and said, "Those guys reminded me of every man who's ever interrupted me in a meeting." A young man on the subway in New York politely said, "Ms. Richards? I saw you testify before Congress. They were so awful—thank you for doing that. Can we take a picture?" I heard countless variations on "How did you sit up there for five hours and answer those questions?" The truth is, there was no other option—not for me or for Planned Parenthood patients and staff at health centers across the country. Besides, anyone who has ever worked at Planned Parenthood is used to dealing with people who don't support what we do. And it's not just the people who are grilling you in the middle of a congressional hearing and trying to shut down Planned Parenthood: the organization's brilliant and brave doctors, nurses, clinic escorts, staff, and supporters are constantly confronted with folks who either don't know any better or don't want to know better. Having the chance to cast a bright light on the hostility and sexism so many members of the Planned Parenthood family experience every day was frankly satisfying.

It was clear that Congressman Chaffetz and his colleagues had unintentionally tapped into something universal. I realized how many people all across the country had been watching and paying attention. So as painful as it had been, the hearing had helped remind people in America about the important work of Planned Parenthood, and it had educated them about who was running Congress.

For me, the experience was remarkable in many ways. I saw firsthand how little interest there was in using hearings for actual information gathering. Most of the remarks by the members were geared toward television that they hoped would play well back home. There was a complete lack of empathy among the Republican members for the patients who rely on Planned Parenthood, and that was sobering.

But the visual that I can't get out of my head is the partisan divide in Congress. On my right, the Republican side of the hearing, the committee members were, almost to a person, white men. In fact they were so desperate to have more diversity that they brought Republican congresswomen not on the committee into the hearing room so that the television coverage would look better (which it did not). On the left, the Democratic delegation was a diverse mix of gender, race, and ethnicity, more like our country in the twenty-first century. The image that day was so clearly the past on one side, and our future on the other.

Most of all, my respect for women in office, which was pretty dang high already, grew by leaps and bounds after sitting through five hours with their colleagues. The sneers, interruptions, and plain rudeness are more than we would ever tolerate from our kids. But like so many women faced with mansplaining and ignorance, they channel their anger and stay focused on what they're there to do.

At one point during the hearing, in the middle of a contentious round of questioning, Congresswoman Tammy Duckworth bravely spoke up. Known for her heroism in combat, a double amputee, marathoner, and mother, she was headed into a very tough race for the US Senate. When her turn came, she adjusted her microphone and said, "I went to college based on student loans and Pell Grants and two jobs, one of which was as a waitress. I couldn't get that waitressing job without getting a health exam. And I couldn't afford to go to a doctor. And the job said, you can start Friday if you come in with a valid health exam. Go to your local Planned Parenthood, they'll do it for you today, and you can start work in two days. It was a lifesaver."

I was proud but not surprised. In the many fights over Planned Parenthood funding, women have gone to the floor of Congress repeatedly and bared their souls. Back in 2011 Congresswoman Gwen Moore from Milwaukee stood up and said, "I just want to tell you about what it's like to not have Planned Parenthood. You have to add water to the formula. You have to give your kids ramen noodles at the end of the month to fill up their little bellies so that they won't cry. You have to give them mayonnaise sandwiches. They get very few fresh fruits and vegetables because they're expensive." When she started talking, members on the floor were chatting and having side conversations. By the time she finished, you could hear a pin drop.

As part of that same debate, after hearing a male colleague's vitriolic anti-abortion rant, Jackie Speier, a congresswoman from California, took the floor. She explained that she had planned to speak about something else, but the past few minutes had put her "stomach in knots." "I am one of those women he spoke about just now. I lost a baby," she said. "But for you to stand on this floor and to suggest as you have that somehow this is a procedure that is either welcomed or done cavalierly or done without any thought is preposterous."

I firmly believe that when half of Congress can get pregnant, we will finally stop arguing about birth control, abortion, and Planned Parenthood—and we might even fully fund women's health care. In the meantime, many women elected officials in Washington and across the country are doing their very best to stand up for an entire under-represented gender. Time and time again they end up sharing their most personal experiences, just to try to evoke a scintilla of sympathy from some of their male colleagues.

A few months before my appearance before the committee, I had read that a state senator in Ohio, Teresa Fedor, told the story of being sexually assaulted and having an abortion. The debate over a particularly cruel bill that would have banned abortion as early as six weeks, with no exceptions for victims of rape and incest, had pushed her to her breaking point. She hadn't talked publicly about her experiences before, especially not on the floor of the state legislature, but she mustered the courage to tell her story even as her voice was shaking with emotion.

It was painful to think of the backlash she was likely facing, so I had picked up the phone and called her. I couldn't imagine what it took for her to tell her story publicly, and wanted her to know that I was grateful that she had been so courageous.

Talking to her reminded me of talking with other women who had spoken truth to power, like Wendy Davis, the Texas state senator whose epic thirteen-hour filibuster of an abortion bill had captured the world's attention. Even when the writing was on the wall, and they knew telling their story wasn't going to stop a horrific piece of legislation from passing, these women spoke out anyway. They hoped that eventually the sum total of so many women's stories would overwhelm the powers that were trying to stifle them. And now, thanks to these brave and defiant women, and thousands more who are coming forward as part of the #MeToo movement, that's finally starting to happen.

Here's what I learned sitting in front of the committee: Focus on the people who are counting on you, not the ones who are trying to drag you down. The Republicans on the panel were simply interested in goading me into a fight, and the more I refused to get down in the mud with them, the more frustrated they became. But that was their problem, not mine. I couldn't control what they did, but I could control how I reacted. At the end of the day, I knew my patience and resolve could outlast their hysteria.

And I'm glad to say that this story has a happy ending. Almost immediately after the hearing, Congressman Chaffetz announced that the committee had found no evidence of wrongdoing by Planned Parenthood (though that hasn't stopped politicians from continuing their efforts to block people from coming to us for care), and the committee disbanded. Later the Center for Medical Progress was indicted on fifteen felony counts. As for Chaffetz, he resigned his seat in Congress. Couldn't have happened to a nicer guy.

CHAPTER 2

Raised to Make Trouble

In a way, I'd been preparing for the showdown on Capitol Hill my whole life. I was raised by troublemakers. Neither of my parents ever backed away from a righteous fight.

My father, David Richards, is a civil rights attorney whose career has been rabble-rousing. And Mom? From her earliest days rebelling against the social norms of Waco to becoming the first woman elected in her own right as governor of Texas, she believed she was on this earth to make a difference. It has been nearly thirty years since she gave her famous keynote address at the 1988 Democratic National Convention in Atlanta, yet people still quote me a line or two as if it were yesterday.

My folks grew up in the hard-core Baptist environment of Waco, Texas, high school sweethearts from different sides of town. Mom's parents were Depression-era survivors, country folk from humble beginnings who worked long and hard for everything they had. Her father—Cecil, for whom I'm named—worked for a wholesale druggist and traveled to small-town drugstores throughout central and western Texas selling his wares. Poppy, as I called him, was well over six feet tall, with a gentle way about him. He never graduated from high school, yet his street smarts and keen sense of people made him a natural salesman. He always had some hilarious way of stating the obvious. "That's no hill for a stepper" was a favorite. In other words, "You can overcome anything if you're determined."

Mom's mother also had little in the way of formal schooling. But she knew how to fend for herself and her family; she made my mother's clothes and grew and canned all her own vegetables. There was never a moment when the deep freezer in the garage didn't have enough food to survive a nuclear holocaust. But not canned tomatoes. Poppy swore he had eaten so many canned tomatoes during the Depression he couldn't bear the sight of them.

Nona, as we called her, was no-nonsense and did not suffer fools. The day my mother was born, going to the hospital was unthinkable; they didn't have the money, and giving birth at home was just the country way. When Nona went into labor she called a neighbor woman to come over and cook for Cecil, as it was unimaginable that he would make his own dinner that night. The story goes that the neighbor was struggling to kill the chicken that was planned for his meal, so my grandmother hoisted herself up on one elbow, reached out her other hand, and wrung that chicken's neck right there from the birthing bed. Mom told that story every chance she got. "Mama is tough," she'd say with a mix of pride and awe. "She isn't scared of anything."

Dad's parents were on the other end of the social spectrum from Mom's. They were Waco society and belonged to the Ridgewood Country Club. They traveled the globe when that was unheard-of in Texas, and it was my grandmother Eleanor who later introduced me to the world. Worried that their only son would fall in love at such a young age with a Waco girl, they shipped my father off to Andover, a prep school in Massachusetts, in hopes of breaking up the romance. My dad rebelled and soon was back at Waco High and back with my mom.

My parents were a "power couple" from the get-go. Mom was the star of the school debate team, and Dad's mother had raised him to hold his own beliefs—which from a young age were progressive by any standards, let alone in 1950s Waco. His favorite book as a child was *The Merry Adventures of Robin Hood*—he loved Little John—and it seemed to inform his politics later in life. On weekends the two of them would see a movie and split a milkshake, then stay out as late as they could, getting into impassioned political arguments. As Dad said later, they were in a rush to grow up and get about the business of life.

Mom and Dad stuck around Waco after high school. They enrolled

Mom and Dad, age sixteen, as Dad gets shipped off from Waco, Texas, to Andover.

at Baylor University, a Baptist school where, in Mom's words, everything was more fun because it was either against the rules or a sin. The singer Marcia Ball jokes that no one at Baylor had sex standing up because someone might think you were trying to dance. It wasn't until the late '90s that the school finally broke down and decided to lift the infamous dancing ban; up to that point, it was basically the provincial town from *Footloose.* For much of my life, Waco's biggest claim to fame was being the home of Dr Pepper and near Abbott, the birthplace of Willie Nelson. Now when people think of Waco, they're more likely to mention the HGTV show *Fixer Upper.*

My parents married in 1953 after their junior year of college. A year later they moved to Austin, where Dad went to law school and Mom took graduate classes for her teaching certificate and taught junior high. She later said it was the hardest job she'd ever had, and the experience solidified her lifelong respect for public school teachers. Once he graduated, Dad took a job with a Dallas law firm known for representing labor unions and taking up civil rights cases—two things few others were doing at the time. Right about then Mom realized she was pregnant with me. She was eager to take on the big city with my father, but Nona was determined that her first grandchild would be born in Waco, where she could be close at hand. So Mom grudgingly moved back home until I was born.

It was 1957. The Supreme Court had recently declared segregated schools unconstitutional in *Brown v. Board of Education*, and the Little Rock Nine enrolled at Central High in Arkansas. It was an exciting time for America and for Dad, but there was Mom: pregnant, living with her parents, and going stir-crazy. Years later she lamented, "David was starting a new career and I was in my old room." As soon as I was born, she hotfooted it out of Waco to join Dad in Dallas and never looked back.

After me came my brothers, Dan and Clark, and later my sister, Ellen. We spent our early years in Dallas, in a house on Lover's Lane. It was small and cramped for the six of us, but Mom spent long hours decorating to try to make it look like the Dallas homes she'd seen in photos; after all, we weren't in Waco anymore. Wallpaper was in fashion, so she put it up in every room: paisley in the tiny kitchen, white with flowers

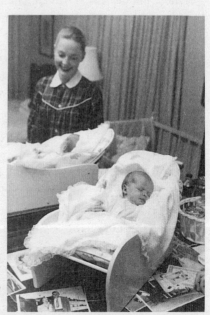

Mom and me in her childhood bedroom.

in the upstairs bedroom. She refinished an old set of dining-room furniture; nothing we had was ever really new, but by the time she was done it looked like it was.

In those days women in our neighborhood were expected to stay home, take care of the family, and help make their husbands successful. Mom pursued her role as a housewife with purpose. While Dad was working on "a big, important case," she baked our birthday cakes from scratch and tried every latest recipe from *Good Housekeeping*. On special days she made chocolate meringue pie; I can still see it sitting on the counter, with beads of sugar forming on top. She drove us to swimming class and took Ellen and me to Brownies and Girl Scouts, made our Halloween costumes, and sewed some of her own clothes. Holidays were epic. We spent days preparing for Easter. Never one to do anything halfway, she'd have us dye dozens of eggs, wrap hundreds of jelly beans in plastic wrap, and throw the biggest Easter egg hunt around. At Christmas she put up the tallest, most elaborately decorated tree. It became an annual tradition: she'd let us all help hang the ornaments, then, true to form, stay up all night disassembling and reassembling to make sure it looked absolutely perfect, tinsel and all. As she once said, "If it was in a glossy magazine, I was doing it!" It was as if every effort was a campaign, soup to nuts. Why go small?

But even early on, I could see that Mom was quietly beginning to revolt against the role she was expected to play. One event in particular is seared into my brain. My father and some friends had planned to take a canoe trip for a few days, and he asked Mom to pack up everything they would need, including their meals. On the day before they left, while Dad was at work, Mom and a friend got together for the afternoon and plotted. They laid out plastic bags and marked each with the day and meal: "Saturday breakfast," "Sunday lunch," and so on. Then they filled them with the absolute worst things they could find. From canned diet drinks for losing weight to stewed prunes, each meal was more unappetizing than the last. Everything was so neatly packaged and labeled—as was Mom's way—that Dad had no idea what was in store until he and his friends got on the river. I don't believe he left her at home with four kids for a canoeing weekend ever again.

People often say to me, "It must have been incredible to have Ann Richards as a mom!" And of course it was. But to paint the picture a bit more clearly, it was not as if this young mother, the only child of working-class parents, sprung fully formed as a feminist icon. That happened over the course of many years. I suspect it was those early days in Dallas, being the perfect wife and mother, that set the stage for her rebellion later on.

Life in Dallas back then is hard to imagine unless you experienced it. The city was segregated and rampant with racism and homophobia. Dad had been working along with others to fight the poll tax, a scheme to prevent African Americans from voting that was finally declared unconstitutional by the Supreme Court in 1966, when I was nine. I recall police raids on movie theaters where gay men were known to congregate, though I was barely conscious of it at the time. Years later my son and I went to see the film *Milk*, which starts with black-and-white footage of raids on gay bars in the '60s and '70s. He turned to me and asked, "Mom, what are the police doing?" I realized then just how different my upbringing in Dallas had been from his world.

Mom shared Dad's passion for progressive causes, but while he fought injustice in the courts, she was bound to us kids and had to find her own ways to resist the status quo. I remember her dragging my brother Dan and me to the local A&P grocery one day. She marched in and made a beeline for the produce aisle, a woman on a mission. As if we didn't already have a reputation for being troublemakers in the conservative, wealthy, University Park neighborhood in Dallas, she walked right up to the young teenager stocking the shelves, a head of lettuce in her hand, and asked, "Where is Mr. Jones?"

Mr. Jones was the manager, and he was unaccustomed to political activities at his store. He approached Mom with a cheerful smile on his face and asked, "How can I help you, Mrs. Richards?"

Mom skipped the pleasantries. "You know there is a lettuce boycott on. Where did this head of lettuce come from?"

"Well, I can't say for sure," he admitted.

"Well, I want to see the crate it came in, because if it doesn't have a United Farmworkers label, I'm not buying," she said.

Mr. Jones, knowing full well the crate didn't have a United Farm-workers label, hemmed and hawed until Mom finally cut him off. She made it clear her family wasn't eating any more iceberg lettuce or any grapes until they had a union label. We didn't have either in the house after that, and I don't eat iceberg lettuce or grapes to this day.

Her keen interest in social issues and politics ended up being what kept Mom sane in those years. With a tree house in the backyard, a basketball hoop in the driveway, and a station wagon parked in the garage, we looked like the quintessential upper-middle-class Dallas family. But while other families bowled, we did politics. Many of Mom and Dad's friends were running for office, mainly trying to beat the Dixiecrats who ran the Democratic Party across the state, and we went all in. At one point my dad ran for precinct chair and toppled an establishment candidate.

While we were growing up, our dinner table was never for eating—it was for sorting precinct lists. The earliest photo I have of me walking is at age two, out on our front lawn with a yard sign advertising the congressional campaign of Barefoot Sanders, a progressive Democrat. Our after-school activities were as likely to include stuffing envelopes at campaign headquarters as they were going to gymnastics or soccer practice.

As time passed and my parents' involvement in local politics expanded, our house on Lover's Lane became the local gathering place for misfits and rabble-rousers, with parties until the wee hours. My parents hosted local progressive politicians, activists, photographers, and writers from the *Texas Observer* and the *New York Times*. Shel Hershorn, the photojournalist who shot iconic photographs of the civil rights movement as well as the picture of Lee Harvey Oswald mortally wounded by Jack Ruby, lived down the street. He and his wife, Connie, were regulars, along with Sam and Virginia Whitten, my parents' best friends. They'd come around to drink and smoke and commiserate about the city's sorry state of affairs, and sometimes play a raucous game of "dirty charades." It was one long continuum of liberal camaraderie, and Mom was the life of the party. It was much later that I realized those early days may have foreshadowed my mother's struggle with alcohol. All of their friends drank,

My first campaign: Barefoot Sanders's run for Congress. Dallas, 1958.

so it never seemed out of the ordinary. Didn't everybody's parents have a few martinis before dinner?

Of course we kids were sleeping during most of those late nights. More than once, my siblings and I would wake up for school in the morning to find some stranger snoring on the couch—the latest traveling reporter or union leader from out of town. Having grown up in that exciting environment, to me, politics never seemed like a chore; it was where the action was.

• • •

Like other progressive Democrats in the 1960s, my parents were in love with the Kennedys. Mom followed everything they did and pledged never to wear white shoes because Jackie Kennedy never would. We even lived in Washington for a couple of years early in the administration, while Dad worked for the Civil Rights Division in the Department of Justice. He was thrilled to be there when the civil rights movement was taking off. Later he told me that change suddenly seemed possible and that Washington had been part of the "new frontier." But the days of that new frontier were coming to an end.

For Mom, finally getting out of Texas was energizing. She loved Washington. We lived on Capitol Hill, traveled to Mount Vernon, and went to the White House Easter Egg Roll. Mom took us to the National Gallery to see Renoir's *Girl with a Watering Can*, a painting she had only ever seen in picture books. She even wrote to Jackie Kennedy to explain that little Caroline and I were the same age, and she thought it would be neat if we could play together. That didn't happen, but for her, the sky was the limit.

Washington was a refreshing respite for all of us, but after two years Dad grew frustrated with the glacial pace of government bureaucracy. He was surrounded by passionate, well-intentioned people, but for all their high hopes, nothing ever seemed to happen. He told Mom it was time to return to Dallas, where he would go back to practicing law, and that was it.

Things were bad back in Dallas—worse than before we'd left. As Dad described it, "Right-wing hysteria seemed to be everywhere." One billboard at the time declared, "Get the U.S. Out of the U.N.," which pretty much summed up the mentality of the city. None of that stopped Mom from throwing herself back into the local political scene—if anything, it spurred her on.

On Friday, November 22, 1963, President John Kennedy and Vice President Lyndon Johnson came to town, greeted by a full-page ad in the local paper accusing them of treason. Mom was at the Adolphus Hotel, along with other Democratic women, waiting to welcome the president and vice president to the lunch they were scheduled to attend. My dad left his downtown office to stand on the street and wave to the motorcade, which passed by right before turning onto Dealey Plaza. Years later Dad talked about that day and how close he was to the president, sitting there in an open car. Dad said he could practically have reached out and touched him.

I was sitting in my first grade classroom that day when a teacher came running in to announce that President Kennedy had been assassinated. The way Mom used to tell it, the kids in the Dallas schools applauded when they heard the news. That may have been true for older kids, but my classmates and I were just six or seven, so I'm not sure any of us really understood what was going on.

They dismissed school early, and by the time I got home, I knew something big was happening. My parents and their friends were glued to the TV, clearly shaken. The death of the president, and within a few days the murder of Oswald on live TV, sent them into despair. They did the only thing they could think to do, which was pack up the family and go camping for the weekend with friends. They were terrified of what Dallas had become and were increasingly convinced that we had to move.

A few years later we decamped to Austin. If Dallas was the heart of right-wing conservatism, Austin was the motherland of the resistance.

• • •

To a twelve-year-old, Austin felt like nirvana. Unlike Dallas, where we never fit in, Austin was full of hippies and protests and love-ins. My brother Dan grew his hair long; we tie-dyed our T-shirts and started a garden in the backyard. Mom ordered hundreds of ladybugs so we could grow vegetables without pesticides, and we planted tomatoes, asparagus, and more. The Vietnam War was raging, and Dad was representing conscientious objectors, defending them from being sent to war against their religious or moral objections. We held benefits at our house for antiwar activists. Mom threw herself into all the things she could never have done in Dallas and seemed to be having a blast.

As was true of so many progressive cities during that era, Austin culture and activism were fused together. It was the 1960s, the decade of hippie counterculture and radical social change; the year of Woodstock, the iconic music festival that brought half a million concertgoers to upstate New York for three straight days of "peace, love, and rock 'n' roll." Early Austin bands like Shiva's Headband and Freda and the Firedogs played at antiwar rallies. My folks were into it. They'd tossed out their Frank Sinatra records in exchange for Jefferson Airplane.

One afternoon their friend Eddie Wilson called and asked them to come over to see a great place he had found, an old abandoned national guard armory just outside downtown Austin. Eddie was lobbying for the beer industry but lived for the music scene, and he was constantly devising wild new ideas. As we wandered through the dusty cobwebbed building that was as big as an airplane hangar, he said he wanted to buy it and turn it into a music hall. It was hard to picture, but Eddie had a vision, and sure enough, he gutted the place, and the Armadillo World Headquarters became a central gathering place for progressives, as well as a must-visit stop for musicians around the country. We saw Frank Zappa, Van Morrison, and Bette Midler. It was magical for me. The Armadillo represented breaking every rule and cultural norm. For the first time in my life, I felt like we were part of the in-crowd.

It was in Austin at age thirteen that I had my most formative run-in with the authorities, so to speak. As they had done in Dallas, my parents hung out at the Unitarian church, less for the religion than for finding a community of other liberals. The kids at church, including my oldest friend, Jill Whitten, whose family had moved to Austin from Dallas a few

My family in Austin, 1970: Mom, Clark, me, Ellen, Dan, and Dad, embracing the hippie culture.

years earlier, had welcomed me to town, and they were up-to-date on all the political activities, especially the antiwar protests. Activists had called for a national Moratorium to End the War in Vietnam, with teach-ins and demonstrations to be held across the country. Kids were planning to wear black armbands to school in solidarity.

Listening to Crosby, Stills & Nash on the record player in my bedroom, I considered whether I too might wear an armband. I was still relatively new to Austin and had spent most of my time just trying to adjust to a new school. We lived in the country, outside of town, and I didn't know how the other kids would react to my political statement. Finally I decided that it was a good thing to do, regardless of what my classmates might think.

Before going to bed, I dug around in Mom's sewing kit and found a piece of black felt. I methodically measured and cut it into an armband big enough that it would be impossible to miss. The next morning I attached it carefully to my sleeve with a safety pin and marched out the door, waving goodbye to my parents. As the oldest child, I had always tried to be perfect, and this felt like the most daring thing I had ever done. The armband might as well have had the word *agitator* sewn onto it. It was sort of thrilling, especially because I was pretty sure I would be the only person in seventh grade at Westlake Junior High to wear one.

Stepping onto the school bus, I glanced around, trying to play it cool, even though my stomach was churning. I found my friend Alison and sat with her. I'm sure lots of kids on the bus had no idea about the moratorium. I knew if there were going to be repercussions, it would be once we got to school. Sure enough, the principal, Tom Hestand, stopped me on my way to third period and asked that I come to his office. I had never been summoned to the principal's office, and I assumed it had something to do with the armband. I followed him and took a seat in the chair across from his desk.

"Cecile, do your parents know what you're doing?" he asked sternly.

I thought about it. "I'm pretty sure they do."

"Well," he said, "surely you won't mind, then, if I give them a call."

I shrugged and watched as he dialed the phone, then listened to it ring and ring. Finally, he hung up. Mom wasn't home—perhaps one of the luckiest moments in Principal Hestand's life. Having tried and failed to censure me, he had no choice but to let me go back to class.

Later that evening, when I recounted the excitement of being taken to the principal's office—escorted by the principal, no less—Mom went ballistic. "Who does Principal Hestand think he is," she fumed, "trying to intimidate you just for standing up for what you believe?" It felt like Mom and I were in a conspiracy together. The rush was exhilarating. Whether he meant to or not, Principal Hestand definitely gets credit for helping to launch my life of activism. I've always wanted to find him and thank him for getting me started!

From then on, it was *Okay, now what can I do? Where can I make a difference?* A few months later, inspired by the first Earth Day in 1970, I started my very first organization with some girlfriends. We named it Youth Against Pollution. We picked up trash in our neighborhood and collected aluminum cans in the lunchroom. Then I enlisted the help of my brother Dan to crush them for recycling.

My family always had lots of dogs, many of which just sort of showed up. I became obsessed with washing out all the dog food cans to recycle them. Dad found me doing it in the kitchen one day and asked me in exasperation, "Cecile, don't you know that it's pointless to wash out all those dog food cans?"

"It's for the environment!" I protested.

Dad did what he so often did when he thought an idea was harebrained: he told me exactly how he felt, in no uncertain terms. "You're not going to save the environment by washing out those goddamn dog food cans," he said, shaking his head. "Don't you know that companies are going to have to start doing this for it to make any difference?"

Dad thought I was nuts, and that wasn't the last time. Despite his idealism, he often let me know how impractical I was—and of course I was so desperate to make him proud. It took decades before I began to understand that he must have felt pride all along, even if he sometimes had trouble expressing it. I'm sure seeking his approval helped drive me to try harder. But it also might have been my first lesson in the importance of doing what feels right and not getting too caught up in what others think—including my father. And I guess in a way we were both right.

Recycling did catch on, but it had to begin somewhere. I like to think it got a jump-start from teenagers washing out dog food cans.

• • •

Even in Austin, the promised land, there were problems. I was really tall, so logically I wanted to play basketball. But this was before Title IX, the federal law that would guarantee equal opportunity for girls in school activities, and the geniuses who determined the rules for junior high sports made us play half-court basketball. The school authorities must have thought girls couldn't run the full court. We played six on six, so three of us were on defense, and once we had the basketball, we could only dribble to half court and then pass it to someone on the other side to shoot.

In Westlake Hills, as in much of Texas, football was the entire focus of our junior high and high school. Since girls' sports were nearly nonexistent, the other option was to be a cheerleader or join the drill team, who performed at halftime at the football games—a sort of high school Rockettes—but I was five-foot-ten, which disqualified me from even trying out for either of them. My mother was outraged, again, but I opted not to take on this fight, since I would rather have died than be a part of the football scene.

Instead, along with friends like Chris Ames, who was a year ahead of me in school and also a troublemaker, we fought against having to go to the weekly pep rallies—demanding a study hall for students who didn't want to cheer on the football team. At Westlake pretty much every teacher was a coach, so history and science and even sex ed were taught by folks whose primary responsibility was coaching football. As you might imagine, I was a thorn in their side.

Coach C doubled as a football coach and my eighth grade history teacher. It was pretty obvious what his first love was, as he used to give us assignments in class while he drew football plays on the blackboard. When he started Current Events Day, asking us to bring in newspaper articles to discuss, I brought in one about a student who was suspended for shining his shoes with an American flag. I was outraged on the student's behalf. "Richards!" Coach C yelled, like I was on his junior varsity team. "That kid got just what he deserved!" I never backed down from a debate with Coach C, and he definitely got me to speak up, since I disagreed with almost everything he believed. He clearly shouldn't have been teaching history. Still, I almost felt bad when he drove the truck full of band instruments under the overhang at the school and peeled the top of the trailer right off.

Although football was the predominant activity in my school, my classmates were also fanatical about hunting. I'd grown up fishing with my grandfather on Lake Waco, catching crappie and frying them for supper. I learned as a young girl how to bait a hook, how to cast and catch a fish. If I caught something worth keeping and eating, Mom insisted I learn how to scale it, gut it, and fillet it. That was the rule, and I followed it. But there was no way I was going to shoot and clean a deer, much less a cow! So I decided in seventh grade that I would eat no more meat, period. I've been a pescatarian ever since.

Westlake High was a dead end for me, and after a while I was spending more time trying to figure out how to skip school and raise hell than anything else. I was a good enough student, so my parents decided to move me to St. Stephen's, a small Episcopal school. It was the first racially integrated school I'd ever attended—and it changed the direction of my life. Suddenly I had the opportunity to learn from really smart teachers alongside kids from different races and backgrounds. It felt like the world was opening up. I threw myself into acting and music and writing—all of which gave me confidence to express opinions and speak in front of others.

Though I loved my family and didn't know much beyond Texas, I couldn't shake the feeling that there had to be more. One of the only times I had ever been out of the state was on a trip to New York City with Dad's mother, Eleanor Richards, when I was in the third grade. We rode the train to St. Louis from Dallas in a sleeper car overnight, and then flew to New York. She took me to the Automat, where you could put in a quarter and get a piece of pie. I had never seen anything like it. We visited the Museum of Modern Art and the United Nations and even went to see Ethel Merman in *Annie Get Your Gun*. Now that was *something*. I can hear her voice still today.

Eleanor grew up at a time when women were expected to stay in the kitchen, but she had seen the world. She had gone to Radcliffe College in Cambridge, Massachusetts, and had been to China and India and Africa. She helped start the League of Women Voters in Texas and fought for integration and civil rights. I loved her. More than anyone in my family, she talked about the world and politics and issues nonstop. Even into her eighties we debated everything under the sun, from Middle East politics to premarital sex, which, by the way, she was all for. She told me, "Shacking up before getting married would have been so much better!"

Momel, as I called her, had big plans for me. When I was still in high school she invited me to go with her to London for a week. No one I knew had been out of the country, unless it was to go across the Texas border for cheap alcohol and Mexican food. My mother had strong opinions about everything, including what I should wear to travel to England. I remember a particular red suit that I wouldn't have been caught dead in anywhere near my friends, but Mom had decided it was what I was wearing.

My grandmother was a big fan of Loehmann's Discount Clothing Store, so between the pair of us, we were a sight in London. Momel wore a black patent leather raincoat with embroidered daisies, so at least I couldn't lose her. Wearing our crazy outfits, we went to the theater, took a boat down the River Thames, and visited Windsor Castle and Buckingham Palace. When I came back from England I told my parents they were not going to believe what was going on outside Texas.

Meanwhile, every movement of the '60s and '70s was coming alive, and it seemed like my parents were into them all. The environmental movement, despite my father's skepticism over the dog food cans, made a huge impression. We began camping and canoeing on the rivers of Texas, which were continually threatened by dams and development. It was on these adventures that we became close friends with the columnist Molly Ivins, an inveterate camper; Bob Armstrong, the Texas land commissioner; and some singer-songwriters and erstwhile politicians. Closer to home, the fight to save Barton Springs, a beloved natural spring and swimming hole, created a whole generation of environmental activists who fundamentally saved Austin from becoming another developer's dream.

It was abundantly clear to all of us that Mom had more than her fair share of pent-up energy. She threw herself into one hobby after another. At one point we even raised chickens in our backyard, until the fateful day that one of our many dogs got into the pen and committed the Great Chicken Massacre. ("But just think how happy that dog was!" Mom consoled my brother Dan.) Everything Mom did was larger than life, a full-scale production. But when she discovered the women's movement, she found her perfect outlet. After all, she'd spent some of her best years taking care of four kids, and she'd volunteered on many campaigns, helping to elect male friends to the legislature. She said that in those days the real sign of a woman's power was measured by the length of her phone cord at the campaign office.

I was sixteen when a young lawyer in Austin named Sarah Weddington decided to run for the state legislature. She came to Mom, asking for help. It was a golden opportunity for Mom and she seized it. She would gather us up in the backseat of the car and take us to Sarah's headquarters, where we further refined our campaign skills, learning to phone-bank and door-knock.

Mom came up with one original idea after another for Sarah's campaign. One of the most ingenious was a new twist on campaigning at the local fair, where voters could enjoy food and music and meet the candidates. Everyone else in the race had a lot more money to spend and they were certain to have more impressive handouts. Mom's idea was to paste "Sarah Weddington" bumper stickers on cheap paper bags for Sarah to autograph, which people could use to hold all the other giveaways. It was a huge success: by the end of the day, people were carrying Sarah sacks all over the fair.

That was a really tough race, and I saw firsthand just how ugly it could be for a woman to run for office. This was especially true for Sarah, who had made a name for herself at the age of twenty-six arguing *Roe v. Wade* before the US Supreme Court, the case that legalized abortion in America. Sexism was widespread in Texas politics; her opponent in the Democratic primary refused to call her by name, instead referring to her as "that sweet little girl." Even some of the local establishment Democrats were organizing against her, doing everything they could to paint her as a radical feminist, literally driving Catholic anti-abortion voters to the polls on Election Day.

Despite all the nastiness, Sarah won the primary and went on to win in the general election by a comfortable margin—the first woman to represent our county in the Texas House of Representatives. Her victory gave Mom the chance to finally get out of the house and go work at the capitol as Sarah's legislative assistant. This was a profound change, because up until then, it was my dad who got all the notoriety and fame. By then he was a big-deal labor and civil rights lawyer. But even we kids could tell Mom was coming into her own, and we were proud of her. After years of organizing the family, she was putting those skills to use organizing political campaigns, and she was really good at it. For the first time, we saw Mom in charge. It seemed like she knew everything.

Increasingly, as Mom was figuring out her path and my father was filling his spare time hanging out with his drinking and lawyering buddies, I was looking ahead. College was a given, but there weren't many people close to me who had been out of Texas. Even though I'd been a good student (besides my scrapes with school authorities, which gave me a bit of a reputation), the college counselor tried to dampen my hopes.

Molly Ivins was one of the few women I knew who had gone away to school. She wanted me to go to Smith, her alma mater and the place where she had "worn black and become a radical." Women's colleges seemed like a logical option. But then I read about Brown University in Providence, Rhode Island, where the Third World Coalition students had taken over a university building and were protesting racism and financial aid cuts. Now that sounded like my kind of place.

Armed with those facts and a copy of the college handbook (my only source of information on the subject), I made an appointment to see the high school guidance counselor, Dean Towner. An imposing presence at school, he always wore a bow tie, and I was not his favorite student.

I sat across from him in his tiny office, excited to tell him what I'd been researching. "Mr. Towner, I've heard about some schools I'd like to apply to. My friend Molly Ivins said I might like Smith, and I've been reading about Brown and Williams. They all sound like they might be the kind of place I would fit in. I was hoping maybe I could get your help."

Mr. Towner looked at me over his glasses with a dubious expression. "Well, Cecile," he replied, "I don't think those are schools that you're likely to get into. So I've put together a list of schools that you should try instead."

Like Principal Hestand, he seemed to be trying to take me down a few notches, and I wasn't going to let him.

"Okay, well, I think I'm going to try anyway," I said. I picked up my college handbook and left. I figured out how to get the applications and put together some recommendations. I was proud of myself for getting it done on my own.

In those days the college acceptance and rejection letters all arrived in mailboxes across America on April 1. When the day arrived, I could hardly breathe as I walked down the road to our mailbox. Inside was a fat letter from Brown. I tore it open and read that I had been accepted.

I was leaving Texas for a chance to see the world and make trouble. And that's just what I did.

CHAPTER 3

Question Authority

Until the day I moved to Providence, Mom and I had never been to Rhode Island or even nearby. Still, she was certain she knew all about East Coast colleges, including what people wore.

Before leaving, we went shopping at the downtown Scarborough's department store in Austin. Mom had lots of rules where clothing was concerned. In junior high I had perfected the art of wearing a mother-approved outfit to the breakfast table before school, then dashing downstairs, throwing on a tie-dyed T-shirt and patched bell bottoms, and racing away on my bike before she could catch me. It was my own personal act of resistance, and it became an ongoing battle once she caught on.

The college shopping trip was her last chance to put her stamp on my appearance. She decided I needed some wool, mid-calf A-line skirts (won't show dirt, go anywhere), and wool turtleneck sweaters. This was a university where the students had recently occupied the administration offices, and we were coming from a state where the temperature never drops below 40 degrees, but that wasn't about to stop Mom. Per usual, I had absolutely no say in the wardrobe decisions.

It was the fall of 1975. Mom's life was changing too. Not long before, the local progressive Democrats had approached my dad about taking on the incumbent county commissioner, Johnny Voudouris, known locally as Johnny Voodoo. He was a classic good old boy. Everyone knew him; he put his name on every trash can in the neighborhood, just so nobody would ever forget he was the county commissioner. Dad knew his own gift for saying exactly what was on his mind with no filter would make him a less than ideal candidate. So in the kitchen one evening, after their friends asked Dad to run, he responded, "Well, why not Ann? She knows everything about political campaigns, certainly more than the rest of us."

Mom recalled that there was dead silence. No one stepped in to say, "Ann, that's a wonderful idea!" or "You'd be a great choice!" She realized no one was going to come begging, not even with her success on Sarah Weddington's campaign. And so, after encouraging countless other women to run for office, Mom decided to take her own advice and give it a shot.

As I left Texas, it was clear to me that even if I returned home, nothing was ever going to be the same. By then Mom was into the women's movement with both feet. She had met lots of other activists around the fight to pass the Equal Rights Amendment, or ERA, which would have guaranteed a constitutional right to women's equality. Once Congress passed it, it would have to be ratified by the states, so women were organizing all across America.

The ERA provided the first window into my mother's and father's different attitudes when it came to so-called women's issues. Dad had spent his entire career fighting for voting rights, civil rights, and expanded opportunities for minorities to serve in office. But even he couldn't see why passing a constitutional amendment guaranteeing women's equality was necessary. He had a wife who raised the kids, took care of every single dog and cat we brought home, threw dinner parties, and grew organic vegetables. Dad had grown up—and was living in—a household where women threw themselves into volunteer work and didn't have careers. I realize now that for him (and so many other men of his generation), the prospect of total upheaval of the domestic scene must have seemed pretty frightening. Suddenly the tumult around women's roles and aspirations wasn't happening just on television; it was happening in our own home.

That women and men are equal might seem obvious to most people, but at the time it was highly controversial. (And of course even now we are living through a political era when men—including our president—are openly questioning women's equality.) At one point during the ERA fight, the conservative activist Phyllis Schlafly threatened that if the amendment passed, women would be drafted into combat and women and men would be going to the same bathroom. As Mom used to say, "Nothing gets conservatives more excited or frothing at the mouth quicker than what's going on in other folks' bedrooms." Or bathrooms, as we're seeing to this day. Eventually the ERA passed in Congress but failed in the states. Out of that disappointing loss came an entire generation of women activists who would go on to pass Title IX, run for office, and keep up the effort to pass the ERA—which continues even now.

In the midst of what was starting to feel like a national identity crisis, and Mom's campaign for county commissioner, I was getting ready to start a new adventure of my own.

The night before we left for Brown, my folks went out to dinner and, as usual, had too much to drink. Mom came by my room, which was just down the hall from theirs, tipsy and teary over my leaving. I got the feeling she was deeply troubled. My parents were struggling in their marriage, but they'd done their best to keep their differences behind closed doors. Though he had encouraged her to run for office, Dad couldn't have anticipated how Mom's ascendancy would shift the balance in their relationship. He was used to being the smartest guy in the room and the center of attention. As her star rose, the marriage was coming apart and her drinking didn't help matters. There was a sadness about both of them that I didn't really understand, but I felt like I was leaving the scene of an accident by going away to school. My brothers were unruly—to say the least—and I had always been the typical first child who tried so hard to keep everything together. Years later my sister, Ellen, who was ten at the time, told me how abandoned she felt when I left. But whatever guilt I carried back then was watered down by relief over getting away—from my family and from Texas.

The next morning Mom and I woke up like nothing had happened and got in the car to head east. Our friend Sarah Meacham had baked us some homemade granola, and I picked out some Joni Mitchell and Carole King cassette tapes to bring along. Without much fanfare, we hit the road for Mom's first and only trip to Brown.

I'd never driven more than a couple of hundred miles with my mother, but suddenly we were off on a cross-country adventure. Both of us were taking a big leap—me finally leaving home and her running for office. In fact she would be elected county commissioner that November. Our lives were about to change forever, but I don't remember our discussing anything more substantial than the weather during those long hours on the road. As I look back, that trip is probably more remarkable for what we didn't talk about: her conflicted marriage and my anxiety about starting over in a place I'd never been, with people I didn't know. We couldn't have helped each other anyway; I didn't know anything about the demands of a marriage, and she knew even less about the journey I was about to undertake. Except for that brief time in Washington, Mom had lived her entire life within two hundred miles of Waco.

When we got to campus, Mom left me at the Wayland Arch on Thayer Street. Saying goodbye was hard for both of us. She was gone, and to say I was lost can't possibly capture it.

My dorm was literally covered in ivy. Since most kids were from the East Coast, their entire families were there, helping them move in. They were unpacking beanbag chairs and mini refrigerators, and all I had was a turntable and a suitcase full of inappropriate clothing. Oh, and an iron my grandfather bought me that he'd hand-engraved with my initials. My friend Jill's mother, Virginia, had even sent me off with a full-length Lanz flannel nightgown that she surely ordered from L.L.Bean—just the thing to impress everyone in the dorms. There wasn't a tortilla in sight, and when I told the other students I was from Texas, I may as well have said I grew up on the Ponderosa Ranch from the TV show *Bonanza*. Which, for the record, was set in Nevada. That's about the extent of what they knew of my home state.

All I wanted was to be cool. But I was the epitome of uncool. It seemed as though everyone else had been to the same summer camps and prep schools. They wore the same clothes, looking effortlessly hip, as though they hadn't given their appearance a second thought. Rugby shirts and Top-Siders had not made it to Texas, but it looked like everyone at Brown had them. There wasn't a wool skirt in sight, so I quickly hid them in the back of the dorm room closet.

From the very beginning I desperately sought out people who played against type at Brown. Amy on my dorm floor was an artist who would go on to be a cartoonist; she was definitely offbeat, with a sardonic wit. Julio, who was Puerto Rican, had been plucked out of his neighborhood in New York and sent to Andover.

There were a handful of other kids from Texas, but they weren't in much better shape than I was. A friend from high school, Jonathan Royston, helped me get a job making sandwiches at the cafeteria, for which I'm forever grateful. My roommate was from Ireland by way of Vermont. She had a boyfriend from West Africa, smoked a lot of dope, and introduced me to all kinds of music, including the Chieftains and John Martyn. God knows she tried to help me out, but it was a tall order. She lent me her clothes until I could find some that didn't make me look like a character out of *Little Women*. That first year she even took me skiing at her home in Woodstock, Vermont, where I nearly froze to death. Unlike the rest of my classmates, I had never gone to a rugby game, never ice-skated, and obviously never skied. Nothing could have prepared me for trying to make it down a mountain in subzero temperatures in enormous borrowed skis without killing myself or another hapless skier. I somehow persuaded someone to rescue me with a ride to Pittsfield, Massachusetts, where I took a bus back to Providence and defrosted.

• • •

If things were shaky for me, life for my family was going from bad to worse. By my second year in college, it was obvious even over the phone that my parents were not happy. Mom and Dad never got on the line together the way other parents did. Even distance couldn't mask the tension between them. They always seemed stilted and preoccupied, and I began dreading every call. It wasn't until shortly before Thanksgiving, when everyone else was going home, that I realized my parents hadn't bought me a plane ticket. I called Mom and asked if it was okay if I came home for the holiday, and of course she agreed that it was. But I knew that for her to forget about me, her mind had to be on something much more pressing than cooking a turkey.

My memories of that Thanksgiving are blurry. I must have been glad to see everyone, but I have no idea how Mom and Dad got through that meal. By this point my mom was a county commissioner, working full time (and then some) outside the house. And she was getting a fair amount of notoriety already. After all, liberal women in public office in Texas were practically unheard-of—especially those in charge of roads and bridges and the county criminal justice system. When her fellow statewide county commissioners got together, Mom didn't call it the "Boots and Bellies Convention" for nothing.

Mom was an anomaly for sure. She was smart and outspoken, and with her trademark Texas hairdo and sparkly blue eyes, you couldn't miss her. She was also a practicing alcoholic. It seems incredible now that we didn't understand what was going on—or maybe we were all in denial?—but alcohol had become a way of getting through her marriage, job, and motherhood. I should have known something was wrong when I came home for Christmas one year and she met me at the airport decked out in a Dolly Parton costume—and I wasn't even surprised. Apparently she wore it later on to the local country music hall, the Broken Spoke, and got quite a few dance offers.

My folks had their hands full at home, and I imagine they were thankful that I'd landed somewhere safe. They were preoccupied with their own troubles, and I was one less thing to worry about. Out of sight, out of mind. It was a strange feeling: coming from a hippie-ish, loving, funky Texas family that seemed to be the perfect progressive nuclear unit, only to realize that everything I'd been led to believe might not be true after all.

So I started building my own life at school. Kids at Brown were smart and self-confident. For lots of them, Brown was just the continuation of prep school; it seemed like pretty much everyone knew someone who knew someone. They even knew the best professors and were playing all the angles to get into the right classes.

A lottery had placed me into a small freshman seminar with Ed Beiser, who I quickly learned was one of the most revered and feared professors on campus. The other students would have paid anything to get into his class on the philosophy of government. We studied Plato, Aristotle, and Locke. Professor Beiser used the Socratic method—meaning, you better read all the homework because, if you didn't, he would instinctively know it and call on you.

One day we were discussing Plato's *Republic*. Some of my classmates had already read it in high school, so this was old hat for them. I had never even heard of it until I saw it on the syllabus. I was incredibly intimidated, which I knew meant it was all but certain Professor Beiser would call on me.

Sure enough: "Ms. Richards? What do you think of Plato's defense of justice?"

I swallowed hard and managed to say something. I desperately hoped it was coherent—to this day, I can't remember what it was. All I know is that when I finished speaking, Professor Beiser nodded and moved on to the next student.

After class, he called me over to his desk. "Ms. Richards, that was a smart point you made today," he told me. "You've got something to say. I wonder, why don't you share your opinion like the other students?"

I was dumbstruck. *Did he really think so?*

He looked me square in the eye. "You are just as smart as any student from an East Coast prep school. Don't be afraid to stand up for what you believe." It was a rare word of encouragement from a man who believed in me more than I believed in myself.

I had the chance to follow Professor Beiser's advice not long after, when the janitors on campus went on strike and suddenly this uber-cool, activist university became a battleground between a rich Ivy League corporation and the folks who cleaned our dorms. The administration told students the strike was uncalled for; they claimed the wages and benefits the janitors were protesting were fair. I felt caught in the middle, and never more than the day I left my dorm and saw Eddie, my freshman-year janitor, walking the picket line. I called my dad and asked what I was supposed to do. I had been raised to never, ever cross a picket line. This was the kind of parental advice Dad probably always dreamed of giving. He said that in all his years of working for unions, he'd learned that the workers never got a fair shake unless they organized. He told me to always support the workers.

Some students were building a support group for the strikers, and so I dove in headfirst, finally feeling I'd found kindred spirits at Brown. We organized support for the janitors, coordinating fellow students to protest in solidarity with them. We handed out leaflets at campus events and demanded to meet with the administration.

Soon the campus librarians also organized and went on strike. One night we held a candlelight vigil. We created a V-formation of students leading up to the Rock, the primary library on campus, so anyone who wanted to get in had to walk through all of us. I guess it was easy enough to support the janitors, or at least no great inconvenience, but now students had to decide whether to cross a picket line of the library staff they depended on in order to do their research. An upperclassman acquaintance, a good guy as far as I knew, walked in that night. I could tell his conscience was bothering him because he muttered something about having to finish his thesis. Not being able to use the library hit some of us harder than others. I was disappointed as I watched people I knew cavalierly cross the line. It hurt, and I lost friendships over it.

To me, though, the choice was clear. The popular button of the day declared "Question Authority," and that's precisely what we were doing. Late at night we would put up strike signs around the university, on electrical posts and the sides of buildings, painting over them with wheat paste, which was basically impossibly sticky glue. It was absolutely prohibited by campus authorities, but it was our best way to call for students to get involved. We also knew that the strikebreakers had to remove all the signs, so that probably added to our motivation. I was afraid to get arrested, but some students weren't. At one point I called my dad and asked, "Just in case I get arrested, can you make sure you can bail me out?" He laughed, but I'm pretty sure he would have been proud if I had—though he would never have said so out loud. Eventually the university settled with the union, and to this day the janitors and librarians at Brown have union representation.

In high school I'd organized food support for strikers at the Longhorn Machine Works in Kyle, Texas, during a bitter labor battle. I'd grown up marching with the farmworkers with my family. But Brown was the first time I'd gotten in so deep, where I really understood the words to the labor anthem "Which Side Are You On?" It was also how I met folks who would become part of my world for the rest of my time at Brown, as we moved on to other battles with the campus administration. In my classes I was learning about the American Revolution and reading *We Shall Be All*, a book about the Industrial Workers of the World. It was dawning on me that history wasn't just something to read about in books—it was being made right in front of us.

Once you start questioning authority, it's hard to stop. The strikes and the aftermath made me question whether Brown and I were meant to be together. Being a student felt like a terrible ethical conflict, and after spending so many months on a nonstop campaign for the janitors and librarians, I couldn't imagine just going back to class. I was one semester into my sophomore year and starting to wonder whether I was supposed to be there at all. I wanted to find a place where I could figure out what I was doing in college, and more than that, what I was supposed to do with my life.

The second semester was rapidly approaching, so I had to figure something out. The ACLU was looking for an intern in Maine, which sounded, well, cold. An organization I'd never heard of was working on Title IX and women's equity in education in Washington, DC. I thought, *I'll give that a try.*

I called my parents and told them I had found something much more important than going to school and was going to drop out. They were shocked.

"What in God's name, Cecile? You are just throwing away your education," said Mom.

Try as I might, I couldn't get them to understand me or the bizarre, conflicted contradictions of life of at Brown. They were embroiled in their own issues and their other kids. Even still, they knew they couldn't stop me.

I moved to Washington, short on street smarts and with zero experience but thrilled to be on my own. With no place to live, and long before the days of Craigslist, I found a note tacked up at the local food co-op advertising for a roommate. I moved into a group house at 1927 S Street—no air-conditioning and totally bare bones. It was so hot in DC that at night, when it became unbearable, we'd go to the movies where at least it was cool.

The internship I'd found was working with the Project on the Status and Education of Women. They were fighting to implement Title IX, which required for the first time that women and men have equal opportunities in education. By dumb luck I had landed in the heart of feminist organizing in America. The world was starting to open up for women, and the women's movement was putting some life-changing wins on the board.

When I arrived in DC in 1977, Title IX was finally starting to have some juice, five years after becoming law. The big fights at the time were over athletics and employment in higher education: at publicly funded universities, women and men now had to have equal opportunities to be professors, and a university that spent $50 million on football had to spend $50 million on women's sports. As a Texan, I knew about the immense resources poured into football, and the thought that the same amount now had to be spent on girls' sports was really exciting. Maybe they could even play full-court basketball!

The women I worked with were making policy and creating opportunities for hundreds of thousands of women and girls across America. I loved what we were doing. It was the first office I'd ever worked in, and it was a hodgepodge of out-there feminist women—led by the iconic Bunny Sandler, one of the early leaders in the women's movement. I'd go to congressional hearings, research legal issues, and generally help out and try to learn what I could. I couldn't have known at age twenty how much the work I was doing would influence my daughters' lives. Decades later, Hannah would be a softball pitcher and soccer player, and Lily would be coxswain of the men's high school crew team, both embodying the change that was ultimately made possible under Title IX.

I met two women at that internship who would be part of my life forever. Judy Lichtman and Marcia Greenberger were the badass lawyers taking on every important feminist cause at the National Women's Law Center and the Women's Legal Defense Fund. They were fearless in fighting the powers that be in Washington, and they still are today. What I saw confirmed my suspicion that there were all kinds of exciting things going on outside of college, which was the reason I had left Texas in the first place. Who knew that instead of just protesting unfair laws, you could go out and change them?

By the time my internship was up that summer, I wasn't the same person I had been when I left Brown, but I knew I was going to go back. It seemed like the right thing to do, I wanted to get my degree, and I had a renewed sense of purpose. Maybe the organizing I did between classes at Brown could actually become my career, even my life. It was clear to me that my path was to take classes by day, but spend all my free time fighting for social justice.

Going back to dorm life, however, was unthinkable. I had been living on my own and cooking for myself, and had a taste of what freedom was like. And I couldn't imagine ever eating another meal in the campus cafeteria. So I moved into the Milhouse Co-op, ironically named after President Richard Milhous Nixon. It was the epitome of the counterculture at Brown—full of artists, proto-hippies, and people who wanted to live in a communal space—the perfect reentry to college for a nonconformist. We did everything together, including cook all our meals. I joyfully learned to make food for twenty-four people. All those years with Mom had made me physically incapable of doing anything halfway, so forget macaroni and cheese—I learned to make eggs Florentine and crepes for two dozen. My biggest fight with our co-op food committee was on the day I demanded they spend the money to get good half-and-half so I could make quiche for the whole house. I was thrilled when people made a point of coming home for dinner on the nights I was on deck; my meals were a nice alternative to the typical vegetarian chili.

I had to work, so within a few months of being back I got a job at the campus coffeehouse. That's where I met the entrepreneurial wizard Sally Stuart, an upperclassman who ran the place and was constantly coming up with new ideas. Sally had wild curly hair, talked with her hands, and had only one speed, which was high-octane. One day she turned to me and asked, "What would you think about starting a food co-op at Brown?"

I thought it sounded like a grand idea. So naturally she got me to run it. We started with fifty households of Brown students, and we called it the Thursday Food Co-op. Each week we'd take grocery orders from everyone. Then, on Thursday mornings, I'd get up at the crack of dawn with Henry, who ran the food co-op in town and had a truck. We'd drive to the produce market that served all the restaurants and groceries in downtown Providence and pack the truck with dozens of crates of tomatoes and lettuce (never iceberg) and whatever was in season. This was heaven! It required a crazy amount of coordination, especially when it came to finding students to fill shifts dividing up oranges and artichokes, weighing peanuts, and cutting cheese into one-pound chunks. Running a food co-op was a perfect job for an organizer: people would stop me on campus saying, "We ran out of cashews!" or "Household 32 never picked up their order!" Food pickup days were chaotic and wonderful and communal—like bringing a little bit of Austin sensibility to the Ivy League.

I was also eager to get back into politics. One day a flyer on a campus billboard caught my eye. Students were organizing support for the global movement to end apartheid in South Africa by pressuring their schools to divest stock in companies that were doing business with the Afrikaner-led government. In my freshman class on South Africa, I had met several African students. While the professor was trying to argue for patience and calm around change in South Africa, these students were knowledgeable and vocal, and brought a deeply personal perspective to everything we were reading and discussing. There was an organizing meeting the next day, and I decided to check it out.

As is true of today's fossil fuel divestment movement, we students were viewed as 100 percent unrealistic. Our critics said it would be financially irresponsible for universities to make investment decisions based on politics, but we didn't care. The international movement against apartheid was growing, and nothing short of full divestment was acceptable. We traveled to Yale to meet with student organizers from other campuses and coordinate strategy and actions.

To raise awareness among the students and create pressure on the administration, we organized protests and held concerts. The great Gil

Scott-Heron came and played in a small chapel off campus. His and Brian Jackson's song "Johannesburg" became an anthem for the movement across the United States. "I know their strugglin' over there ain't gonna free me, but we all need to be strugglin' if we're gonna be free," he sang.

It seemed impossible to impact a movement that was oceans away, but we were gaining momentum and we knew it. I felt so passionately that later, on my graduation day, while the rest of my classmates accepted their diplomas, I volunteered to unfurl the "Free South Africa" banner from the second floor of Sayles Hall. Someone had to do it!

At the time we had no idea if the organizing would pay off, but in fact Brown became one of the first universities to divest. Several others followed suit, and now, as the history has been uncovered and written, it's fascinating to learn how important the international pressure was to overturning apartheid. The genius of Oliver Tambo, the revolutionary leader in exile, was his understanding of how effective it would be to make the imprisoned Nelson Mandela the face of the inhumanity of this horrific regime. In light of our fights with the university, I found it was incredibly meaningful to return to campus and receive an honorary degree from Brown in 2010, the year Mandela was awarded the same.

• • •

As an equal opportunity agitator, I didn't pass up any chance to make a commotion. During the summer of my junior year, the environmental movement was in its heyday, which is how I found myself signing up for the Clamshell Alliance along with my surfer boyfriend. The "clams," as they were known, were a Quaker-led group fighting against nuclear power. The big target of the moment was the planned Seabrook nuclear plant, which was being built in New Hampshire. The fight over Seabrook had been going on for a few years, and this felt like a last-ditch opportunity to raise public awareness of the danger of nuclear power and hopefully stop the construction.

Every detail of the occupation had to be planned by consensus; that was how the Quakers rolled. We would be camping overnight, so the entire group had to agree on all kinds of weighty issues, like whether to bring crunchy peanut butter or smooth. Our group had to organize the tents and gear—perfect for me, being a veteran camper. But we had also been warned to get gas masks, since folks were pretty sure that the police would teargas anyone who tried to break into the construction site.

I called my friend Vicki, who was the only person I knew with a running car, and asked, "Would you be up for a trip to the Cape?" She agreed immediately, and I went on: "There's an army navy surplus store, and I'm in the market for gas masks for the Seabrook occupation." Vicki was always game, so we drove out to Provincetown and picked up gas masks for the group at a bargain price, along with some industrial-grade wire cutters and utility gloves for taking down the fence at the nuclear site. I've always wondered what the army navy store manager thought of these two college students buying equipment for what could have been a bank robbery.

Soon we resolved all lingering matters and were off. I left a sign on the door of the campus coffeehouse I was managing: "Gone to Seabrook!" We made the two-hour journey in beat-up old cars, armed with tents, snacks, and homemade signs that said *Split wood, not atoms!*, *Fishing, not fission!*, and *No nukes!* (It was the '70s, after all.) Folks were coming from all over the Northeast, as part of the larger movement—the Ocean State Alliance, the Granite State Alliance—and meeting near the Seabrook construction site.

It was gray and rainy when we arrived, and the land around the site was a wet mess as far as the eye could see—which, it turned out, wasn't very far through the small window on my gas mask.

The odds against us were ridiculous. Although there were hundreds of us, we were taking on the nuclear power industry and the state police. Still, it felt satisfying. There were plenty of organizing ventures I'd participated in, where, if we ever actually stopped and thought about our chances of success, we never would have done it. Seabrook definitely fell into that category.

We made camp, then trudged through the mud, making our way to the chain-link fence. As a Quaker group, we practiced nonviolence, but that did not apply to property. The people armed with wire cutters made their way to the front. There was a loud *snip*, and we let out a cheer.

We had just begun to tear down portions of the fence when suddenly the state police were on us. They ripped the gas mask off my head and confiscated it—they must have figured that was simpler than teargassing the hundreds of protesters. I was outraged—I bought that gas mask fair and square!

We had hoped for arrests—unlike the days of the janitors' strike, I was no longer afraid to go to jail—but the police refused to take us into custody given the limited accommodations of the Seabrook city lockup. Since we weren't going to get arrested, and we'd been routed away from the nuclear site, it was time to come up with Plan B.

Before everyone scattered and went our separate ways, we decided we couldn't let our protest signs or our enthusiasm go to waste. We stopped in Concord, New Hampshire, and held a makeshift march outside the capitol. We were proud to have taken a stand against the plant, and it was gratifying to be part of the movement to resist nuclear power. As one of our protest signs said, "Better active now than radioactive tomorrow!"

Seabrook wound up being one of my less successful ventures. The plant was up and running by 1990 and is to this day one of the biggest nuclear plants in New England. I knew taking on an entire industry with my fellow "clams" wasn't going to change the course of history, but we had set out to make a statement, and that's just what we had done. It felt so much more rewarding to go out and do something about environmental policy instead of just talking about it in class.

• • •

As college was winding down, I began talking to my co-conspirators at Brown about what to do next. We were on our way to massive social change, I just knew it. We had developed our organizing skills, and now we would be set loose in the world. But to my total disbelief, most of the folks I had been in the trenches with were actually going straight! They were heading to law school, becoming psychiatrists like their parents, or going to New York to work in publishing. What about the revolution we were building? What about all the issues we had fought for and were committed to?

Right around this time I read *Living My Life*, the autobiography of the 1930s radical Emma Goldman. Goldman would travel the country, lecturing on college campuses and urging students to recognize their privilege. In no uncertain terms, she would tell them that they would not be where they were without the blood and sweat of working people who had sacrificed for them. Reading her words, I felt she was talking right to me: I was in college because my grandfather, who had owned an Iowa seed company, had put aside the money for my tuition, and I wanted to pay back the opportunity I'd been given.

I had no idea how I'd make a living, but by now I'd seen enough people fighting for social good that I knew it was the life for me. Applying to law school like my dad was not in the cards; sitting in more classrooms was near the bottom of the list of ways I wanted to spend my time. I decided that my path would be to get an organizing job with a union. I had no idea how tough that would be and soon learned that organizing jobs were few and far between. Most labor organizers had come up through the ranks of their unions, so it was hard for outsiders to break in.

Part of the challenge was (and still is) that no one was traveling to college campuses looking for gregarious young activists to hire. Recruiters had come to Brown from every law firm and graduate school, and even from Wall Street. But no one had showed up to enlist organizers. For most of my classmates, organizing was a passing phase—a part of college life they were ready to leave behind as they moved on to adulthood. In a way it was understandable that so many of my fellow students were taking what I saw as the easy route. I couldn't blame them. Being a troublemaker wasn't exactly a career, and nobody's folks paid for four years at Brown University to have their child choose that path. There were certainly exceptions: Tom Israel and Rich Pepper, for instance, joined the labor movement and continue as organizers to this day. Like them, I wasn't ready to give up. With help from my dad, I sent letter after letter to unions. They began, "I am interested in any openings you have for union organizers, anywhere in the country. I can start immediately and I speak Spanish."

As I watched my friends pack up and move to new places for new jobs or, more often, move back to where they came from, I felt the familiar pangs of being an outsider who just couldn't take the conventional route. I was restless and eager for my next adventure. Brown had actually prepared me for the career I wanted: I may have majored in history, but I minored in agitating. I learned something from each thing I did—organizing with the janitors, supporting the librarians, protesting in Seabrook, even running the campus coffeehouse and food co-op. My time in college taught me a lesson I have carried through my life: Don't sit around and wait for the perfect opportunity to come along—find something and *make* it an opportunity.

CHAPTER 4

It's Not the Work, It's Who You Work With

I met Kirk Adams on Memorial Day in 1981 when he walked into the United Labor Union offices at 628 Baronne Street in downtown New Orleans. The first thing I noticed was his outfit: neatly creased khaki pants, button-down shirt, lace-up brown shoes. He reminded me of a Jesuit missionary. (I didn't know it then, but he *had* been an altar boy and brought with him the best parts of the social justice Catholic tradition.) I took one look at him and thought, *Great-looking guy, nice smile. He'll last a week.* Kirk remembers that I had on a leotard top, a jeans skirt, and flats, which had all been bought at the secondhand clothing store, my go-to in those days. The way he tells it, he fell in love at first sight.

I'd been at the ULU for about a year by then. It was my second union organizing job. The first didn't work out quite the way I'd hoped; the union had been less than enthusiastic about a young woman who came in questioning everything. The ULU, on the other hand, was a scrappy upstart dedicated to organizing low-wage workers for better pay and working conditions. In New Orleans that meant hotel workers. By the time Kirk showed up, I'd seen many would-be organizers come through town, but few stuck it out. I was in charge of newcomers, so I gave him a list of hotel workers to visit and put him on a bus to the Desire housing projects. He not only came back—he was hugely successful in getting folks to think about starting a union, after they figured out he wasn't a cop or selling insurance.

Kirk came to us from Massachusetts, where he'd worked on a campaign to unionize home health aides in Boston, primarily women who took care of the elderly and disabled for less than minimum wage. It turned out he was a great listener with enormous empathy. He related well to the people we were organizing, who sensed his sincerity and commitment. That was no coincidence: Kirk's mom had worked the midnight shift at the post office, and his father was a milkman. Kirk knew what it was like for working-class families because he had come from one himself.

As a gritty little organizing team, we were constantly putting up traveling staff and anyone we could convince to join our merry band. That's how Kirk ended up staying at my house when he first arrived in town. He didn't know anyone, so I said he could sleep on my living-room couch until he found a place.

By then I was subletting an apartment in Mid-City from a wild artist who made life-size stuffed puppets. They were scattered all over the apartment, along with about seventy house plants that, in exchange for cheap rent, I was supposed to keep alive.

I learned a few things about Kirk during those first weeks. He would happily eat cereal three meals a day, and sometimes did. He used shoe trees, which my sister, Ellen, always found suspect. And he had no bad habits, except for betting on the occasional basketball game with his brother Jeff, a bar owner in western Massachusetts. In short, Kirk was the most respectable guy I'd met in years, but he fit right in with the rest of us and never blinked at the crazy life we were living. And underneath that button-down shirt, he was a troublemaker at heart.

If union organizing is a foreign concept to you, here's a quick 101: Unions are one of the main ways workers can fight for good wages and benefits. Employers have a whole lot of power on their side, and the best way for workers to bargain with them is if they all stand together. And by the way, having strong unions doesn't just make things better for union members: if you enjoy affordable health care, an eight-hour workday, and weekends, thank the labor movement in America.

To win a union campaign, two things usually have to happen. First, employees show their interest by signing a union card or petition, which means they want to unionize. Then, often, a government-run secret-ballot election is held to see if their coworkers feel the same way, with a representative of the federal National Labor Relations Board coming out to monitor the vote. If a majority of workers vote for the union, the employer has to bargain with the employees in order to reach a labor contract, spelling out wages, hours, and working conditions.

That's union organizing in theory. In practice it's an uphill battle and frequently risky for the workers who are willing to stick out their necks to fight for a decent wage. During the process, employees are often harassed or fired, or they quit due to the pressure. It can be incredibly hard to win a union election, and even harder to get someone's job back when he or she is illegally terminated. It might take years for an employee to win his or her case, by which time the union campaign is usually long over. That's especially true for workers earning the minimum wage.

When I was starting out, union organizing wasn't much different from the movie *Norma Rae*. In the climactic scene, Sally Field as the title character climbs up on a table in the garment shop where she works, holding a handmade sign with the word UNION scrawled in Magic Marker, while, one by one, her coworkers shut down their machines in a show of solidarity. While I never witnessed anything quite that dramatic, I worked with countless women leaders who were every bit as gutsy.

As organizers, our job was to go to workplaces—from hotels to hospitals—and talk with folks about forming a union. As you might expect, employers don't exactly roll out the red carpet when they see an organizer coming, so we wound up spending most of our time waiting around to talk to employees when they got off work.

At my first job I hung around outside a garment factory in Texas and made conversation with the primarily Latina workers either on lunch break or after the workday ended. It's crazy now to think of grown women, most of them supporting kids and sometimes their own parents as well, talking to me about starting a union. What did an Anglo kid fresh out of college know about the world? It was as humbling as it was eye-opening. Many of these women had already risked so much to come to the United States. They knew they were not being treated fairly on the job, and they could write volumes about their experiences with sexual harassment. Whatever apprehension they felt about talking to me was outweighed by their desire to make something better for themselves and, more important, for their kids. They didn't want their daughters to end up sewing jeans for $3.35 an hour.

Back when Mom was starting to get into politics, she often reminded me, "People don't do things for *your* reasons—they do things for *their* reasons." What I learned in that first year, sitting in trailers in rural Texas or at the local church or coffee shop, is that the women I met would do just about anything to improve their lives, including talking to me about banding together with their fellow workers.

On my first day at the ULU, I was hanging around outside the Warwick Hotel in downtown New Orleans when I spotted a young woman dressed in a housekeeping uniform. She looked determined, like her shift had just ended and she was out of there—just the kind of person I was hoping to talk to. As she headed toward the bus stop, I intercepted her and introduced myself. "I've heard that the wages and working conditions at the Warwick are pretty tough, and I wanted to see if we can do something about it," I said. Glancing over her shoulder to make sure no one from the hotel was watching, she asked for my phone number. "I'll call you later," she promised, running for her bus.

In my short career as an organizer, I'd had plenty of similar conversations that never actually resulted in the promised call. So I was surprised when the phone rang later that day, and it was the young woman. She told me that working in the hotel was a horror. Hotels were notorious for putting white male employees in the cushy "front of the house" jobs, staffing the front desk or working as a bellman, where they got tips. Like most African American women in the service industry, she was relegated to housekeeping, working long hours for terrible pay. When Mardi Gras or the Sugar Bowl was on, rooms were full and she had to pull double shifts. But in the slow season she didn't work enough to make ends meet. There were no guarantees of a weekly paycheck, and when she did work, she was cleaning fourteen rooms a day.

After that initial call, we started getting together after work. She said she had friends who wanted to talk too. Soon we were meeting with other housekeepers, busboys, janitors, and cooks from the hotel—all of whom were working for low pay with no hope of advancement. They weren't naïve; they knew just talking to us could cost them their jobs, but that was a chance they were willing to take. Sure enough, management started firing and harassing people right and left. I quickly realized the hotel owners were not going to make it easy for their employees to improve their lot—and the workers realized it too. One day a cook named Eugene had finally had enough. He decided to go out with a bang, literally. He paraded through the well-attired lunchtime crowd at the Warwick, pounding on a gumbo pot and yelling, "We don't even have a pot to piss in!"

One of the many wise workers I met was Charles Husband, a maintenance employee at the Warwick and a natural philosopher. The young guys at work looked up to him, and though he knew our odds of successfully forming a union were almost nonexistent, he believed that standing up for himself and his coworkers was worth taking the chance. It was from listening to Charles that I learned a fundamental truth about organizing: despite the terrible wages and working conditions, what mattered most to the workers was gaining respect from their boss. And if they lost their job in the process, as Charles would say, "I was looking for a job when I got this one." In other words, there was always going to be more work, but nothing was going to change unless someone was willing to stand up and fight back.

I had never worked so hard in my life, yet I had it easy compared to the women pulling a double shift cleaning hotel rooms. I wouldn't trade those days for anything—working seven days a week, often from early in the morning until late at night. There was no such thing as a time clock or a regular schedule; we followed the schedules of the service workers. I witnessed firsthand the enormous challenges they faced both at work and in their personal lives. The women in particular weren't just figuring out how to make it until payday. They were the ones tasked with finding someone to take their kids when they got called in at the last minute or looking for a ride to get their mom to church on Sunday. Their jobs didn't end when they punched out; they just changed venues.

For all the time and effort we put in, we were hardly what you would call successful. The union was running on a shoestring, as were we. We knew all the best deals in town—from $1.25 beans and rice at the original

Buster's on Burgundy Street in the French Quarter to the oyster-dressing special at Eddie's on Law Street in Gentilly to the fact that you could get any beer for $1.00 at the Saturn Bar in the Ninth Ward, with the best neon sign in town. George Porter from the original Meters played every Thursday night at Tyler's on Magazine Street. My coworker and roommate, Nancy Cohen, waited tables there, which meant she could get us in for free. Everyone had a side hustle and a way to get free tickets or free food. My fellow organizer Jon Barton figured out that if you kept the "all you can eat" salad plate from Wendy's, you could just keep coming back day after day. If nothing else, we were a resourceful bunch.

In between organizing twelve hours a day, our team did whatever we could think of to keep the union afloat. We'd get the hotel workers to run fish suppers on Fridays. We took orders; set up an assembly-line frying station; packed bags with donated Hostess Twinkies, some potato salad, and fried fish; then drove all over town delivering them. This was where Kirk put us all to shame. If a group turned away their lunches because we showed up an hour late, he wasn't about to let them go to waste; he'd hock them at a construction site on the way back. "Kirk, what happened to the last order? They called and said not to bother!" we'd ask. "Don't worry about it, I found another taker," he'd answer, and drop the money on the table. He could out-work and out-hustle anybody.

We ate, slept, and breathed the union. We fundraised on street corners all around New Orleans—it was really more like organized begging—and canvassed door to door, which was more respectable but even more uncomfortable. (Nothing is quite so humiliating as asking for money and having the door slammed in your face.) We even made our own advertising flyer for downtown business; we'd sell ads on the flyer and pay kids to pass them out on street corners. I learned quickly that I would never starve, though some days we came a little too close for comfort.

We all found ourselves doing things we might not have pictured. One of my favorite Kirk stories was the time he was standing on a street corner at Claiborne and Carrollton Avenues in New Orleans, looking so clean-cut, shaking a can to raise money for the union. A guy drove up and rolled down his window at the intersection: it was one of Kirk's classmates from Wesleyan University. Kirk said hi and explained to his surprised classmate what he was doing. At least the guy gave him a dollar—our goal was "No contribution that clinked." It was a little embarrassing for Kirk, but he took it in stride. Three months later Kirk went back to Boston to help out on a home care organizing campaign for the union. They too were trying to make ends meet, and he was shaking a can on Massachusetts Avenue when the same guy pulled up again. Kirk explained sheepishly that he was an expert at can shaking, so he had gone national.

Somewhere along the way Kirk and I went from roommates to friends and ended up dating—although he never technically asked me out on a date. He recalls that a seminal moment in our relationship was when he got arrested on a Friday night for driving without a license, without insurance, and without an inspection sticker. These were details he hadn't taken care of, probably because the moment he got to New Orleans we had put him to work knocking on doors. He was cooling his heels in the general lockup, otherwise known as the drunk tank, at the New Orleans City jail and facing a very long weekend. I called around and we found a judge to bail him out. Kirk says that when I arrived, it was like the line in The Band's song "Up on Cripple Creek": "a drunkard's dream if I ever did see one."

• • •

By the spring of 1982, when it was obvious that we were serious, I brought Kirk home to spend Easter with my family and friends in Austin. That meant he had to:

1. Experience the intensity of a Richards holiday.
2. Wear bunny ears like everyone else.
3. Be cross-examined not only by my mother, which was hard enough, but also by Jane Hickie, Mom's trusted friend and first lieutenant. (Ultimately Jane announced, "He's a keeper.")

After Kirk passed the test in Texas, it was my turn to meet his family in Massachusetts. We went up that summer to see his dad and brothers at his sister's house in Scituate. Kirk had lost his mom several years earlier from a stroke; it is the heartbreak of my life that I never met Marion

Adams. The black-and-white photos show a woman with gorgeous cheekbones, just like Kirk. She was usually holding a cigarette in a glamorous '50's movie star kind of way and drinking—she apparently loved her whiskey. She was a working-class mother of four who had enormous compassion for others. With pride in his voice, Kirk described his mother as an early feminist. At the post office where she worked, and at church on Sundays, she saw that women were getting a raw deal. She used to open their home to young, unmarried pregnant women who came to her and needed a place to stay until they gave birth. His father, Bill, was a shy guy who worked as a milkman and always held down at least two jobs all his life. I credit him with Kirk's unmatched work ethic. It was watching his father toiling for decades to support his family that drew Kirk to the labor movement.

With the parents often pulling double shifts, everyone in the Adams family had to fend for themselves. Kirk's dad cooked at least as much as his mom did. Every weeknight had its own routine—who had time to think up something new? Monday night was meatloaf, Tuesday was macaroni and cheese, and Friday was "tuna wiggle." This was before Vatican II, when Catholics couldn't eat meat on Fridays. Food and cooking were such a big deal in my house growing up that I could hardly imagine eating the same thing each week. That was just one early sign of the culture clash between a Texas Unitarian liberal upbringing and that of a shanty Irish Catholic from western Massachusetts.

There were no hoops to jump through for me, no Hercules-type trials, and certainly no bunny ears with the Adamses. It's hard to find many similarities between our two families, but one thing was true: both supported our work unconditionally, even if they were slightly mystified by the lives we'd chosen for ourselves. As Kirk's dad would say to him, shaking his head: "I can't believe they pay you to make trouble."

• • •

After two years in New Orleans—one year for Kirk—we were ready for a change. For all of our enthusiasm, our team's organizing efforts weren't succeeding. We had taken on the second largest industry in the city, tourism, with a popgun. To organize the thousands of hotel workers in the city effectively, we would have needed at least two dozen organizers and a better way to finance the operation than selling fish suppers. Even the established labor movement, representing the waterfront and the building trades, saw us as a bunch of leftist upstarts—which, for all intents and purposes, we were.

One day Gerry Shea, a big shot with the Service Employees Union, came through New Orleans. They were going to try to organize a union for workers at the largest for-profit nursing home chain in the country. The chain, Beverly Enterprises, had made a fortune buying up nursing homes and cutting wages to the bone—and one of the crown jewels was Texas. Gerry hired both of us. So not long afterward Kirk and I loaded up the Lynx, tying our futon on top. Everything we owned was in that car. (Well, almost everything. We had to leave the toaster oven behind; we just didn't have the space.) With that, we headed to Houston.

From the moment we started our new jobs we were on the road, traveling all over East Texas. It seemed like every small town had a Beverly nursing home, and we set out to unionize them all. The women we worked with were doing the Lord's work taking care of the elderly, but making less than $4.00 an hour, which was only slightly more than minimum wage.

I soon learned that there were three kinds of nursing home workers: those who had been working there for years, who were dedicated, patient, and loved by the residents and their coworkers; those who stayed on until they could get a job somewhere else, where they didn't have to handle the incredibly tough working conditions and frequent abuse by family members and residents; and those who quickly figured out there was no way they were working there. One of the employee leaders we met described this last group as women who on their first day said they were going on break to buy cigarettes and never came back.

Most of the places we organized were in deep East Texas, which was as segregated a world as I'd ever seen. After a few months Kirk and I migrated to Tyler, where there were many more women to organize. We moved into a small redbrick house where we could live in the back and hold union meetings in the front. The house was on Houston Street, in the middle of town, pretty much right on the racial divide between north and south Tyler. The day we arrived, our neighbors came over to bring us some fresh-cut Tyler roses in a mason jar.

"We're so glad you moved in," they said, "because before you, there was a Negro family living here." My jaw dropped.

Much to their dismay, our house became the central gathering spot for African American nursing home workers. Women pulled up in their run-down Chevrolets and parked in the front yard, before and after their shifts. We had our union meetings in the living room, and often they'd bring a cold one in a brown paper bag. Tyler was a dry county, so you couldn't buy liquor unless you drove thirty miles to the county line at Big Sandy. As a result folks drank more in Tyler than anywhere I've ever lived; as long as you were driving a half hour, you sure as hell weren't going to come back with just a six-pack.

Kirk and I made fast friends with a bunch of progressive lawyers, including Larry Daves, Rick Levy, and Martha Owen, who ran a law firm that kept busy suing all kinds of folks for employment discrimination, wage and hour violations, and any other social justice issue. They often helped us out on the many labor issues we were dealing with at Beverly. And every year a new crop of law clerks would arrive in Tyler from around the country to work for Judge William Wayne Justice, famous for championing the rights of low-income folks, minorities, and people who had no one to stand up for them.

There wasn't much to do in Tyler, so we made our own fun. Social outings usually revolved around food and beer and music. This is where I reinvented the Richards family tradition of "all-come" dinner parties—everyone was invited. It was also in Tyler that I began my lifelong love affair with pie—a food group that the local café, Cox's Grill, had perfected. There was coconut cream, cherry, chess pie—you name it. You could even have pie for breakfast.

Most important, Tyler was where I learned that, even in the midst of soul-crushing poverty, people could celebrate and love life. East Texas was a tough place to live—especially if you were African American, and a woman to boot. When we won a union election, it was time to rent a room at the Ramada Inn, get somebody's son to DJ, and have at it. Those years were full of Luther Vandross's "Bad Boy / Having a Party" and Lionel Richie's "All Night Long." Even though the days were hard, some of our very best times were celebrating with the amazing women employee leaders of East Texas.

The years we spent in East Texas reminded me of a question the longtime farmworker organizer Marshall Ganz had posed years earlier: *What's the definition of a leader?* His answer: *Someone who has followers.* The women we organized with didn't have money or political influence, but everybody looked up to them. Jeril was raising her daughters on her minimum-wage salary from the nursing home in Bryan, and her apartment in the projects was the center of the community. Vicki in Texas City was constantly taking second jobs so she could finally buy a home of her own. She never missed a day's work, and she was committed to her patients. And Georgia Landry in Beaumont was everyone's grandmother, working the graveyard shift and encouraging the younger new employees to stick with the job. These were women who had earned the respect of their coworkers and, more often than not, the unspoken admiration of their employers.

The organizing campaigns were ugly, and they were tough. Folks were threatened and fired, but they persevered. We held elections in town after town and had the best winning streak in the union. Our leaders took photos with Instamatic cameras, and we produced "Why I'm Voting YES" posters that they passed around to their coworkers. After we won the election, Kirk worked with the employees to bargain for the first time on their union contract.

Beverly Enterprises was as cheap as dirt, and the contracts provided barely more than what the workers were earning before we started. But the women wanted respect and recognition for the work they did, and organizing a union accomplished that. Their boss had to sit across the table from them as equals and talk about wages and working conditions, and that had never happened before.

• • •

After we'd been in Texas for a while, it was time to fish or cut bait, so Kirk and I decided to get married at my mom's house in Austin. I don't remember any grand proposal or sweeping gesture; we were in love and I was impatient, and it seemed like a good thing to do. I was twenty-seven, Kirk was thirty-four, and we were ready. For us, getting married was more of a continuation of our organizing life, with the added commitment that it seemed we would now be doing this forever. There wasn't much time to plan a wedding in between nursing home elections, so we just picked a weekend in June. We obviously didn't think ahead or we never would have done *anything* in June in Texas—it was hot as blazes! But it was a great chance to bring together our organizing buddies, my Texas family, and Kirk's relatives from Massachusetts. In those days we didn't need much to have a celebration—just a date, a band, good friends, and good food.

Mom's house wasn't big, but she put up a tent in the side yard and threw a party. The wedding was hot and raucous; the highlight was a rousing chorus of the labor anthem "Solidarity Forever," led by the civil rights lawyer Jim Youngdahl. By that point Mom was the state treasurer, so the gathering also included politicians and longtime family friends such as Molly Ivins and Congressman Lloyd Doggett—a progressive lovefest in more ways than one! I wore a white lace dress Mom and I bought off the

rack, which later became a dress-up costume for my kids, and some crazy beaded headpiece my mother had bought. Kirk and I wrote our own vows, my sister was my maid of honor, and Kirk's best friend, Dave Keith, was his best man. Mom had told us that if we wanted a band, we'd have to find one ourselves, so we booked Beto y los Fairlanes and shared our first dance to "String of Pearls." Everyone hit the dance floor after that, and we carried on until the neighbors shut us down. It was only years later that my father told me he had been hurt when I didn't ask him to give me away. *Give me away?* I had been on my own for years, and, anyway, no one was giving me to anyone! It was not a traditional wedding in anyone's book. Looking back now, I realize that the misunderstanding with my father happened because of a personality trait he and I share: we both believe that our way of thinking is always the only way, and we are often completely oblivious when we've upset someone as a result.

As soon as the "I dos" were finished, we raced to Beaumont in Southeast Texas to prepare for the biggest nursing home strike in Texas history. A few years earlier the women at the Schlesinger nursing home had organized and bargained a union contract with the best wages in the state. But when it came time to renegotiate, the employer decided to try to break the union and force the women to go out on strike or work for lower wages. It was against the law, but employers got away with it all the time. We decided there was no option but to strike, and Beaumont was an ideal place. The area was home to industrial unions, since it was in the heart of the petrochemical plants. It was as union-friendly a town as you could find in Texas, and these women's cause was just.

The women were incredible. Jim Youngdahl came down from Little Rock to do the lawyering; he was brilliant and irrepressible. Jim was a large man, and he loved the ladies. One night after a particularly hard day on the picket line, we all wound up at a bar in Beaumont. Using very bad judgment, we let Jim and the women strikers participate in the bar's tug-of-war, which consisted of Jim on one side and a dozen large women on the other. Despite Jim's girth, the women won. The whole ordeal ended with him crashing to the floor.

We threw everything we had at Schlesinger, but they wouldn't budge. Our last-gasp effort was to create as much bad publicity for the employer and public uproar as possible. So we printed a gigantic banner and signs that shouted "Justice Comes to Beaumont!" We organized a march and even persuaded Congressman John Lewis of Georgia to come and lead us. It was at least 100 degrees that day, but he marched the entire way, and I have loved him ever since.

Sadly, in the words of my friend the late Ray Abernathy, who masterminded the campaign, "Justice may have come to Beaumont, but it left the next day." We lost the strike, and it was a bitter ending. The company had hired replacement workers in order to keep the nursing home open. Our women stayed out on strike, but once employers break the union, they get to decide who they're going to bring back. Some women got their jobs back, but others did not. Even if we had won, the women we were organizing were never going to get rich or even make it into the middle class. At its core the campaign had been a fight for dignity—a way for the women to finally have their boss treat them as an equal, to sit down and bargain with them. Now they were back at square one. I learned a very tough lesson that my dad had admonished me about before: Never go out on strike unless you have a plan to get back in.

There's no way to minimize the responsibility Kirk and I felt. It was a deeply personal loss for so many people who had been counting on us, and for everyone who had worked on the campaign. In a low moment I wondered whether it would have been better not to have fought at all. But while I didn't know what the outcome would be when we started, I knew for certain what it would have been if we'd never even tried. That is as true today as it was in Beaumont.

After we had run union elections in pretty much every Beverly nursing home in East Texas, the union approached us about moving to Los Angeles, where they needed more organizing talent. By this point we were used to moving every couple of years, so we accepted the job and I flew out to look for a place to live. Someone had recommended I check out Venice Beach. After segregated, Bible-thumping Tyler, Venice was another world. I had to call Kirk. "You aren't going to believe it. The beach is integrated, and there are women in bikinis Rollerblading down the boardwalk!"

We packed up the car and moved to L.A., where we would run the most important union organizing campaigns of our careers. Kirk was hired to organize seventy-two thousand home care workers, something no one had ever done before. And I became part of the "Justice for Janitors" campaign, with the goal of unionizing the immigrant workers who cleaned the high-rise office buildings downtown.

Here my Spanish came in handy. Eric Porras, originally from Guatemala, and Jono Shaffer, from California, were my partners in the campaign. Eric was a born leader and could talk to anyone. He had worked in and around the janitorial industry and so knew plenty of folks and, it seemed, pretty much everyone from Guatemala. He was tall, dark-haired, and good-looking and could hold a crowd. Jono had been organizing public workers but was looking for something with more energy. He matched Eric in height and his Spanish was perfect—they were an amazing duo. We soon added Rocio Saenz, a young immigrant from Mexico, and Ana Navarette, from El Salvador. Ana called me *la chingona*, which means "big boss"—I took it as a term of endearment. She was short but mighty, and she was as fierce an organizer on the doors as anyone I've ever met. Rafael Estrada, or Rafa, as we called him, was the only mild-mannered one of the bunch, a total sweetheart.

The idea of the campaign was pretty simple: we needed to get the attention of the downtown building owners and shame them into granting better wages and working conditions to the cleaning crews. There were dozens of nonunion buildings housing the most prestigious banks and law firms in town, from O'Melveny and Myers to Citibank.

The janitors worked at night, usually long after all the office workers had gone home, so we would meet them outside at the food trucks at ten p.m., on their dinner break. We would flyer the building lobbies during the day with pictures of the janitors, who cleaned the buildings for minimum wage and no benefits, and their families. The mad genius of it all, Stephen Lerner, was the organizing director for the Service Employees International Union, based in Washington. He was constantly thinking up new ways for us to get in the news and increase the pressure on the building owners. We marched through banks and law firms during the lunch hour, carrying mops and brooms and banging on enormous drums. We used every possible stunt to get in the news, which isn't easy in Los Angeles. If it wasn't a ten-car pileup on the Santa Monica Freeway, you almost never made the TV. Fortunately Spanish-language television loved our stunts. For Thanksgiving we would dress someone in a turkey costume and present "Turkey of the Year" awards to the worst building owners.

At this point our first daughter, Lily, had arrived, so she was raised from the start on the picket line. I'd show up at night at the buildings with her in a backpack; she was at more union meetings before she could walk than most people in their entire lives. While Kirk and I ran our organizing campaigns, Jono and the rest of the team became her surrogate parents, and she would roll around the office in a baby walker.

It was clear from the beginning that we weren't in Tyler anymore. The Latino community in Los Angeles was powerful: there were Latino elected officials, activist priests, and respected community leaders. We were able to get all kinds of political support. There were janitor leaders in every downtown building, the face of the tale of two cities: a booming economy that was supported by janitors making minimum wage.

We decided to escalate, and after one of many building sit-ins, with more than one hundred people occupying the lobby of the O'Melveny and Myers Building, three of us—me, Jono, and a baby-faced Episcopalian priest named Phillip Lance, who was carrying a large crucifix—refused to leave. We had planned this, since we couldn't have any undocumented janitors getting arrested. We had put together such a mighty campaign; now we just had to tip it over the edge. I was more than ready to go. It was my first arrest, for disturbing the peace. After sitting in the city lockup for a few hours, we were released, but I never forgot the humiliation of being fingerprinted and having a mug shot. Nothing about jail is glamorous.

We succeeded in letting the building owners know we were serious—and more important, we raised the profile of the campaign and highlighted the injustice of the wages and conditions of the downtown janitors. There were many more chapters and arrests to come, but ultimately the Justice for Janitors campaign in Los Angeles was a success in getting union contracts downtown and eventually all across the city.

Seeing the chances that our leaders took—being public and bold, putting a human face on the inequity in the city, potentially losing their jobs (which many did) to fight for respect and decent conditions—still inspires me today.

Whenever I asked the janitors about the risks involved, they would tell me what they had already sacrificed to come to the United States. Most were from Central America and had traveled by land hundreds of miles, paying *coyotes* to smuggle them across the border. Many had left their parents, children, or spouses behind. Despite the shamefully low pay, many counted on their minimum-wage jobs to send money back home. More than any folks I've ever worked with, they understood that life is what you make of it, and they were determined to take every opportunity they had to make something better. It was a family endeavor for all of us; there were kids at every march and protest, wearing union T-shirts, carrying balloons, and holding signs.

As for my partners from that campaign, Jono Shaffer is still at it today, organizing service workers in California. Rocio Saenz went on to run one of the largest local unions in the country, in Boston, and later became a national officer for SEIU. And I never work in a building without knowing the janitors. In most cities they are truly the invisible ones, who work long after most people have gone home and do work that no one else would do. I always remember to thank them and make sure they are earning a living wage.

• • •

Kirk and I were on a high. Up until then we had been organizing small, one-off campaigns in which we weren't actually shifting the power or changing the situation for the workers. Now we were fundamentally changing the landscape, fighting for real equity instead of just fighting for a nickel an hour. Lily was two years old, we were settled into our neighborhood in Venice, living right near the beach, and there was organizing as far as the eye could see, from hospital workers and janitors to home health aides. Our whole life was the fight for respect and justice for the most overworked and underpaid folks in the city. We loved it.

But life happens when you're making other plans. My mother called to say she needed us back in Texas, so we were soon packing up our California memories to head back home.

Kirk and me as union organizers, saying goodbye to janitors, health care workers, and friends in Los Angeles as we moved back to Austin.

CHAPTER 5

Going for Broke in Texas

"We want Ann!" came a chant from the crowd in Atlanta, followed by raucous applause. I looked out from the gigantic, ocean-liner-size stage where I sat alongside my brothers, Clark and Dan, and my sister, Ellen, taking in the scene. It was classic convention-style pandemonium: folks were throwing beach balls, wearing crazy hats, and blowing horns. In a few days Michael Dukakis would accept the 1988 Democratic nomination for president from this very stage. But right now the entire convention was focused on the woman of the hour, my mom.

True to form, from the moment she had gotten the call inviting her to deliver the keynote speech at the Democratic National Convention, Mom had approached the task with military precision, right down to the eye-catching blue dress she knew would look just right on television. We had spent the days before holed up in her hotel room, as she worked on her speech. It was both thrilling and nerve-racking. Everyone on her team was suggesting lines, making edits, crossing things out, and making notes in the margins. Suzanne Coleman, who had written for Mom since she first got into politics, was the primary writer. Suzanne had the driest wit imaginable, knew Mom's voice, and could tell a story and think up a great line better than anyone. Jane Hickie was with us, along with Mary Beth Rogers, Mom's political guru. Kirk and I were offering suggestions and advice, and Lily Tomlin and Jane Wagner were faxing in lines from Los Angeles. We went through draft after draft and, as always, finished at the last possible second.

Finally the moment had arrived, and I found myself onstage at the

Omni Coliseum, sitting on the edge of my seat and waiting for Mom to appear. I looked to my left and caught sight of Kirk and Lily in the audience. Lily was sitting on Kirk's lap, and I thought how wonderful it was that Mom's granddaughter was getting to see this in person.

This was not Mom's first time on the national stage, but it was the most significant. Four years earlier, at the Democratic National Convention in San Francisco, she had given a speech seconding Walter Mondale's nomination for president. But her speech was totally unremarkable and landed like a lead balloon. Sitting through that first convention speech, she and I learned two important lessons: first, no one in the convention hall pays attention to what's happening onstage in the midst of all the chaos and noise in the audience; second, you can't hope to speak to the conventioneers—your audience is the millions of people watching back home.

As a result Mom had just one request of the convention organizers in Atlanta: to bring the house lights down for her speech. The organizers were worried that the networks would balk at this, but Mom prevailed. Sure enough, when the lights dimmed, a hush fell over the crowd. People settled in to listen, just like she knew they would.

I heard Mom coming before I saw her. She entered to the song "Deep in the Heart of Texas." The second she came around the corner, thousands of conventioneers stood and cheered, holding signs reading "Democrats ♥ Ann Richards." Kirk had his buddies in the labor movement print them and pass them out—it was such a boost. And then, of course, she gave the speech of a lifetime. "Twelve years ago, Barbara Jordan, another Texas woman, made the keynote address to this convention, and two women in about 160 years is about par for the course," she began. "But if you give us a chance, we can perform. After all, Ginger Rogers did everything that Fred Astaire did. She just did it backwards and in high heels!"

This is nothing like San Francisco, I thought, and I knew that my brothers and sister were thinking the same thing. The speech was perfect, better than anyone could have hoped. Mom was landing every line with the audience, and they were captivated. Her speeches were always better in person than on paper, and this was no exception. She brought the house down when she talked about George H. W. Bush, who, after two terms as Ronald Reagan's vice president, was now the Republican candidate for president. "And for eight straight years George Bush hasn't displayed the slightest interest in anything we care about. And now that he's after a job that he can't get appointed to, he's like Columbus discovering America—he's found child care, he's found education. . . . Poor George, he can't help it—he was born with a silver foot in his mouth." The crowd roared.

We were all beaming with pride by the time Mom got to the closing section. Turning sentimental, she said, "I'm a grandmother now. And I have one nearly perfect granddaughter named Lily. And when I hold that grandbaby, I feel the continuity of life that unites us, that binds generation to generation, that ties us with each other. . . . And as I look at Lily, I know that it is within families that we learn both the need to respect individual human dignity and to work together for our common good. Within our families, within our nation, it is the same." I looked out into the audience again. Kirk, who has never been a crier, had tears in his eyes. He was bouncing Lily up and down, knowing she was too young to understand why her grandmother was up on the stage in the first place.

Someone had brought Mom's parents to their local TV station in Waco, and they streamed in live to talk with Mom after the speech. The news announcer turned to Poppy, my grandfather, and said, "Well, Mr. Willis, when you told your daughter that she could do anything she wanted to do if she just worked hard enough, did you ever dream that she would be doing something like this?" Poppy laughed and said, "Why, hell, I didn't even know there *was* a this!"

Dukakis went on to a crushing defeat, but the speech made Mom a household name. (I still run into students who study it in communications class. In fact when Lily was in college, her political science class watched it to analyze public speaking, and she had to fess up that Ann Richards was her grandmother.) Candidates asked her to help them with their campaigns. Women everywhere wrote letters, asking her to run for governor of Texas, or better yet, president of the United States. Her whole world was opening up, and nothing would ever be the same.

• • •

The '80s had brought enormous changes for Mom, and the most life-changing of these was that she had gotten sober. Drinking had been such a big part of my parents' social scene that I didn't think much of it until I was in high school. I would learn only later that when I was quite young, Mom had asked her doctor if she might have a drinking problem.

"I don't think so, Ann. Why? How much do you drink?" he asked.

"Well, I usually have two or three martinis before dinner."

"Oh, that's nothing to worry about," he reassured her. "I drink that much myself!"

I was home from college one Christmas when a friend brought her a present. As soon as Mom unwrapped it, she burst into tears. It was a light sculpture by a local artist, and it flashed in pink and white, "I'm okay, you're okay." She was definitely not okay. It was hard to see Mom so sad, and have no idea how to fix it.

In those days there was no easy way to publicly declare your addiction and go for treatment. It wasn't something people talked about, let alone did. I'm not sure who finally decided to break that unspoken code, but some of her friends consulted with a couple who specialized in interventions—a miserable process where loved ones confront the addict at a group meeting to persuade him or her to get help.

As with so many unpleasant things in life, the details of that day are hazy, except for this: it was horrible. I have never been good at keeping secrets, and it felt awful to plot this whole event behind Mom's back. As the oldest child, then in my early twenties, I was in on it, along with Dad and many of Mom's good friends. We gathered in someone's living room, though I cannot remember whose, and she arrived under some other pretense. We sat down in a circle of chairs, and Mom had to sit and listen to each of us tell how her drinking had affected us. "I was scared to get into the car with you when you were drinking," I told her, "and scared for the other kids too." That was all I could get out, but it was enough.

She heard so many hard and heartbreaking statements that day that she left for treatment in Minneapolis—she called it "drunk school"—the same afternoon. Later we spent a week with her to do family therapy. It was a sad time for everyone, especially Mom. I know how terrible it must have been and how ashamed she felt. But she took on therapy like everything else she'd ever done, full-on, and she never had another drink in her life. She later said that getting sober saved her life, but I don't think she ever forgave any of us for the way we went about it.

When Mom went away for treatment, she predicted that it would be the end of her marriage. She was right: she was sober for less than six months when Dad moved out, and though she saw it coming, she was crushed.

At the time, I was working in Texas at my first union organizing job. Mom wanted companionship more than anything else as she was beginning the slow adjustment to living on her own for the first time, so we decided I'd move in with her. Who would have thought we'd be making dinner and watching bad TV together at that point in our lives? It was an awkward transfer of roles: she was staying at home in the evenings, and I was going out with friends, after making sure she had dinner and was going to be okay for the night.

It was a temporary arrangement, and I was anxious to get on with my life. As for Mom, she eventually got used to living alone. More than that, she came to love her newfound independence. She dated Bud Shrake, the Texas sportswriter and author, for many years, but she never wanted to live with a man again. That way, she explained, they could go out and have a good time, but she didn't have to take care of anybody. Most men her age wanted someone to be their cook, nursemaid, and support system—and once Mom came into her own, she wasn't about to go back. She felt free.

When she ran for state treasurer in 1982—her first state office— Mom made a decision that while she would talk about recovery, she was not going to answer the onslaught of questions she knew were coming: *Who did you drink with? Were you ever drunk in public? Did you endanger your kids?* Because she refused to open that can of worms, her opponents used every opportunity to speculate about the extent of her addiction and what other substances she might have used along the way.

Despite the personal attacks, she was elected treasurer, becoming the first woman to hold statewide office in Texas in more than fifty years. During her two terms, she brought the job into the twenty-first century. When she started, there were drawers full of checks that hadn't been cashed. She computerized the agency, cashed the checks, and, lo and behold, actually made money for the state. To most of the men who made up the Democratic Party establishment, the job seemed like appropriate women's work: nonthreatening, out of sight, kind of like keeping track of the family budget.

In Texas, being too big for your britches is just about the worst thing you can be, and that goes double if you're a woman. There was a long list of Democratic men who had been angling for the governor's job for a while, and they would have been happy for Mom to stay where she was. Her male counterparts in the Texas Democratic Party saw her as a colorful addition to the statewide team, but they didn't think of her as their competition, and certainly not as their leader. But after her star turn at the Democratic National Convention, and eight years sober, she was starting to think seriously about taking on what was certain to be an even more grueling campaign for governor. She gave us fair warning that if she decided to run, she'd need our help.

When my phone rang a few months after the convention, I was at home in California, working, raising a toddler, and about as far removed from Texas politics as you can get. I wasn't ready for what she was about to ask.

"Cecile, I'm gonna do it," she said, cutting right to the chase.

I took a deep breath.

"The women are on fire," she continued. "But I'm going to have a tough Democratic primary. Really tough. They are going to say I'm a drug addict and hassle me about being divorced. But if I don't do it, I will always wonder, *What if?* I just can't live with that."

As independent as Mom was, she had the same human frailties that we all do. After my parents' marriage unraveled, Mom had come to lean on her kids for her emotional support. My mother was a very complicated person, and although she was enormously competent and driven, she was also unsure of herself. She was always struggling to overcome the insecurities of her upbringing, trying to prove she was just as smart as the other kids. On top of that, she was trying to succeed in a political environment that was inherently hostile to women.

For her to be as fearless and unflappable as she was in public, she needed a private place to retreat—somewhere she could be honest and open about her anxieties and fears—and that was with her family.

Now she was counting on us to be there for her during what promised to be her most daunting challenge yet, both in the Democratic primary and in the general election. Leave it to Kirk to put everything in perspective. "If your mom needs us, we have to go back home," he said. I loved him for that.

It was never a question of *if* we would go, but the decision came with regrets. Kirk and I both felt loyalty toward our teams and worried we were letting them down. At the same time, as I packed to move to Texas, I thought about how improbable and extraordinary this was—that someone who had spent so much of her life as a housewife and had only recently gotten into politics not only wanted to be governor but actually thought she could win.

Of course, it was not lost on me that men take these chances all the time. They say, "I work for an advertising firm and have never been in public office, but I'm going to run for Congress." Women, on the other hand, say, "I was thinking about applying for that job, but I haven't finished my PhD yet." Even my daughter Lily, when she was steadily working her way up the career ladder, doing grunt work on campaign after campaign, couldn't believe that her male classmates were already planning to run for office or applying to jobs they clearly weren't prepared for. It breaks my heart that young women who should have all the confidence in the world still hold themselves back.

My mother decided she wasn't going to wait until she had the perfect résumé, and she certainly wasn't going to wait until she was guaranteed success. Every political race she'd gotten into, it was because she knew that she was qualified and could do a better job than the incumbent, even if she was the only one who thought so.

• • •

Mom's campaigns always brought together family and friends in a way that resembled a Judy Garland–Mickey Rooney "Let's put on a show" performance, and the governor's race was no exception. So for Kirk, Lily, and me, our family life became consumed by the campaign.

Practically overnight, campaign headquarters became our home away from home. It was a dump, but it reminded Kirk and me of the places where we had worked before, the makeshift union halls and organizing offices. We started there first thing every morning and didn't leave until late at night. We never even unpacked all of our boxes at the house we rented in Texas, and we never set foot in the backyard.

Lily was two and a half. Our routine was to drop her off at day care the moment it opened and pick her up a minute before it closed (on a good day). Afterward we'd bring her back to the office for pizza while we spent the evening making phone calls to potential volunteers and county coordinators. These may not have been ideal circumstances for other young families, but we were in our element. It was the ultimate organizing challenge; we knew the only way we could win the election was to build a grassroots operation in every part of the state. Texas has 254 counties, and our first priority was finding a coordinator for each of them, a herculean task.

Mom was an upstart candidate, and the people who ran her campaign were a combination of family and friends, plus women and political types who were intrigued by the idea of her running. We didn't have the establishment kingmakers, but we had a lot of talent. Mom's longtime support system, including Mary Beth Rogers and Jane Hickie, were on board, along with Suzanne Coleman, who was writing speeches as fast as she could. Jack Martin was a trusted adviser throughout, and slowly but surely we built a statewide team. Her best friend, Virginia Whitten, organized meals that volunteers would leave for Mom in her fridge every week. Kirk was the de facto field director, overseeing the volunteers and staff responsible for running the campaign at the local level and getting voters to the polls on Election Day. And my brother Dan was Mom's traveling aide and "purse carrier," as she called him, though in reality he was so much more.

Lily and I became stand-ins for Mom, along with my sister. Geographically Texas is bigger than France. Campaigning in a state that size is overwhelming, even for someone as relentless as Ann Richards. Mom took to heart the words of the legendary speaker of the US House of Representatives Sam Rayburn: *If they can't meet the candidate, they want to meet the candidate's family.* The Richards clan was out in force.

The Ann Richards campaign for governor, featuring Lily, who traveled nearly as many miles as the candidate.

Our car was like a mobile campaign unit, jammed with stickers and yard signs. On many days, early in the morning, I'd throw Lily, still in her pajamas, in the backseat and we'd hit the road, stopping to change at the local Dairy Queen. Food on the road was in short supply. Out of necessity I learned the location of every Whataburger across Texas, where I could get a fish sandwich and even top it with jalapeños—that was a good day! The definition of dressing up was stopping at the local 7-Eleven to buy a new pair of panty hose in "suntan" on the way to a speech.

Because Kirk and I had lived in Tyler, I knew East Texas like the back of my hand. I drove to every county fair and barbecue. Every town I went to, I hit the local café or the courthouse to shake hands. Did you know there is an annual tamale toss in Del Rio? Oh, there is.

There was no crowd too small to hand out "Ann Richards for Governor" cards. A lot of people had voted for Mom for treasurer, but they didn't know much about her. Our goal was to defang this wild idea of electing a progressive woman and to let them know that Mom was just like them. It was exciting; retail politics was as good as it got. Getting to do the color commentary for the Jasper High School baseball game on local radio—what could beat that?

Best of all were the women I met along the way. You better believe the Cass County Democratic Women in Atlanta, Texas, had been waiting for a chance like this all their lives. Women had been behind the scenes, running Democratic campaigns across the state, for as long as anyone could remember—making the calls, dividing up the block-walk lists, organizing the fundraisers and chili suppers. Now they were doing it all for a woman, and that was a great big deal. Everywhere I went, women my mother's age and often with her hairdo would grab me by the arm, their eyes shining, and say, "I never thought I'd see the day!" Mom said that being a woman running for governor was like being a three-headed dog at the carnival: she was a novelty, so we got a crowd pretty much wherever we went.

The worst part of campaigning was dealing with the negative press, the rumors and personal attacks on Mom. When the news started off with "Today Ann Richards was accused of . . ." I'd turn off the TV. My job was to be the most enthusiastic warrior I could be, and that often required fielding questions from reporters that were based on half-truths and rumors. I've found that you have to decide what it is that makes you a good organizer, and what saps your strength and energy. For me, television news has always been the latter.

It's easy to get caught up in the press and assume everyone else is as well, but I discovered that in most towns, people were busy just living their lives. In those places we could make a big impact just by meeting people and listening to their concerns. There's no better way to refute false attacks than to have a conversation with people and tell them what you know to be the truth.

Not everyone was a fan—witness the homecoming parade at Baylor University in Waco, Mom's alma mater. My brother Dan had decked out his '57 Ford pickup with bunting on the sides and hay bales in the back. We climbed up into the truck. Lily sat on the hay, the center of it all, dressed in a darling red, white, and blue dress, and threw candy to the paradegoers. She had become a bit of a campaign mascot—whether she was riding on a float for a Cinco de Mayo parade in Laredo or handing out Ann Richards campaign materials at the annual Luling Watermelon Thump. She had learned early on to look someone in the eye and shake their hand, and people were charmed by her. But even Lily's winning personality wasn't always enough. We got a few scowls in the homecoming procession—it was conservative territory, after all, so we weren't expecting a welcoming committee. But it was too much when an older gentleman, dressed in a checkered shirt and jeans, stepped up and shot the finger at my toddler. *Welcome to hard-knuckle politics*, I thought.

The primary was our first big test. Mom's Democratic opponents were former governor Mark White and Attorney General Jim Mattox. Mattox had taken on every corporate special interest while in Congress and campaigned for his current role in a retired Hostess Twinkie bread truck with "The People's Lawyer" painted on the sides. He was the one to beat. He was constantly planting bogus stories in the media and would do anything for attention. I'd been to more than one wedding reception where he was standing in the receiving line right after the bride and groom. At one point he issued a press statement saying he had a poll that showed him in the lead, which he wasn't. The press called, asking us for a comment. Our press secretary, Monte Williams, faxed them back an article from the *National Enquirer* attesting that 62 percent of Americans believed Elvis was still alive.

The one key for any Democrat in the primary was getting the labor endorsement, because it guaranteed money, workers, and a statewide campaign organization. Mattox had been labor's go-to guy, and everyone thought he had the endorsement in the bag. But we had one card to play, and that was Mom's support from the public employees union. AFSCME leaders like Dee Simpson bucked the rest of organized labor; their union was made up primarily of women and people of color, and they were up for the fight.

The state labor convention was make-or-break time. Kirk and I went into high gear, with one goal: block Mattox from getting the endorsement. This is where our past experience running dozens of union elections helped: we knew how to count votes. We walked the convention floor along with a Texas state representative, Lena Guerrero, and an underground network of women labor leaders and, with their help, managed to keep labor from endorsing any candidate. The papers covered it as a huge win for us and a serious blow for Mattox.

Besides labor, there was one other group that swooped in to help us. The legendary Ellen Malcolm had recently started a national organization, based out of Washington, called EMILY's List, which stood for Early Money Is Like Yeast (it makes the dough rise). They knew full well that this would be an uphill race, but they sensed Mom's potential early on. Without them, I'm not sure we would have made it through the primary. They called on women around the country to contribute to Mom's campaign, and women did. They were the financial lifeblood of the early days of the campaign, and thank goodness.

Texas has an outsize law-and-order kind of culture, and this campaign was no exception. Mattox's slogan was "Texas Tough!" Both of Mom's opponents had been attorneys general, and the primary campaign became a classic pissing match over which one had been more successful at executing inmates on the state's robust death row. Both men actually ran competing ads that showed face after face of men they had executed, each one trying to outdo the other. The campaigns were so over-the-top that *Saturday Night Live* ran an unforgettable parody featuring a Texas gubernatorial candidate sitting on a pile of coffins. The obvious implication of the original ads, and an undercurrent running through the entire campaign, was that a woman wasn't tough enough to keep Texas safe.

Everything is considered fair game in politics—even if it isn't true. Mom's very public recovery from alcoholism opened the door for her opponents to accuse her of being an addict who couldn't be trusted to hold office. The fact that she was unmarried allowed for all kinds of public speculation about her sex life. As Mom would say, "They said I couldn't get a man, couldn't keep a man, or didn't go with men."

The attacks were hard on everyone, but they especially stung my sister and me. I hadn't realized how fiercely protective I was of Mom until I saw her attacked on television night after night. Whether or not I intended to, I fell into the role of her biggest defender. At times I pulled myself out of a campaign meeting, saying I'd rather be on the road at some county fair instead of in a back room making cutthroat decisions about how to respond to the latest ad against her. I was just too close to the situation.

Fortunately Kirk was more cool-headed, as was my brother Dan, who traveled with Mom on the campaign trail. Dan and Mom had always been particularly close. If I was the insufferable first child, always striving to be perfect, Dan was the easygoing, fun-loving second kid who brought joy to everyone, and to Mom in particular. He has always been a car nut, and growing up there was always a car in some state of disrepair on our front lawn. One sat for so long that Mom strung Christmas lights over it for the holiday to make her point. They both laughed over that.

Mom could be acerbic with staff, and no one took more of the heat than Dan. On those long, tough days, he had to absorb all of her fear and frustration. He was so loyal, and I was always impressed by the way he seemed to take it in stride. It wasn't until recently that he confessed he had once been pushed almost to his breaking point. It had been another exhausting day on the road, with event after event. They were sharing a hotel room in Houston—there was never enough money for everyone to have their own room—and she lit into him about something or other. Dan quit talking and quietly decided he couldn't do it anymore—he was leaving the campaign. When they woke up the next morning, before he could say anything, Mom apologized. "I'm sorry," she said. "I really need you." Dan stayed on. As devoted as he was to our mother, he had the ability to field the relentless attacks on her while keeping his own emotions in check. I don't know how he held up.

By the skin of our teeth we got through the primary. The grassroots organizing paid off, and the network of volunteers and supporters we built across the state gave us the edge. It was a campaign that radiated intensity and excitement. But of course it was Mom who clinched it. What people remembered when it was time to vote wasn't so much policy or a position statement; it was how Mom had made them feel. She wasn't afraid to be who she was, warts and all.

· · ·

The general election meant facing Republican candidate Clayton Williams, a Texas oilman and classic sexist pig. Williams had never held public office, and he loved to make crude comments about women. (Sound familiar?) He joked about going across the border to Laredo to get "serviced" by prostitutes, and once told reporters that rape was like bad weather: since you couldn't do anything about it, you may as well lie back and enjoy it. He was awful. Every chance he got, he'd try to physically intimidate Mom and put her off her game by looming over her or pointing his finger right into her face. My brother once asked how she managed to stay calm when dealing with Williams. "You know," she said, "my blood pressure drops. I go into cool mode. Here he is, another guy who lives a privileged life and doesn't give a damn about women. Now I get to expose that to the world. He doesn't get under my skin any more than the rest of the people I've dealt with all my life."

As the campaign went on, the days got longer and the pace picked up. With Lily in tow, I just kept campaigning, speaking to teachers, union meetings, and students from the Rio Grande border to Texarkana. Even Texas A&M University, known for being conservative, had its own student group, and boy, were they bold. On that campus, simply being a Democrat was gutsy enough, let alone working to elect a progressive

Ann Richards versus Clayton Williams: He was a classic good old boy who wanted to put women in their place. It didn't work.

Democratic woman. But they wore their "Aggies for Ann" T-shirts with pride. The great homecoming parade incident notwithstanding, Baylor was home to some of our very best organizers, including David Miller, a fearless student who organized volunteer phone banks, rallies, and more.

Everywhere I went I made a point to stop by the local paper; in those days there was one in every town. I could drop by, get a picture in the next day's edition, and talk about Mom. I'd drive up with bumper stickers and yard signs in the backseat, along with a change of clothes and the names of the newspaper editors from the *Palestine Daily Herald* or the *Corsicana Daily Sun*. Sometimes I had an appointment, but sometimes I just had to knock and ask, "Is anybody home?"

If I got really lucky, I'd be able to go to the radio station next door and do an impromptu interview. I'd introduce myself: "Hi, I'm Cecile Richards, my mom is running for governor, and I just wanted to stop by and say hello." More often than not they'd put me on the air right away. It wasn't like today, where you have to know everything about every issue to go out and speak about a candidate. They didn't have in-depth questions about health care policy or the rice subsidy; they just wanted to know why Mom was running for governor and what she was like. I was an expert in those areas.

In the middle of it all, I discovered I was pregnant. My doctor called while I was busy campaigning to tell me I'd had an abnormal blood test, which meant I either had a complication or was looking at a multiple birth. I was incredibly anxious. Everyone was busy, but my sister came with me for my follow-up appointment. I was on the exam table, mid-ultrasound, when my doctor looked up and said, "Well, it looks like you're having twins!" Ellen and I just looked at each other, dumbfounded.

Kirk called me from the East Texas headquarters to see how the appointment had gone, and I gave him the big news. "Ann," he said, calling Mom over to the phone, "you're going to want to hear this for yourself!"

Mom was delighted. Later that day, she informed the press that she had just learned she had twin grandbabies on the way. "I told my daughter, 'Great, you can name them Darryl and Darryl!'" she cracked. These were characters on *The Bob Newhart Show*.

My last months on the campaign I traveled through the state, large as a barge. You haven't lived until you've been on a float for the Gilmer Yamboree, the annual celebration of the yam, eating for three and looking like it too. Every morning I'd hook myself up to a fetal heart rate monitor, which sent readings to my doctor's office, then go about business as usual. One day Kirk walked into the office to find me plugged into the monitor while shouting into the phone about some urgent situation: "Who's introducing Mom at the fundraiser in Dallas?" or "The radio station in Lufkin doesn't have the ads that are supposed to be running!" or "Who can drive to Houston and pick up those four-by-six highway signs?" He told me later he wondered what kind of readings were coming through on the other end. But maybe all the chaos helped prepare my twins for the world they'd inhabit.

The campaign went on through the summer and fall, with polls routinely showing us 20 points behind. Then one night Mom took the stage for a debate with Williams. She turned in a rock-solid performance—it was clear to all in attendance that she had won. Afterward she walked up to him and held out her hand; he looked her in the eye, turned on his heel, and walked away. Mom tried to laugh it off, saying to the person next to her, "Well, that wasn't very sportsmanlike." Ironically, after everything else he had done, *that* was the moment when some people began to question whether he had the temperament to be governor.

Still, come fall, this crude, inexperienced businessman was the favorite to win. Things were looking bleak for us—that is, until he made a gaffe even he couldn't recover from.

For months one of the major sticking points of the Williams campaign had been his refusal to release his income tax returns, and folks were starting to wonder. Was he hiding shady financial dealings? Had he even paid his taxes? Why wouldn't he do what years' worth of candidates had done and disclose his returns? (Does *this* sound familiar?)

He trotted out every excuse in the book. He even tried to claim that as a successful businessman, his returns were just too long and complicated for the average person to understand. He must have been feeling pretty cocky when, a week before the election, yet another reporter asked why he hadn't released his taxes. Exasperated, he explained that he always paid his taxes. It was *just that one year* when he didn't pay any. That was it. Even he knew he had messed up.

In the days before internet access, before social media, before a million competing narratives, that, with five days left, gave us the opening we needed. We made copy after copy of radio and TV ads that we then ran around the state, Pony Express–style, hoping they would strike a chord with hardworking, taxpaying Texans.

On Election Day, Mom stuck to her usual good luck rituals: she took Lily for a walk around Town Lake in the morning, then got together with her friends for a game of bridge. Her parents came up from Waco and joined us at campaign headquarters, where they sat watching the chaos, a little wide-eyed.

At regular intervals throughout the day—9:00 a.m., noon, and 3:00 p.m.—calls came into the office with precinct reports, letting us know how many people had walked into the local polling place to cast a ballot. If numbers were low, we'd send out more folks to knock on doors and get people to the polls. If numbers were high, we'd send our organizers somewhere else. It was all a question of turnout.

Matthew Dowd, a data expert who knew Texas inside and out, was tracking all the numbers on a massive paper spreadsheet. He had identified a magic number we needed to reach in key precincts—if we could get there, we'd win. All day long we hovered around him, asking for the latest counts. At 7:00 that evening, when they started collecting the ballot boxes from the precincts and taking them to be counted, the calls took on a new urgency.

"How many boxes?" Kirk would ask the person on the other end. A pause. "They've got twelve hundred," he'd shout, and Matthew would write it on the spreadsheet.

Matthew was the first to realize we'd done it, before any of the networks had called the race. He quietly gathered us together and announced, "That's it. Ann, you won."

It looked like Matthew was right, but Mom decided not to say anything until she heard from Williams. We went to the hotel where volunteers were gathered, and as Mom was waiting in a stairwell to go onstage, he called to concede.

I was eight months pregnant, and as we headed into the supporter rally, I just hoped I wouldn't go into labor from the excitement of it all. By the time we arrived in the ballroom, people had been partying for hours, and they were worked up into a frenzy. The theme song to *Chariots of Fire* played when Mom walked onstage, and the place erupted. As we looked up on the TV screen, CBS flashed "Richards Wins Texas Governor's Race." The cheers were so loud that Lily, who was in Kirk's arms, put her hands over her ears. Standing there, basking in her win, Mom held up a T-shirt that someone had handed her: "A Woman's Place Is In The Dome."

It was truly an organizers' victory. We had beaten the odds and elected a divorced, recovering alcoholic, feminist, progressive woman to be governor of Texas. In the end it was the determination of our volunteers that pulled us over the line. We never had a poll showing that we could win—never—and had the election taken place two days earlier or two days later, we probably wouldn't have. Still, we always believed it was possible.

Over the years plenty of folks have asked me if there are lessons to be learned from Mom's race. Aside from never putting your toddler in the middle of a college homecoming parade, I can think of two big ones.

First, you can't win unless you compete. For all the people who told Mom she'd never win, she knew that the one way to guarantee that outcome was not to run in the first place. Second, politics at its best is about a lot more than expensive TV ads and polling. It is a contest of wills between folks who are satisfied with how things are and those who are passionate about what could be better. In our case it was a battle between the mostly white, male political establishment desperate to hang on to power, and those who wanted to widen the circle of opportunity for all Texans.

We had built a progressive grassroots army, and they knew that it was their work—every door they had knocked on, every phone call they had made—that put Mom in the governor's mansion.

• • •

On Inauguration Day we held a march up Congress Avenue to take back the capitol for the people of Texas, and tens of thousands of Texans showed up. It was the kind of sunny day you can get in January in Austin, with an enormous clear blue sky. Women from all across the state—and many more from around the country—came to march. There were student organizers, farmworkers, teachers, you name it. It felt like the people of Texas were back in charge of the state, even if for a fleeting moment. As we marched along, people leaned out the windows of office buildings up and down Congress Avenue and cheered.

Mom's inaugural speech was one for the books. She welcomed folks to the "new Texas," and said, "Today we have a vision of a Texas where opportunity knows no race, no gender, no color—a glimpse of what can happen in government if we simply open the doors and let the people in."

At that point, I had twins at home, and taking care of them was a full-time job. Kirk went to work for Mom, running her political operation across the state. And Mom rolled up her sleeves and got about the business of governing. In Texas the governor's job isn't actually all that complicated—you mainly appoint people and approve executions. But Mom was a big believer that you have to make hay while the sun shines, and she used the office to fight for what she believed in. Through the Department of Health she started midnight raids on nursing homes to bust bad actors. She deinstitutionalized thousands of people who had been relegated to state schools and facilities. She began drug and alcohol treatment programs in jails, knowing how many incarcerated people in America are struggling with addiction.

Perhaps most important, she changed the face of state government by appointing more women, people of color, LGBTQ Texans, and regular citizens to boards and commissions than any previous governor had. For the first time there was an environmentalist, Terry Hershey, on the Parks and Wildlife Commission, historically made up of hunters. Ellen Halbert was the first crime victim appointed to serve on the powerful Criminal Justice Board. And Reverend Zan Wesley Holmes Jr. became the first African American ever appointed to the prestigious University of Texas Board of Regents.

Those appointments made a difference, and best of all, they opened the door for a new generation of public servants, many of whom are still involved in government. Ron Kirk, who was Mom's secretary of state, went on to become mayor of Dallas and, later, a US trade representative for President Obama. Glen Maxey, a prominent LGBTQ activist and campaign organizer, won his race for the state house and became the first openly gay member to serve. Former congresswoman Barbara Jordan was appointed the state ethics adviser and set an entirely new tone for the government of Texas.

Mom was popular as governor, and her Dairy Queen–swirl hairdo made her instantly recognizable. By the time she came up for reelection, there were Ann Richards doppelgängers in cafés all across Texas. She was officially a rock star. But there was nothing she loved more than hiding in the movie theater with a box of popcorn, or taking us all down to the beach in South Padre, where she could shake off the challenges of governing and just be with her friends and family. She took pains to teach Lily how to play gin rummy, instructing her, "Never pick up a face card."

Mom faced plenty of tough decisions along the way, but one of the toughest was whether to veto a bill that would have allowed people to carry concealed handguns. She received letter after letter from family members who had lost loved ones to gun violence, talked with law enforcement officers across the state, and did her fair share of soul-searching. Ultimately she decided that vetoing the bill was the right thing to do. Arguments for the other side ran the gamut, from fearmongering to the absurd. At one point someone suggested that women needed to keep guns in their handbags in case they were attacked. Mom replied, "I don't know a single woman who can find a hairbrush in her purse in an emergency, much less a handgun." She knew her decision was the right one, despite what it might cost her—and in the end it may have cost her a second term.

On election night in 1994 Matthew Dowd, who had called the race the night we won, was the first to realize we had lost to George W. Bush.

It was such an emotional loss. We all felt we'd let our volunteers down, not to mention all those folks who had poured their heart into Mom's race and her tenure in Austin. For Mom, that was the hardest part; she hated to disappoint anyone. We were overwhelmed with regret, wondering whether, if we'd just done this or that, things would have turned out differently. And of course there were plenty of people lining up to question every decision. It would take months before we realized we had been part of a wave election and a watershed moment for politics in America.

Just like that, Mom had gone from catapulting onto the national scene to feeling lower than low. Ironically she was the most pragmatic of all of us: she knew that beating Bush was going to be harder than most people thought. She was a hard-nosed political realist who knew beating Williams had taken not only our hard work but also his own mistakes. Bush never opened the door in the same way.

Kirk helped pull together meetings in every part of the state to get all the volunteers together and encourage them to stay the course and even think about running themselves. Meanwhile Mom was focused on the staff of her administration, trying to help them get jobs. And of course we had to figure out how to pay off the campaign debt. It was a heartbreaking exercise, so different from what we'd experienced four years earlier.

After the loss the whole family went down to South Padre Island, fantasizing that if we just cut the state in two, Mom could be the governor of South Texas, which she had won handily. Lily, who was seven by then, and had campaigned like a pro, turned to Mom and asked, "Does this mean you don't have a job anymore?"

In classic Ann Richards fashion, Mom replied, "Honey, this means everybody you know doesn't have a job."

But she was still a national icon, and not long after the election she got a call from Frito-Lay to see if she would appear in a Super Bowl ad with her friend, the former governor of New York Mario Cuomo. Like Mom, Governor Cuomo had also lost his reelection bid that year. It sounded crazy, but they would get paid a lot for sitting on a couch, eating Doritos.

I encouraged her to do it. The ad was hilarious and showed all over the country during halftime. A few weeks later Mom and I were in an elevator in New York, and I heard a woman behind me whisper to her friend, "That woman with the big hair—she used to be the governor of Texas!"

Her friend corrected her: "Nope, that's the lady in the Doritos commercial."

As an organizer, that was a moment of revelation: maybe instead of running political ads against Bush, we should have just been running Doritos commercials. Apparently those were breaking through in a way we never could. In fact, afterward a poll showed that most Americans could name only three governors: Ann Richards, Mario Cuomo, and their own.

. . .

We were picking ourselves up from the loss and packing up for Mom to move out of the governor's mansion in January when an invitation came from Carlos Salinas, the outgoing president of Mexico, for the inauguration of the newly elected Ernesto Zedillo. As governor, Mom had worked to build stronger Texas-Mexico relations. Salinas was popular and had brought renewed economic prosperity to the country. (Later it was discovered that he had presided over a huge corruption network, falsely inflated the peso, created a massive financial crisis, and even had someone murdered in the process. But we didn't know that then.)

I begged Mom to go and to take me with her. Just being invited proved what I knew in my heart: that she was more than a former governor of Texas; she was on the national and international scene. She lost the race, but they had invited her anyway. She had ideas, she had drive, and people still saw her as a leader. So she agreed, and we headed off to what turned out to be the first of many memorable adventures together around the world.

The night promised to be a fabulous gathering of Latin American leaders, and it did not disappoint. The apex of the trip was a dinner at Los Pinos, the official residence of the president. It was the most spectacularly beautiful night I can remember. Murals by Diego Rivera covered the walls, mariachi bands played, and the tables held towers of fruit: pomegranates, oranges, limes, lemons.

Presidents from across the continent were there, but the person everyone wanted to meet was Fidel Castro, who was attending in full military regalia. Practically no one in America had ever seen or met him. When the dinner was breaking up, I found Mom and insisted we had to at least meet Castro. She was horrified. "If I go up to Fidel Castro, it's going to be splashed on the front page of the *Dallas Morning News*, and God knows where else! I don't have a job, Cecile, and that will make it even harder to get one."

"Mom, if you don't do it, you will always wonder, *What if?* And you just won't be able to live with that." I was channeling Ann Richards, and she knew it. I was determined, and so, on the way out, we muscled our way over to say hello.

"Gobernadora Richards!" Castro exclaimed, and he gave her a big *abrazo*. Whatever else he was, the man had charm.

Sure enough, the next day in the Mexico City paper a big photo appeared of Mom, Castro, and me—though I'm misidentified as Princess Astrid of Belgium (maybe that's how I got into the dinner after all). Thankfully, the *Dallas Morning News* missed the story, but that photo is still one of my prized possessions.

Now that Mom was liberated from being governor, she took advantage of other opportunities that came her way. She was making up for lost time. We traveled together to all seven continents. She was genuinely curious to see the world and to experience everything she could for herself.

As much as we tried to make the most of it, the election was a brutal loss. Beyond the pain and hurt I felt on a personal level, it was recognition that the state I loved was not the progressive home I thought we were

integrantes del nuevo gabinete en la ceremonia de toma de posesión de Ernesto Zedillo Ponce d

DURANTE LA CENA

La gobernadora de Texas, Ann Richards; el presidente cubano, Fidel Castro, y la princesa de Bélgica, Sar Astrid, intercambian opiniones

■ El regente ordenó una investigación exhaustiva

building. Something was happening, and it was about more than Mom's election loss.

I'd had inklings of this during the campaign. A few weeks before the election, I was sent to hand out Ann Richards material at a plant gate in Beaumont, a place I knew well, since it was the scene of the Schlesinger nursing home strike years earlier. Of all the folks on the campaign, I was the logical one to go—this was my territory.

The general idea was that you showed up early, as folks were going to work, and gave them a campaign flyer with Mom's photo and a reminder to vote on Election Day. It was a way to create a sense of urgency and enthusiasm as we were getting down to the wire—not the most intellectually stimulating task, but a lot of organizing really comes down to hard, even thankless work. I liked doing it because I learned a lot from seeing hundreds of people and hearing what was on their minds.

What I heard that day, as I stood outside the gates, was frightening. Grown men in hard hats with union stickers on their lunch pails cursed and snarled at me. "There is no way I'm going to vote for Ann Richards or any other left-winger who wants to take away my guns!" Or a variation: "She's a baby-killer." It was as if they were reading from a script—and a familiar one at that.

We'd heard this kind of rhetoric from our opponents plenty of times before. The National Rifle Association had always hated Mom, even more so since the concealed carry veto, and we knew they were out for her. And the antichoice folks were after her because she was unapologetic in her support for abortion rights—no surprise there. But these union guys? They were our people! They were the same folks who had carried her to victory four years earlier, and by any measure Mom had done right by working people and built economic opportunity in Texas. She had stood up for collective bargaining, helped enforce laws that guaranteed union wages on public works projects, and more. What was going on?

At the height of the election we knew that Bush's political strategists were injecting homophobia into the campaign. Many gay and lesbian leaders were openly and proudly serving in Mom's administration, and that opened the door for yet another disgusting line of attacks. At one point Rick Perry, then a candidate for lieutenant governor, even accused Mom of being supported by "Hollywood thespians," a nod and a wink to his own grotesque ignorance and that of his audience.

This kind of political character assassination had been commonplace for years. But this time the rumors and hostility were actually gaining traction. The effect was not only to defeat Mom and several candidates across the state, but also to cement the ownership of the extreme right wing of the Texas Republican Party, which carries on to this day. Political hack Perry later became governor and went on to create what has become one of the most reactionary state governments in the country (before his time on *Dancing with the Stars*, of course). And George W. Bush? He was elected president of the United States. But that would all come later.

Talk about taking risks: Mom left office with no job, no house, no car, and definitely no one to fall back on. As she said, she was the ultimate ex: ex-wife, ex-governor, and ex-politician. She'd had plenty of defeats and overcome them all. Fortunately she knew that being governor had been her job, not her entire identity, and she was determined to look forward, not back. Her motto was "No regrets."

She hustled up a job pretty quickly. As she told us kids, "I do not want to end up living in Ellen's driveway in a trailer." Poverty had been such a part of her upbringing that she was determined not to end up back where she had started. That's how she found herself working as a lobbyist and consultant for a Washington law firm, translating legalese into plain-spoken English along with teaching lawyers how government works. Her skills were in high demand.

The rest of us were at sea. Kirk went back into union organizing, and everyone else hit the pavement. Austin was the kind of town where there were only a few decent progressive jobs, and folks died before giving them up. Which meant there was a glut of talented do-gooders hoping to find what was next.

I had to work, but I couldn't imagine going back into organizing with the labor movement. I had three small kids, and as my organizer friend Madeline Talbott used to say, "I'm too old to door-knock, too young to die!"

Given the total wipeout of the Democratic Party in Texas that election, there was an opening to run for party chair, and folks asked me to think about it. As an organizing challenge, it was certainly compelling: there was enormous rebuilding to do. But it was unclear whether the Democratic Party, which had plenty of baggage, was ready for radical change.

Most of all, I just couldn't stop thinking about my experience in Beaumont. I remembered an email I'd gotten a few weeks before the election from someone in California, telling me that we better be on the lookout for a newly formed group called the Christian Coalition. She said they were organizing through churches, using extreme social issues and rhetoric to boost turnout in the elections. At the time it had sounded like a lot of other conspiracy theories that show up in the last days of an election. I figured that, at any rate, it was too late in the game to do much about it.

Despite the name, the Christian Coalition was not a religious organization. It was a political organization, designed to elect candidates and build political power. Across the country they had quietly launched a targeted culture war to demonize politicians who supported women's rights,

LGBTQ rights, and gun safety reform—casting supposed "God-fearing" candidates against everyone else.

Up to that point the business community had led Republicans in Texas and pretty much everywhere else. While they had supporters among the Far Right, that element had never dominated the party, and most of the Republican issues related to lowering taxes and smaller government. But in 1994, the year Mom lost, the party took a hard right turn. The Newt Gingrich "Contract with America," helped elect dozens of ultraconservative members to Congress. This was bigger than Mom. In fact it was bigger than any of us.

As I weighed what to do next, I thought of a question a reporter had asked Mom after she lost the election: "What would you have done differently if you knew you were going to be a one-term governor?" She had just grinned and answered, "Oh, I probably would have raised more hell." I decided it was time for me to start raising some hell of my own.

CHAPTER 6

Don't Wait for Instructions

"We believe that Langston Hughes's poems must be removed from the books, as he was a known Communist," declared a voice from the front of the room.

It was hour 2 of the State Board of Education meeting, and I was riveted. This rather bland-sounding body was responsible for approving textbooks and setting curriculum standards for more than three million public school kids across Texas. Though it was 1995, I felt like I had traveled back in time to the 1950s.

A new day had dawned in Texas politics after the November election. The same right-wing agenda that swept George W. Bush into the governor's mansion also changed the balance of power on the fifteen-member state board of education, with three new members that one newspaper called representatives of "the sex-obsessed shock troops of the religious right."

A week earlier I'd been with my friend Harriet Peppel, who had been following the state board of education. She turned to me with her eyes as big as saucers and said, "Cecile, you are not going to *believe* it. The only way to understand what is going on is to come with me to the next public meeting."

Now we were there and I could barely comprehend what I was hearing. I scanned the room, looking for allies. The audience was disappointingly sparse. There were some representatives of the teachers' organizations and the superintendents and school boards. But most of those in attendance were lobbyists for the textbook industry, and they were simply trying to figure out how to sell books. As one of those lobby-ists later told me, "I can hit a curve ball, a slider, or a fast ball—I just have to know what game we're playing." In other words, he wasn't going to fight these nuts; he was going to make sure that the book publishers de-leted whatever the right wing objected to so that they had the best chance of getting their books approved for the lucrative Texas textbook market.

The most active participants in the audience were Melvin and Norma Gabler, an East Texas couple who read every single textbook put forward for adoption and wrote up page after page of complaints. They objected not only to the poems of the great Harlem Renaissance writer Langston Hughes but also to anything that smacked of equal rights for women, environmentalism, or negative portrayals of slavery, to name just a few.

When I couldn't take any more, I ripped a page out of my notebook and passed a note to Harriet. It read, simply, "It's so much worse than I believed!"

I had started reading up on the Christian Coalition and learned a lot from Harriet, who was working for People for the American Way, a group started by the sitcom producer and writer Norman Lear to moni-tor the activities of the right wing.

Getting up to speed on the Christian Coalition was like running down a rabbit hole. The more I discovered, the more it became clear that none of what was happening at the State Board of Education was a one-off. Ideas that were once relegated to the wackiest late-night televan-gelists had now moved into the realm of politics. Pat Robertson's preach-ing that feminism was "a socialist, anti-family political movement that encourages women to leave their husbands, kill their children, practice witchcraft, destroy capitalism, and become lesbians" summed up the phi-losophy of the Christian Coalition. Reverend Jerry Falwell made the case directly, evangelizing, "I hope I live to see the day when, as in the early days of our country, we won't have any public schools. The churches will have taken them over again and Christians will be running them."

The worst part was that they were well on their way to achieving that goal. One of the most under-the-radar efforts in the Texas elections was the targeting of two mainstream State Board of Education members, Mary Perkins and Patsy Johnson, who had devoted their lives to public schools. Like Mom, Patsy and Mary were both defeated in November, the victims of a truly vicious direct-mail campaign. The headline of the most infamous mailing sent to voters screamed, "Is this what you want your children to see?," with a large photo of two naked men embracing and kissing. It repeated scandalous claims by the Christian Coalition, including that the State Board of Education was peddling instructions in gay sex to high school students. Mary and Patsy were replaced by two Christian Coalition–supported candidates, who proceeded to take on every curriculum and textbook issue with a vengeance. At this point I had three kids in the public schools. It was alarming to think that this crew of far-right political strategists wanted to determine what my kids were reading and studying—let alone decide what went in textbooks across Texas and across the country.

I was on fire. I wanted to turn to people and say, "Does everybody know what's going on? Isn't somebody going to do something about this?"

Then I realized: *What if that somebody was me?* I'd never started anything other than the odd food co-op and antipollution group, but I realized that if I didn't do it, it probably wasn't going to happen.

Here, dear reader, is something worth considering before committing to a spouse or partner: there are only certain people who would hear that and say, "Hey, that's great! We have no savings and no house and three kids in school, but do your dream!" That's Kirk. I've had a lot of harebrained schemes in my life, and he's gone along with every one of them.

Without any idea how to start an organization, I made up a name, the Texas Freedom Alliance, and typed up a mission statement. I was going to organize Texans in support of public education and religious liberty. I found a group in Washington, the Alliance for Justice, that helped folks start nonprofits. (If you're thinking about branching out on your own, they're still a great place to start.)

We started out in my living room, then found someone to temporarily donate a tiny office. I convinced Peter Shakow, a friend from Mom's campaign, to help out for the first few months. My grandmother Nona wrote our first check, for $100. It has to be the only check she ever wrote in her life for that much money. My kids were some of our earliest vol-

Austin, 1995, with the first volunteers for the Texas Freedom Network.

unteers, helping put together flyers and mailing them out to people we knew. My sister held the first house party, and we were off.

I had just the beginnings of a plan, but every time I had to explain it to someone, it got a little bit clearer. Our new organization wasn't rolling in money, but we were rolling in opportunity—speaking to education groups, teachers, anybody. A local synagogue invited me to come and speak to their congregation, and that is where we got the first non-family-member donation and our first two non-family volunteers, Ethyl and Manny Rosenblatt. They were tremendous, and didn't care if we were making it up as we went along. Like a lot of other Texans, they were frustrated with the rightward political drift and looking for a place to pitch in.

Our unofficial motto was "Wherever two or more are gathered together!" Harriet and I drove all over Texas and, fortunately, joined forces with Janis Pinelli, another former Ann Richards volunteer. Not only did Janis have a car big enough for all three of us to ride around (and change clothes) in; she was also a licensed CPA and helped me figure out how to set up the books and create a board of directors.

After meeting Mary Perkins and Patsy Johnson, the two Board of Education members who had been ousted, we began to connect with others who had similar horror stories at the local level, including one close to home.

Round Rock, Texas, is a suburb of Austin, known for having an excellent public school system. People would move there and commute to Austin just so their kids could go to the Round Rock public schools. That made them a prime target for the Right. The same families that had come to Round Rock for the schools were now watching in horror as the superintendent was fired, school board members were tossed out, and reading lists were rewritten. Up to that point the parents we talked to wouldn't have been at the top of anybody's list to become political activists, but now they were angry and determined to fight back against what was happening.

Coincidentally Round Rock had a well-known, well-respected young adult author right there in the district: Louis Sachar. Louis was a kindly, older, soft-spoken guy, and one of his books, *The Boy Who Lost His Face*, was on a school reading list. But the newly elected school board members banned the book, claiming it was profane. Louis would go on to win the Newbery Medal for his book *Holes*, which was made into a very popular young adult movie. But here in his hometown, the local school board was trying to prevent young people from reading his work.

The craziness of what was happening in Round Rock was so profound, combined with the shenanigans in other suburban communities and at the State Board, that we decided to make a documentary. Campaign friends Mark McKinnon and Margie Becker made it for next to nothing, and we then had an excuse to speak to groups. We showed them this ten-minute film, then gave our spiel and tried to recruit members.

Folks were definitely starting to take notice, and not just our supporters. I arrived at the office one morning to get a certified letter from the attorney of none other than Colonel Oliver North, infamous for having illegally funded the contras during the Nicaraguan Civil War. Apparently North's right-wing organization was called the Freedom Alliance, and his attorney threatened that we must "cease and desist" using our name lest the two be confused.

It was incredible! Our scrappy group in Texas was on the radar of the Right Wing! Even better, being threatened by Oliver North gave us a great chance to start a statewide renaming contest and get some free press. That is how we became the Texas Freedom Network and picked up some new supporters in the process.

It was exciting and fulfilling to build something from nothing—especially something that might actually make a difference. Everywhere we went we met people who were eager to help. By bringing together teachers, PTA activists, and progressives across the state, our motley crew began to stand up for public schools. We did battle at textbook hearings, bringing scientists to testify on the importance of accurate science books, and blasting out the most outrageous statements by board members to the press. At one point some board members wanted to remove a photograph from a textbook of a nicely dressed woman walking out the door of her house, carrying a briefcase and waving to her family, saying it encouraged women to leave their children. We tipped off the *Today* show, and it made for great television.

We also started organizing an unexpected group: religious leaders. What was being done in the name of religion was so appalling that one of the most common bumper stickers at the time read, "God, please protect me from your followers." We started the Texas Faith Network with Baptist preachers who had been fighting the takeover of the southern Baptist Convention by the Far Right. At that point the Texas Baptist Convention was led by mainstream preachers who saw their faith as fundamentally and critically disconnected from the government.

For a statewide convention of Texas public school teachers, I had asked one of our clergy leaders to address the growing challenges to our public schools. Reverend Larry Bethune of University Baptist Church in Austin was not only an eloquent orator; what he said was relevant to many teachers who were deeply religious and involved in their church. Afterward a woman came up to him with tears in her eyes and said, "I'm so glad you were here. I'm a Christian and a public school teacher, and it was so important to hear a man of faith tell me that what I do is good and not the work of the devil."

One of the most extraordinary religious leaders I got to know was

Don Sinclair of the Bering Memorial United Methodist Church in Houston. Reverend Sinclair was at the end of his career, and his gentle, grandfatherly countenance immediately put people at ease, even when he was taking on his harshest critics. One day, sitting with him at a radio station where I had asked him to do a live interview, I could hear the difference it made to have him, rather than me, on the airwaves. No one could out-scripture Don Sinclair.

The clergy became so critical to our organizing efforts that they were in demand in the press, speaking out about everything from LGBTQ rights to support for public education. Bill Davis, a Catholic priest from Houston, would ask me before such events, "Are we supposed to wear our sin-fighting suits?" Bill always came in his collar unless otherwise notified.

Along the way I made my fair share of mistakes and learned just how hard it can be to get an organization off the ground. It's one thing to raise money for a candidate; it's another to fundraise for your own organization. I soon learned the truth of the adage "If you want money, ask someone for advice. If you want advice, ask someone for money." There were plenty of folks (especially men) who didn't want to write a check but were happy to tell me how *they* would have done it.

That fall, we were out of cash. Harriet and Janis and I put thousands of miles on Janis's Buick looking for anyone to hold a fundraiser. We had heard about a woman in Dallas who seemed keen, so we piled in Janis's car and drove four hours just to see her. We met on the sun porch of her lovely North Dallas home. The backyard looked like it went on for days, and the whole place screamed "fundraising party" to me. We were desperate and ready to pull something together right then.

"I really love what you are doing," she said. "It is so urgent that we stand up to anyone who would be trying to harm the public schools." (Though from her expansive home and neighborhood, it seemed unlikely anyone in her immediate family had any personal familiarity with the public schools.) "I would love to do something next spring. That's when the azaleas are in bloom, and the yard really looks its best."

My heart fell into my stomach. Next spring? That was six months away. It may as well have been next century. We needed someone to help now—like *yesterday*. Janis and Harriet and I stopped by the Dairy Queen on the road back to Austin to drown our sorrows in chocolate dip cones. An eight-hour round-trip drive to Dallas just to be pushed off to next spring. I felt lower than a snake. Still, I didn't regret making the trip. We were a start-up and desperate, and this was what it took to build something from scratch. On the way home I lamented, "Coming across a wealthy person who agrees with what we're doing is like finding a needle in a haystack! It would be easier to go find a donor, and ask them what kind of organization they want us to form!"

TFN was barely six months old when a call came that changed our fortunes and our future. It was Halloween, and I was in costume. I'd just come back from the kids' elementary school, having learned from my mother that there's nothing like embarrassing your children on Halloween. I was wearing my Maleficent headdress with entwined horns and a sweeping black cape, with black and purple eye makeup, when the phone rang at the TFN office.

"I'm calling for Cecile, from the Leland Fikes Foundation in Dallas," said the voice on the other end, who turned out to be Nancy Solana. Suddenly I remembered that one of the many requests for support we'd sent had been to the Fikes Foundation. I didn't know them, but a friend had said to give them a try. I took off my horns and quickly switched from my alter ego to say yes, this was she.

"We received your grant proposal, and I just have one question: What font did you use?"

Was this a trick question? Crazily enough, I knew. It was Footlight MT Bold. I've always had a thing for fonts, and this was before the days when the internet gave you a million options. It was important to me that anything we sent out looked good, and the font I'd picked was clean and classy. That's the beauty of running your own organization: you get to weigh in on everything from the logo to how to arrange the chairs at a meeting. I'd learned from Mom that there were a million ways to do something, but only one right way. So I told her.

"Great!" she said. "I love that font. I want to use it. Oh, and by the way, the foundation approved your grant. We'll send you the paperwork and have a check to you in a couple of weeks."

"YESSSS!" I screamed at the office. This was our first legitimate grant. It meant we could make payroll through the end of the year, and maybe even be on the road to survival. Lee and Amy Fikes, the most unassuming, wonderful people, became our strongest supporters. That phone call gave me the confidence that we could keep going.

There was no guarantee when I started the Texas Freedom Network in my living room months earlier that it would ever make it. But if I hadn't given it a shot, I would have spent the rest of my life wondering what might have been. I stayed for three years and built it into a small but mighty organization.

Eventually, though, I started to feel that it was time to move on. Kirk and I were ready to leave town for the next challenge. It was hard being in Texas after Mom's loss, which felt like a betrayal, and we'd stuck it out as long as we could. I guess I should have realized how angry I was when a guy came to mow my lawn, long after the election. He was driving a beat-up truck with an old bumper sticker on the back from the days when Mom was in office: *Gee, I Sure Miss Governor Clements* (the jerk who was governor before Mom). I walked up to him and said, "I am going to pay you, but you'll have to leave." He looked dumbfounded. "Why?" he asked. "I haven't even gotten out my mower." "I just can't have you out in front of my house," I replied. It was then I knew I hadn't gotten over it.

When Kirk got an opportunity to go to Washington for the AFL-CIO, it seemed like a good place to make a new start. I'd started TFN from scratch and built it to a point where I knew someone else could take over. We had an office, staff, and (hallelujah!) a year's budget in the bank. Fortunately I knew a brilliant organizer, a Texan named Samantha Smoot, who was out in California working for EMILY's List. Somehow I convinced her that running TFN was a great opportunity, and thank God the board agreed. Sam moved back to Austin and took the TFN to the next level. Years later she handed it back to Kathy Miller, our original deputy director, who made it her own. Today the Texas Freedom Network is a key force for good in the fight for public school funding, LGBTQ rights, and immigrant and voting rights. And best of all, they've begun training hundreds of young leaders across the state. That's another important lesson: Once you leave, let go! Sam and Kathy each had their own vision, and the organization changed and grew with their leadership. It has been wonderful to see what they have built.

• • •

If there's one common theme that runs throughout my life, it's strong, kick-ass women. My grandmothers, each in their own very different ways, were tough and pioneering. My mother broke the mold. And at every job I've ever had, I've tried to work for someone who could teach me something—and more often than not, that someone has been a woman. For all of these inspiring women, it wasn't as if the world just threw open the door and invited them in. Each one has been a disrupter in one way or another. They've made trouble, broken the rules, and challenged authority—and no one more than the US House Democratic leader and former speaker Nancy Pelosi.

I'd been living in Washington for a while when my friend Gina Glantz, who had tried to hire me to work on Bill Bradley's campaign for president, called with another crazy idea. Congresswoman Nancy Pelosi had just been elected Democratic whip—the highest-ranking woman ever to serve in Congress—and Gina saw her rise as a huge opportunity. Gina had the unerring ability to peek around the corner and imagine what could be, instead of just seeing what was. And she was right about Nancy.

"Nancy will have her pick of talented folks who come from Capitol Hill," Gina explained, "but she needs someone who can help make sure her agenda is understood outside of Washington. She understands organizing and wants someone who can bridge the gap between the grassroots out in the states and what is going on in the Capitol."

Up until that point it had never occurred to me to work on the Hill. At the time I was working for Ted Turner and Jane Fonda, traveling around the country and giving away money from their foundation to groups working for reproductive rights. It was a great job. But rather than funding other people's work, I wanted to be doing the work myself.

I had not the foggiest idea what Gina was actually proposing—she was describing a position that didn't yet exist, and I had never even met Nancy Pelosi. The people I did know on the Hill had all been there for years and knew the ropes. That whole world was a mystery to me. But George W. Bush was in the White House by then, and it seemed like we were settling in for a rough few years. I wanted to be somewhere I could have a greater impact, so I decided to give it a try.

I interviewed with George Crawford, a Capitol Hill veteran who was putting together Nancy's staff. The whole time, I was thinking, *This is crazy—why would they hire me when anyone would kill for this job?* But George seemed to think my knowledge of the progressive organizing world would come in handy, and he brought me on, along with the brainiest bunch of people I've ever worked with.

We worked cheek to jowl in a small office; you couldn't so much as sharpen your pencil without everyone else noticing. I was constantly aware of my shortcomings, though none of my colleagues ever made me feel that way. I was in awe of them; they seemed to know everything about government, from the requirements of a "motion to recommit" to who had been where in the last race for speaker of the House.

No one gets to be the highest ranking woman in the history of our country without being enormously driven and willing to upset every convention, including the notion that men are forever destined to be in charge. As Democratic whip, Nancy was second in command to the Democratic leader, Congressman Dick Gephardt from Missouri. She was also the ranking Democrat on the House Intelligence Committee and part of the so-called Gang of Eight—the group of members of Congress who received private intelligence briefings from the CIA, Defense Department, State Department, and the White House. She was intimately aware of all foreign policy issues, and on top of that, she was an incredibly hard worker. She read every briefing memo, every policy paper, every headline—and expected her staff to do the same. Somehow she managed not only to beat us all to work in the morning but also to keep on top of all five of her kids, their spouses, and every grandkid. She would implore us at the end of the day, "Go home and see your family! Get out!," even though she never did.

In the fall of 2002, just a few months after I started, President Bush declared that intelligence reports showed that Iraq had weapons of mass destruction, and he wanted a vote by Congress approving military action.

Capitol Hill began a contentious debate on the proposal, but not long after, Gephardt appeared with Bush in the Rose Garden and endorsed the president's plan to go to war. I was angry that the Democrats were in any way going to support us going to war with Iraq. It made me wonder whether working in Congress was even a good idea; I had been used to speaking my mind, not toeing a party line.

The topic had consumed our office, and I was pretty sure that Nancy was not at all convinced that Iraq had weapons of mass destruction. She took a declaration of war seriously, as all members of Congress should. As she often reminded us, it was perhaps the most important vote you could ever take. I was still new, and I didn't work on intelligence issues, so I was an observer, like everyone else, waiting to see what would happen.

A couple of days later, at the next meeting of the House Democratic Caucus, I got my answer. Each week the entire caucus would cram into a tiny basement meeting room and get their marching orders for the week: what's coming up, what they needed to know. Gephardt defended the resolution to support the Iraq war. Then Nancy got up to speak.

"I am aware of all the intelligence reports," she said. "I strongly believe there is not adequate rationale to support this war with Iraq, and I will vote against it."

I was standing in the back of the room with the others from our office, and I was stunned. I knew that Nancy was strongly against the war, but she had just spoken against the position of the Democratic leader and of the president. This was a closed meeting: no press and very few staff. She didn't do this for attention or to be a heroine; she did it because she genuinely believed it was the right thing to do. It seemed like a staggering act of courage. I was so proud to work for her that day.

Here's the thing about Nancy Pelosi: she backed up those inspiring words with action. She provided information and helped persuade other members of Congress that this was critically important. By the time of the vote on October 11, 2002, she had convinced a majority of Democrats in the House to vote against the war. That was no small feat, considering that the majority of Democrats in the Senate voted for it.

That was the Nancy Pelosi I have experienced time and time again, who knows her mind and does not back down. I remember feeling I would do anything to make sure people in the country knew the battles she was taking on. It was difficult to convey the complexity and importance of what was happening on the Hill, but that became my main assignment for the next several months. It was a puzzle: How could people who lived in Ohio or West Texas be made aware of the fight the Democrats in Congress were waging back in Washington?

Even though at times I felt like I was in over my head, I also felt at home working for Nancy. She reminded me so much of Mom. Both had raised kids and done what society expected of them before they had the chance to become political leaders. Both were impatient to make sure that the next generation of women did not have to wait so long.

My mother said often, "Life isn't fair, but government should be." There are countless stories of women who run for office because they believe exactly that—like Congresswoman Jan Schakowsky of Illinois, who got her start as a young housewife leading a campaign to put expiration dates on food in the grocery store, and Congresswoman Stephanie Murphy of Florida, who was inspired to challenge an NRA-endorsed incumbent after the 2016 Pulse nightclub massacre. Women aren't usually in it for the glory; they're in it to get something done.

And it's a good thing they are, because Congress on the whole is a macho, "guys hanging out with guys" kind of place. When Barbara Boxer was elected to the US Senate, there wasn't even a women's bathroom near the Senate floor—and that was in 1993! For many women in Congress, once they leave work for the day, they're back at their house, doing homework with their kids or catching up on the legislation they want to pass. But the men, even with their partisan differences, drink together, work out together; in Texas they hunt and fish together. There is no harder social circle to break into. Senate Minority Leader Chuck Schumer, a Democrat, often boasts of working out in the congressional gym early in the morning and catching up with his Republican counterparts over the free weights or in the locker room. How are Senators Kamala Harris and Kirsten Gillibrand supposed to pull that off?

Like a lot of women in office, Nancy didn't get where she is because

someone picked her; she got there because she decided to run and then
was determined to succeed. She knew the caucus intimately, knew the
members' districts, and understood the difference between what Jack
Murtha, a Vietnam veteran from Pennsylvania, needed for his constituents and what John Spratt from South Carolina needed for his. She usually knew the members' spouses, their kids, and what issues they were
passionate about. She fundamentally understood how to connect with
her colleagues as people, and she showed them every day how much she
cared about them.

When Congressman Gephardt retired, Nancy decided to run for
Democratic leader, the highest-ranking position for the party in the minority. Even though she had served as whip, her election was not a sure
thing. She ran against Texan Martin Frost, a fellow progressive, and a for-
midable opponent. Nancy had strong support from women in the House,
but there weren't nearly enough of them to build a majority.

I watched in awe as Nancy designed her campaign plan and executed
it like clockwork. Morning, noon, and night she did outreach to caucus
members and got commitments to support her. It was a race with plenty
of plot twists. After a contentious year-long battle, with just days before
the vote, Congressman Frost realized he couldn't win and dropped out.
Young Harold Ford Jr. of Tennessee jumped in. But Nancy just kept at it.
Three of us in her office were responsible for being able to account for
every member of the House on the day of the secret ballot. I studied the
photographs and was stunned again at how many white men were in
our caucus. It was another reminder of how tough the odds were against
Nancy.

But when they counted the votes, Nancy had won. Like Mom's inauguration, it was a day I'll never forget: the first woman ever to lead
her party in Congress! And wouldn't you know, when they did the final
tally of the votes, the result was exactly what Nancy had predicted. She
knew something I had learned early on in union organizing: Assume any
wavering vote is a no until you get a firm commitment. It seems like a
simple thing, but this is one of Nancy's most important skills: whether
as speaker or as minority leader, she has been able to hold her caucus
together and predict where the votes are. Time and time again, no matter

which party is in charge of Congress, it's usually Nancy who can round up the Democratic votes needed to pass crucial legislation.

Nancy has an incredible grasp of history and an enormous respect for the institutions of government and Congress. The day she was elected Democratic leader, she also became part of the congressional leadership made up of the two highest-ranking members of each party in the House and Senate. As is customary, the president invited the group to the White House. When Nancy came to work the next day, she was still processing what her election meant. Back in her offices on the second floor of the Capitol, she described the emotion of going to the meeting with the president. I've never forgotten what she told us that day. "I was so aware, walking through the gates and into the White House, of the hard work and sacrifice of prior generations of women," she said. "The suffragists, and all the women who broke barriers. As I sat at the table with the president and the top leaders of Congress, I realized that it was the very first time a woman had ever been at this table. It was as if women from throughout history, women who had made this possible, were there with me. And all around me, I felt their presence."

I heard her tell that story to countless women, looking them straight in the eye, underscoring that they too were picking up the torch from generations who came before. She often quoted Congresswoman Lindy Boggs from Louisiana, a mentor of hers, who implored women, "Know thy power!"

To the surprise of no one, Nancy's workday did not end at 5:00 p.m. She spent every additional waking hour helping her colleagues stay in Congress—flying out to help them in their districts, organizing private lunches for them, and advising them in the way only she could. She was also a prodigious fundraiser, and many aspiring candidates beat a path to her door. Accompanying her to these meetings, I learned lessons about politics that have stayed with me ever since.

One day Nancy and I were at the Democratic Congressional Campaign Committee offices, meeting with a young man with stars in his eyes. He settled in across the table from us and launched into his talking points. "I am a really good fit for my district," he said. "I have the money I need to be competitive, and I think it's the right next move for me."

I fought the urge to roll my eyes. Nancy, however, was always gracious and inordinately patient. She listened to his spiel, then asked, "Who is really interested in you being in Congress?"

He looked a bit dumbstruck and stammered, "Well, the business community will support me, and I'm on very good terms with the labor unions."

"Here's what I suggest," Nancy said. "Find one thousand people in your district who care enough about your candidacy that they will write you a check and volunteer, and then come back and see me. If you can do that, I'll know you can actually win a race."

I heard that conversation, or a close facsimile, many times. Nancy believed in the importance of grassroots democracy. If you could show her your campaign wasn't about just you, she would move heaven and earth to help. No matter your gender, race, or ethnicity, she believed what mattered was your commitment and connection to your community. She believed that if you were going to come to Congress, you better be ready to work for the folks back home. Besides which, she knew that this was the only way Congress would ever look like the people of America.

· · ·

I had been on Capitol Hill for less than two years when the organizing bug bit once again. By then it was 2004. President Bush was up for reelection. His success was far from settled—between the war in Iraq and the Patriot Act, progressives hoped this would be their chance to make him a one-term president.

A friend from my organizing days, Steve Rosenthal, was the political director for the labor movement, and he was getting ready to run one of the biggest voter outreach efforts in history. But first he did a study: he asked progressive voters in Colorado to keep a stack of all the mail they had received in the last two weeks before Election Day. The results? Voters got dozens of pieces of mail, from many different organizations, all asking them to vote. There was mail from Planned Parenthood, the environmental movement, the AFL-CIO, and of course the candidates and the Democratic Party. It was not only a huge waste of money; it risked turning voters off to the whole process. As Steve said, "Each night, progressive voters came home to a pile of political mailers which they then threw directly in the trash. It's a disaster!"

Steve and I were talking about what progressives could do to be smarter this time around, when Gina Glantz had an idea. "What if all the major progressive organizations actually talked to each other," she suggested, "and planned together what they were going to do in elections, instead of all focusing on the same voters?" Gina is the queen of the elegant solution. It made perfect sense, but someone would actually have to do it.

That's how I found myself starting what became America Votes, the largest collection of progressive grassroots organizations working together to register, educate, and turn out voters. It was a daunting task, but a worthy one. Despite having vowed to never again create something from whole cloth (Never say never!), I realized once more how useless it was to sit around and wait for someone else to build the organization we needed. I took a deep breath and dove back in, telling myself that at least this time I was older and wiser.

I won't pretend it was all smooth sailing. Putting together that first meeting was a real bear. Carl Pope at the Sierra Club, Andy Stern at SEIU, and Ellen Malcolm at EMILY's List all thought it was a good idea. Perhaps even more important, so did everyone underneath them, the people who were going to be responsible for voter contact in the election. But coordinating progressive leaders is like keeping puppies in a basket. Just when they are all in, someone jumps out. A male head of a major labor union never got over the fact that he wasn't in on the original conversation and wound up trying to undermine the plan of bringing all these groups together to collaborate. Just like the song from the musical *Hamilton*, it seemed like what mattered most to some people was simply being in "The Room Where It Happens."

The thorniest parts of getting started had nothing to do with the mission or the work. Organizational differences, whether on issues or tactics, got in the way. There were groups that didn't like the idea of having to share lists or volunteers, or who wanted to be the one to take credit. But gradually, progressive organizations learned that helping each other actually made everyone stronger, even if it meant taking a stand on something that had never been their issue before. In the end we all agreed that it would help everyone if we could determine who was working in Michigan, who was taking on Florida, and how in the world we were going to split up the Philadelphia suburbs. Beating an incumbent president was going to be nearly impossible, and the only way we could succeed was to expand the number of people we were talking to and make the best use of our time and money.

For the very first time organizers sat at the same table and divided up precincts, counties, and phone calls. Even when folks bickered at our headquarters in Washington, in states like Colorado and Pennsylvania and Michigan, working together became second nature. For the people on the ground, it was a dream come true. They knew they had more in common than not, and with limited resources and volunteers, it was a lot smarter to divide up the work. In Pittsburgh, Pennsylvania, the Planned Parenthood volunteers knocked on doors for the United Steelworkers, who had economic campaign issues that were more salient that year. And in the Philadelphia suburbs, where many pro-choice Republican women would cross over, labor activists distributed Planned Parenthood literature.

The even more exciting result was that for the first time all the progressive leaders got to know each other. It's still crazy to think that it took organizing America Votes for the heads of the Sierra Club, Planned Parenthood, and the NAACP to get together. What's more, they all learned the power of grassroots organizing. The president of one national political organization actually knocked on her first door during that election in Ohio. There's nothing quite like doing the work yourself, talking to voters one on one, to appreciate what is happening in the country.

In starting America Votes, I learned one of the most important lessons of my life: Don't wait for all the boats to get in the flotilla—just start moving. You may lose a few people, and others may join up along the way, but if you wait until everyone is 100 percent on board, you'll never get going. At a certain point you have to quit talking about it and start doing it.

There was one really tough setback, of course: We lost the 2004 presidential election by 118,000 votes in Ohio. But the fact that we had built up a national progressive community helped everyone weather the loss. When the blaming began, no one was going to let any single group take the hit. And for every election since then, the major progressive organizations across America have continued to work together.

I meet people all the time who are considering starting their own organizations, whether a student group on a college campus or a national initiative. If you're thinking of giving it a shot, here are a few of the things I learned so you don't have to.

First, be practical: Set a goal so you can achieve something concrete. In the beginning it's going to be the small wins. I knew I could not start the Texas Freedom Network by myself, so my initial goal was to raise enough money in the first three months to pay an assistant and myself.

Second, you have to be willing to ask for money. And believe me, it's a great skill to have. It tests your proof of concept: if you can find people willing to pitch in $25, then you are onto something. And there aren't any shortcuts worth taking. How many nonprofit meetings have I been in when someone says, "Maybe we could get Oprah or Matt Damon or Beyoncé to do a fundraiser for us." That's just not how it works. Raising money isn't only about getting an influx of cash; it's about being able to prove that other people support the idea you're working on. It's about building a following.

Third, for better or worse, when you start and run your own organization, you own all the successes and all the failures. Big risk, big gain. It's like being an entrepreneur, only you're not trying to make a profit.

Fourth, master the organizing rules of the road: Always have a room that's half the size you need, with half the chairs you need, so you can guarantee meetings will be standing room only. When you are starting out with new leaders, make sure everyone has the chance to speak. That will be the single best test of whether the meeting went well: Did they get a chance to give their point of view? Besides, you learn more from listening than from speaking. Of course, getting people in a room is 20 percent of the work; the other 80 percent is having something meaningful for them to do after they walk out the door. And no matter what you do, never forget the basics: Provide name tags and food; start on time and end on time; have a next step; have fun. Remember, "If I can't dance, I don't want to be part of your revolution."

There are a ton of great ideas floating around the universe, but the ones that end up becoming reality are those someone commits to doing, no matter what. Why not you?

CHAPTER 7

Everything You Need to Know in Life, You Can Learn on a Campaign (and Other Lessons on Raising Activist Kids)

Our tiny New York apartment is crammed with folding tables and enough chairs to seat twenty-six (one year there were twenty-eight—the more the merrier—except that no one had enough room to get up for more pie). All three kids are home, because this is our holiday, the one where everyone shows up, no matter what. More than a few girlfriends and boyfriends have heard from my kids, "Nope, can't go to your place for Thanksgiving." It's been this way for as long as I can remember. We plan for months, and after one Thanksgiving finishes, we start thinking about whether we should switch up the pies for next year. *Were the two pecan pies really necessary, or should we do something wild and have a pumpkin cheesecake?* Before we get together, recipes are dug out, swapped, and edited. The cheese grits recipe that my friend Jill dictated twenty-five years ago is still written in felt-tip pen on a note card. I hate to think what would happen if we lost it.

Our Thanksgiving might not be the fanciest, but it's the best time—a time when all are welcome. We have regulars, folks who have become part of our extended family, and occasionally my siblings will arrive from Texas, or island friends will come down from Maine. We play charades and often our favorite game, where everyone has the name of a famous (or infamous) person taped to their back and has to guess who it is before we can eat. Sometimes my sister brings tamales from back home. My friend Joe Armstrong, who lived nearby, used to prepare the bird and do an annual turkey handoff to Kirk at the corner of Eighty-first Street and Central Park. From one Thanksgiving to the next, you never know exactly what's going to happen.

On Thanksgiving or any other day of the year it doesn't take much for our family to have a great time—all we need is a campsite and decent weather. I swore no child of mine would leave home without being able to pitch a tent, catch and clean a fish, and make a campfire, so whenever we could, we've squeezed in camping out and cooking over an open fire, from the Shenandoah Mountains to Big Bend National Park. To make sure they'd never starve, the kids learned to deep-fry, a dying art that we southerners are determined to preserve, and to make their own pie crust from scratch. All three kids are great cooks. Our most common group text is to figure out who has the recipe for barbecue shrimp.

· · ·

When I discovered I was pregnant with Lily, I worried how on earth I was going to work as a union organizer and also be a mom. Kirk and I were living in California, both working eighteen-hour days. We had planned on having kids, but just not then. Like so many people, I was using birth control, but it wasn't always reliable, nor was I. When I told Kirk I was pregnant, we both just sort of sat there, excited and stunned. How could we make this work? Was I going to drive across Los Angeles visiting janitors and walking picket lines with a baby strapped to my back? (The answer, as it turned out, was yes.) In the end we came to the same conclusion millions of people do: there was never going to be a "perfect" time to have kids, but just like everything else, we'd figure it out. Just as folks have done for centuries.

I was enthralled with the idea of natural childbirth, but a home birth was 100 percent out of the question. How could we birth a baby in our one-room, chaotic apartment? So I visited a natural birthing center. I was okay until I saw the birthing stool that was used to help the baby drop out. It looked like some kind of medieval torture device.

The wonderful midwife giving the tour said, "You know, sometimes everything doesn't go as planned, so we also have a doctor for backup."

Between the birthing stool and the image of being frantically rushed to the hospital if things went wrong, I was starting to question this whole notion. I thought fast. "Okay, well, who is the doctor?" His name was Dr. Wu, just like the Steely Dan song. I wasn't interested in leaving anything to chance, so I immediately made an appointment with Dr. Wu, and he became my obstetrician.

There were several points of contention between Kirk and me, and naming this new baby was one of them. We didn't know whether we were having a boy or a girl, but I loved the name Georgia. Georgia Landry was one of my favorite nursing home leaders in Beaumont—loving but tough as a boot. Kirk, the Massachusetts native who had married into some major southern influences, put his foot down. I was equally alarmed that he wanted to name a boy Derek. All I could picture was a hockey player who had lost all his teeth. No way.

Then one day Mom met me in San Francisco, where we went to see Lily Tomlin in her one-woman play, *The Search for Signs of Intelligent Life in the Universe.* Her play touched me in a way that can only happen when you are seven months pregnant. Her brilliant collaborator (and now wife) Jane Wagner wrote the script, which included such gems as "I made some studies, and reality is the leading cause of stress amongst those in touch with it." Kirk and I agreed: Lily was the perfect name for a daughter. If it was a son, I was holding out for Woodrow. But as fate would have it, we put that argument off for the next go-around.

The arrival of our Lily was lifesaving. Until then we were round-the-clock activists and organizers. We didn't even have a goldfish or a guinea pig. We barely owned a potted plant. For the first time we had to think about something other than a union meeting or staying at the office until the wee hours of the morning. When the twins came along three years later, we had three somethings to think about.

Parenting isn't for everyone, and I will fight to my last breath to protect every person's right to decide whether or not to have children. But raising our three kids—Lily, Hannah, and Daniel—is, bar none, the absolute best thing I've ever done. I give it my highest recommendation. Suddenly everything made more sense: my work, my life, the world around me, even my own parents. And my priorities changed to accommodate this new, awesome responsibility.

As every parent learns, so much about raising kids is out of your control. Kirk and I were fortunate that all of our kids were healthy, even if each of them managed to make a trip to the emergency room for stitches before their second birthday. Many people have so much more on their parental plate than I ever did that all of the following must be taken with a grain of salt. I didn't know—and never quite figured out—how to get my kids to make good grades, keep their rooms clean, or stick with piano lessons. Instead, these are the lessons I learned while trying to give them self-confidence and encourage them to chart their own paths and stand up for what they believe.

1. Child-rearing is a team sport

Nothing could have prepared me for how humbling the experience of parenting would be. It was a big transition to go from running an organizing campaign to having these three little people running just about everything else in my life. Time is precious, and I couldn't be everywhere at once. The biggest lesson I've learned from raising three kids is that you never do it on your own.

For all Kirk's and my luck, I was slightly jealous of folks who had grandparents who would take the kids for a week—or even for a night! My mom often reminded us, "I'm not the baking-cookies kind of grandma," and she was right. And by the time Lily arrived, my father was remarried and had a newborn of his own. Take it from me: there are few weirder conversations with your father than comparing your respective success and failure at toilet training.

Fortunately we had other options. Lily grew up at the campaign office, surrounded by a clan of staff and volunteers. Legions of folks helped raise her—in fact I learned recently that one of her earliest sitters is now a nurse at Planned Parenthood—and after that she never met a stranger. Our three kids, like most, were raised by a community of caregivers— family, friends, coworkers—all of whom influenced them at least as much as their parents did.

One summer, when the twins were barely tall enough to see above the kitchen table, our friends Jennifer and Dawn were cooking hamburgers on the stove, something my kids had never seen since I don't eat meat and do pretty much all the cooking. Hannah and Daniel peered up at the frying pan as if its contents were an exotic food from a foreign land and moments later sunk their teeth into their very first burger. They cried out in unison, "Mom, you have to try this!" I like to think having so many people around all the time expanded their horizons.

2. Pick your battles, and your kids will learn to pick theirs

Once you have kids, you are never *not* a parent again—if you are fortunate, this child-raising stuff is pretty much a lifelong activity. You know that feeling, like you have no idea what you're doing? In my experience, it never goes away. Half the time you realize you are falling back on some deeply ingrained, often bizarre and inexplicable memories from your own childhood. Honestly, are mothers and daughters genetically programmed to fight about hairstyles? I think not, but if I didn't catch myself, it was easy to repeat verbatim things my mother said to me. "You look so pretty when I can see your eyes!" Meaning: *If you don't get your hair out of your face, I'm going to go nuts.*

My mom had a lot of rules to obey when she was a child. After a hardscrabble beginning, my grandmother was determined to make sure Mom fit in with the rich kids at her school. Which included wearing the "right clothes." My grandmother had taken in sewing during the Depression, and she made much of what Mom wore, making sure that the seams matched and that everything fit just so.

Mom carried on this tradition with me, making sure I always had the right outfit. Once, when I was in fifth grade, she relented and agreed to take me shopping to get something that looked more like what other girls my age wore for an upcoming slumber party. The red bell-bottom jeans with white polka dots and a robin's-egg-blue jumpsuit I picked out were my first expressions of liberation. But special occasions still were her purview, and many of those outfits are permanently etched into my brain—including a truly hideous orange Christmas jacket-and-skirt combo in junior high made of what can only be described as faux Naugahyde.

In keeping with her family tradition, on holidays Mom was hell-bent on ensuring that all three of my kids would be decked out in perfectly coordinated matching outfits, from their hats to their socks. When she was governor, it was hard to object when she wanted every child in a denim jumper with a matching red cowboy hat for the photos with the pony. At Christmas she would try to get them all in a photo looking nice. That lasted about three years.

The rest of the time I was adamant that they be able to wear whatever they wanted. That resulted in some bold fashion choices, like Hannah wearing a pair of red cowboy boots with white stars nonstop for at least a year before moving on to a phase of tucking sweatshirts into her leggings. That's how she got the nickname "Tuck" from my friend Jennifer. Lily always wanted to have long flowing hair, which she did not. So she took to wearing elastic-banded skirts on her head, which was the closest she could get to golden tresses. This was a unique look when we went to the grocery store. And then there was Daniel, who wound up wearing little to no clothing pretty much whenever he felt like it. Why do boys like to run around naked and pee outside? I'm not sure, but that was his preference. There is an infamous photo of Daniel on an early camping trip, riding a bike and wearing only a helmet and sneakers. At least we did enforce necessary safety measures.

Beyond some basic standards, it was live and let live when it came to wardrobe decisions. I like to think it freed up some mental space for us all to focus on other things.

One of the other mantras drilled into me as a child was you must try everything on your plate. Why? I have no idea. But it seemed like an immutable rule that I needed to preserve in order to raise well-rounded children. There was an unforgettable standoff between Daniel and me one evening, when I insisted that he at least try the just-picked-from-the-garden homegrown tomato at dinner. (If you have not eaten a home-grown Texas tomato, you must before you die. Or at least listen to Guy Clark's ode to the same, which is aptly titled "Homegrown Tomatoes.") When Daniel refused, I was going to show him who was boss! "Well then, we are just going to sit here at the table until you try it," I declared. The girls exchanged a "Who does she think she is kidding?" look. We all ate dinner, and everyone else finished. The rest of the family was excused and went to wash up, but Daniel and I remained, locked in a celebrity death match.

Daniel was five, loved staying up all night, and didn't have anything else to do. As far as he was concerned, this was great. So we sat there for another two hours. Finally I said something really stupid like, "Well, I have to go to work in the morning to take care of the family, so we're just going to see next time."

Daniel didn't gloat—he never was that kind of kid—but he had definitely gotten the better of me. It helped me learn that arbitrary rules are made to be broken or, at the very least, questioned.

We tried hard to let the kids express themselves at an early age and to challenge convention and rules that exist just because "we've always done it that way." This is how kids learn independence and to stand up for what they believe—even if they're standing up to a tomato.

3. Raising kids is the ultimate serenity prayer

One lesson I learned immediately was how little impact parenting can have. You can do everything right, provide love and encouragement, and yet still raise a child who becomes a right-wing fanatic just to spite you—every progressive parent's nightmare. Luckily, unless someone's life takes a dramatic turn, I managed to avoid dealing with that particular scenario.

Having girl and boy twins is an ongoing social experiment. How could two children raised in the same family, with the same values, turn out so differently? It's true they are fraternal twins, though if I had a nickel for every person who has asked Hannah and Daniel if they are identical twins I'd be a rich woman! (That's actually not possible for a girl and boy. Think about it.) I quickly saw that they also had their own unique approaches to life.

Hannah was, from the jump, a thoughtful observer. She still is to this day, which makes her a great organizer. She was always strategizing, figuring out how to make her ice-cream cone last the entire car ride home, while her brother and sister scarfed theirs down in the first few minutes. She worked hard at school and was up for anything. My friend Sandra Castellanos said on practically the day she was born, "Hannah is an old soul. This is not her first time around in the world."

Daniel, on the other hand, wanted to do only what he wanted to do, which mainly consisted of running around outside and watching TV. In fact it seemed like there was a microchip in his brain that directly connected to the television, and for several years before he decided to read, this was his source of all information. One morning he walked into the kitchen while I was getting breakfast ready and asked, "Mom, did you know there is a chocolate cereal?"

"No, Daniel, I guess not."

"Well, there is, and it's part of a complete breakfast." Kellogg's advertising was created for Daniel.

Later that year we were buying Christmas presents for a family we had adopted for the holidays. Reading through the list of what their kids were hoping for, I asked, "Hannah and Daniel, the girl in this family wants a Teacher Barbie—have you heard of that?"

Daniel didn't miss a beat. "Yes, I have! Teacher Barbie comes with two outfits, batteries sold separately."

Once they started school, it was abundantly clear Hannah was made for kindergarten, and Daniel wasn't quite ready for so many rules. Sitting in one place and paying attention ran contrary to every instinct he had. When I was called in for Daniel's parent-teacher conference I was told there was a big problem: Daniel refused to learn his colors. He was five.

I don't know why she felt so strongly, but his teacher was definitely disturbed. I was amused. "Well," I said, "I'm pretty sure he is going to learn them when he wants to, and definitely before he goes to college." The same was true with learning to read, doing homework, and paying attention in class. *All the way through high school.* Daniel just did things in his own sweet time. Eventually he did learn his colors. Not only that—he became a chemist, and he's now studying for his PhD. The irony is not lost on any of us that he's the most educated person in the family.

4. Gender roles are alive and well, and they start early

My mother grew up in a time when most women didn't have many options; you could be a teacher, a secretary, a domestic worker, or a nurse, and that was pretty much it. My kids, though, grew up seeing women in charge. Our life was such a matriarchy that when Daniel was three he said, "When I grow up, I want to be a woman." This was less gender confusion than gender envy. The women he knew were in power, doing important and cool things.

While I grew up playing half-court basketball, the twins were nine months old and in a Snugli when they began going to see the University of Texas Lady Longhorns basketball team. Lily and her friend Amanda even had the honor of wiping up the basketball court floor during time-outs. At the time, the longest-serving women's basketball coach, Jody Conradt, had the winningest record for a college women's team. We were season ticket holders, as was everyone we knew. In those days, if they had dropped a bomb on the Erwin Center during a Lady Longhorns game, every lesbian and progressive in Austin would have perished.

Mom and her friend Barbara Jordan, then in a wheelchair, would sit courtside and cheer like teenagers. Barbara took the sport seriously and did not go easy on the women when their game was off. You could hear her voice thundering from the sidelines, just as if she were back in the middle of the Watergate hearings: "Women, can we not shoot any better than this?" It wasn't until they were much older that the twins learned men played basketball too.

Still, as far as we had come, the stereotyping of boys and girls from the earliest age was heartbreaking. The teacher in Hannah and Daniel's kindergarten class gave out "awards" at the end of the year. For

Texas Lady Longhorns fans Congresswoman Barbara Jordan, Governor Ann Richards, and Lily Adams. They were regular and relentless cheerleaders.

the girls? "Most helpful to the teacher" and "Friendliest student." The boys' diplomas were very different: "Most likely to invent something" and "Best in math." It was maddening, part of a pattern we fought hard to break.

When we moved to Washington, DC, Hannah joined the Girl Scouts. I too had been a member back in the day, and my memories were of camping and working for badges, in addition to sewing baby blankets for the local hospital. Hannah, though, spent the Girl Scout year doing three things: getting ready for the cookie sale, selling the cookies, and tabulating the sales. I'm sure this is not the experience of every Girl Scout troop, but meanwhile Daniel was in the Cub Scouts, and he didn't have to sell a thing. Daniel and I carved a car for the Pinewood Derby and competed with Cub Scouts from all around the area. His den was taking bike rides along the C&O Canal, learning about rocket ships from astronauts, and volunteering at Loaves and Fishes, the local soup kitchen. When the Cub Scouts decided to discriminate against LGBTQ kids and leaders and we decided to drop out, Daniel was disappointed, but I was devastated—I lived for those Pinewood Derby competitions!

Finally one day I'd had it. I said to Hannah, "What if we started our own organization, one where we didn't have to sell cookies and could do the cool kinds of things the Cub Scouts do?"

Hannah was game, so along with a half dozen of her friends from her fourth grade class, we got ourselves organized. The girls met and determined they needed a name and a T-shirt. They decided to call themselves the Future Women Presidents, and one of the artistic moms in the group, Cindy Jaffe, designed the shirts. They went camping and learned how to make a fire and cook outdoors. They painted a mural at a community center. They hiked, recycled, visited the Museum of Women in the Arts, and then, through a miraculous series of events, got to visit the White House and even the press briefing room. It seemed only fitting for the Future Women Presidents!

As the girls moved out of elementary school and into junior high, the FWP dissolved. I still think if we had stuck with it, we could have gone national. I recently came across an old photo of the Future Women Presidents, now all women in their twenties. It's nice to think that early on they had the chance to think big thoughts, learn some self-sufficiency, and be proud of the women they would become. One just received her master's degree in public health, working on reproductive health care. Another is working with a food kitchen. They are scattered from San Francisco to South Africa, and it has been wonderful to see them grow into confident women. And the Girl Scouts? These days they're on the move, teaching girls math and science, business and leadership skills.

5. Get comfortable making others uncomfortable

I know all three kids secretly wished that at least once, on "career day" at Lafayette Elementary School, one of their parents was a firefighter or librarian or something they knew how to explain to their friends. By that time Kirk was neck-deep in labor organizing and I was fighting for reproductive rights. We were always going up against some tough adversary, and the dinner table conversation was usually about some injustice somewhere or our overwhelming frustration with the political scene in Washington. George W. Bush was president, and had recently nominated Samuel Alito and John Roberts to the Supreme Court, so we were in constant battle.

One day Daniel came home and announced that his third grade classroom had been talking about what they wanted to be when they grew up. He had decided he wanted to be a potter.

Daniel had not shown the slightest talent or interest in anything artistic. "That's great, Daniel!" I said. "What a fascinating thing to do. How did you decide that?"

"Because, Mom, nobody doesn't like a potter."

A little bit of my heart broke that night, and I realized how much he and his sisters had internalized some of the toughest parts of life as an activist. Daniel was learning that going up against the powers that be means there will always be someone who doesn't like what you're doing. That's the life Kirk and I chose. As a result the kids learned that not everyone is going to love you, and that's okay.

Years later, instead of becoming a potter, Daniel headed off to Allegheny College in rural western Pennsylvania. He also became an activist and learned to stand up for his beliefs, which didn't always match up with the beliefs of his classmates or the campus administration. I'm pretty sure he is the first and only Allegheny student to both chair his fraternity's social committee and serve as the vice president of the reproductive rights organization. One of his proudest moments (and mine) was his fight to get reproductive health services on campus. Daniel called me to say he'd met with the head of the school clinic. "We went in to talk to her, because, Mom, they won't even prescribe birth control for students, and it's hard to get it off campus. I told her that, honestly, kids weren't breaking their legs every weekend, but they were having sex."

Eventually the campus agreed to provide prescriptions for birth control for students, a major win. Daniel went on to help organize "slut walks" and the sex fair at Allegheny, where they attracted the attention of the *Drudge Report* for holding a session on female orgasm in the school chapel. I called Daniel to congratulate him when I saw the headline. His explanation? "She was the most popular speaker, and the chapel was the biggest meeting space we could find." That's my boy!

6. Work-life balance is a myth

My life as a mom did not break neatly into "work" and "parenting." For many years it was just one big blur. Like so many parents, I put my kids in day care the minute it was a possibility. Working for the union, I had three months of unpaid leave, though Kirk had none. As soon as my leave ended, I had to go back to work. I wasn't ready. In fact driving away after dropping Lily off at the sitter that first morning, I wept uncontrollably. And I was one of the lucky ones. It is unconscionable that this country still has no paid parental leave.

I remember leaving the twins at day care one morning, only to hear on NPR as I drove away about a new study confirming that 90 percent of how your kids will turn out is determined in the first three years of life. I slammed on the brakes, thinking, "I've got to go back and get them right now, before it's too late to make a difference!" But then I realized that because they were then nearly three and a half, it was likely a lost cause already.

Kirk and I moved to Washington in 1998 because we both agreed it was time to see something other than Texas. (The children wept when we said we were moving across the country, but after we moved, they had a whole new set of friends and experiences, and it was fine.) There wasn't an obvious job for me in DC. One day I sat all three kids down and asked, "What do you guys think about me maybe not going back to work? I could be here in the afternoon when you got off from school. We could do stuff together!"

They looked horrified. I'm sure they could count on one hand the days I had taken off from work to be with them, and the thought of my being at home was crazy. They had been raised to be independent and take care of each other, and they weren't interested in giving up their freedom. I certainly couldn't blame them for that. Besides, I think they knew, even at that young age, that it was in nobody's best interest for me to have extra time on my hands. So that answered that.

Still, until I found a job, it was hard to be an organizer with nothing to organize. So I volunteered to make the costumes for the sixth grade play, *The Wiz*. Every sixth grader had to be in it—it was not optional. Since she could sing, Lily scored a plum role as Glinda and would share the stage with about sixty other kids. Everyone had multiple roles (requiring multiple costumes), which meant, among other feats, securing ten leather jackets for the Winged Monkeys and hot-gluing glitter and felt stars to dozens of T-shirts for the grand finale. I was in organizing heaven!

Just a week before the performance, I got a call from former senator Tim Wirth of Colorado, asking if I could meet with him and a couple of people about a possible job. I didn't know him and had no idea how he'd gotten my number, but as they say, the show must go on. "Sure, that would be great," I replied, "but it would need to be Thursday, because today I'm getting ready for dress rehearsal, and the Munchkin costumes aren't finished."

There was silence on the other end of the line. "Well, I guess we can wait. We'll see you tomorrow then," said the senator.

I rushed downtown Thursday right after a less-than-perfect dress rehearsal. There was still glitter all over my hands from last-minute touch-up work, and I realized too late that I didn't have a pair of panty hose without a run in them. Looking pretty much the worse for wear, and still preoccupied with how I was going to attach all those wings to the leather jackets for the monkeys, I walked into Wirth's office. Sitting in the room with him were Ted Turner and Jane Fonda. They were looking for an organizer to work on reproductive rights for their foundation. I'm not certain whether the organizing skills I'd demonstrated by corralling all those sixth graders into costumes clinched it, but that couldn't have hurt, because they hired me on the spot. That crazy day confirmed one of my mom's favorite admonishments: Never turn down a new opportunity. And for every parent who has organized a PTA meeting or coordinated volunteer shifts for the silent auction, know this: Those skills will serve you well.

7. Someone always has to be the mom

I know even as I write this that some people aren't going to like it. But this is the truth: No matter how evolved you are, no matter your family makeup or the gender roles in your home, in any family with kids, someone has to remember birthdays, make lunches, keep track of doctor's appointments, give pep talks, and coordinate after-school activities and holidays. For most of history, and often to this day, the default expectation has been that those responsibilities are women's work.

There are all kinds of families. Sometimes "the mom" isn't a mom at all. Sometimes it's a dad or a grandparent, an uncle, an older brother, or a sister. The point is, someone has to keep the wheels on the whole operation. If you're a man reading this and thinking, *That has nothing to do with gender*, ask the women in your life if it sounds familiar.

Kirk and I agreed from the get-go that we were going to take turns, and for the most part it has worked. At different junctures in our careers, one of us has been the one to work regular hours, uproot their life for the other one's job, rush to pick up a sick kid from school. And honestly, more often than not it has been Kirk. Those responsibilities are always there, and someone is always going to assume the lion's share. And if you can find someone who recognizes that and is willing to trade off with you, you've got it made.

8. Everything you need to know in life you can learn on a campaign

Lily never had a choice. At age three she went straight from janitors' picket lines in Los Angeles to the middle of Mom's campaign for governor. Our life was at work with her grandmother, or Mammy, as she called her. Letters to the Tooth Fairy were written on a typewriter in the campaign office, and she was probably the only preschooler who entertained herself by signing "Ann Richards" over and over again with the autopen.

Though Hannah and Daniel didn't arrive until after Mom's election, they made up for lost time, as everyone around them either worked for the governor or on an issue she was embroiled in. By the time they were old enough to read, they were helping out at the Texas Freedom Network office, stuffing envelopes or making copies. Campaign offices are chaotic places, and so was TFN; there were always volunteers dropping by, mailings to be sent out, or lists of people to call.

When you think about it, a campaign is a great place to pick up new skills. Early on, kids can learn to alphabetize, since there is nothing like sorting a mailing list to nail the ABCs. And then there are the essential etiquette and people skills. As Daniel, an experienced phone-banker, will tell you, people may not always be happy to hear from you if you're the twelfth call they have gotten reminding them to vote. Remaining cheerful and persistent, despite verbal abuse, will always come in handy. And recruiting volunteers and raising money are evergreen skills no matter your future path.

I believe every kid should know how to speak in front of people, especially at their door, about supporting a candidate or cause they believe in. When Hannah was in high school she and I went door to door for President Obama during the final week of the 2008 campaign in Florida. It was an hour before the polls closed on Election Day, and Hannah had just one more door to knock on. The man who answered told her Barack Obama was born in Africa, and he was *not* getting his vote. Hannah's eyes welled up with tears as she explained that he was actually born in Hawaii.

"Well, I'm not going to vote for him anyway," he said, and stomped back inside. Nothing like a door slamming in your face to toughen you up.

Campaigning teaches you about winning and losing and, probably most important, that you never get ahead unless you try. Lily still says it was Mom's first campaign that taught her anything is possible if you're willing to step up and give it a shot. No one thought Ann Richards could overcome the odds and become governor. The only reason she did is because she, and a bunch of others, never gave up. From her second campaign we learned that you don't always win, but it's worth the fight. And of course the greatest thing about working on campaigns, marching, and organizing is getting to do something important with people who share your passion.

One of my best memories is marching with my mom and kids in Washington with the Texas delegation at the national March for Women's Lives in 2004. Today there is nothing much better than seeing parents at a Planned Parenthood rally with a little kid in tow. I can't help but smile to think of the stories that kid will be able to tell one day about learning to take a stand even before they could walk. Children learn not from what you tell them, but from what they see you do, how you spend your days and what you do with your life. I'm glad Lily, Hannah, and Daniel got to see early on that politics works best when it's not a spectator sport.

9. Nothing is more motivating than seeing generational progress through your kids' eyes

Having a mom who worked for Planned Parenthood came in handy for my kids more than once. At the very least, by the time they were in high school, our apartment was where one could always find condoms.

It was also Planned Parenthood that provided the twins their first organizing opportunities. In 2011, when Congress turned on us and the efforts to shut down Planned Parenthood really took off in Washington (with a little help from Congressman Mike Pence, who will always have a special place in my heart), both Hannah and Daniel were in college.

Hannah called me, agitated. "Everyone at school is really upset about this defunding of Planned Parenthood, but I don't really know what to do. We just have to do something."

"Students all over the country are getting involved right now. How about you organize something on campus?" I suggested.

We hung up, and the next week I got a notice that the students at Wesleyan were holding a rally of support for Planned Parenthood. I knew right away: that was Hannah. She'd just gotten it together—created a Facebook event, hung posters around campus, told everyone she knew, and remembered to call some reporters a day or two before the event. Hundreds of people packed into a hall on campus, plus overflow rooms.

Senator Richard Blumenthal and the school president, Michael Roth, even showed up to speak. After the rally a bunch of Wesleyan students made an amazing video in support of Planned Parenthood, titled *I Have Sex*—you better believe it went viral.

Daniel knew what was happening from the news, but that was about all I was sure of. One Saturday I was racing downtown in New York to speak at a Planned Parenthood rally when I got a text. "Hey Mom, I'm in a car with some kids from Allegheny. We're driving to Ohio to a rally for Planned Parenthood. I love you." It was from Daniel.

My first reaction was totally emotional: here was my happy-go-lucky son, getting in a car to spend his weekend fighting for Planned Parenthood. But my second thought was *Wow, if Daniel is driving to Ohio, then this is a movement, and we are going to win.* (Which we did, thanks in no small part to young people who organized on campuses across the country.) Today Daniel is a chemist, but also a lifelong political activist, and proud of it.

Hannah decided to become a full-time organizer, working on environmental justice and commonsense gun reform, among other causes. If anyone is taking up the family business, it's her. She's experienced the pains of coalition building just as Kirk and I did when we were trying to organize New Orleans back in the day. How do you get groups to see their shared interest on some issue when they may have nothing else in common? Every now and then I get a call from her ahead of some big community hearing or after an organizing mishap, and my heart skips a beat. We are constantly brainstorming organizing strategies, and I wouldn't have it any other way. I have such enormous love and respect for her.

And Lily? Well, she picked up where her grandmother left off. I tease her that her public profile peaked at age one and a half, when Mom mentioned her in the Democratic keynote speech in Atlanta. That night Kirk was wandering around the convention hall wearing a homemade button that said "Lily's Dad." Mom, meanwhile, was eager to pass on all the important life skills she had spent years learning: If you can't remember someone's name, you can always call them "honey." Never wear patterns on TV. And for heaven's sake, before you name your kid, think about how it will look on a bumper sticker or billboard.

Lily remembers those Ann Richards lessons like nobody I know, and they've served her well in politics. She's worked for US senators, worked on campaigns, won and lost. And who could have guessed that her early experience at Baylor would turn out to be such good training when, in her twenties, she found herself a target of Rush Limbaugh on his radio show. Now that's a story. Limbaugh had said that men shouldn't be criticized for ogling women's breasts, but should instead tell women, "Will you please ask your breasts to stop staring at my eyes?" Lily was working at the Democratic National Committee and sent an email calling on Republican leaders to stop going on Limbaugh's show. Next thing we knew, Rush was yelling about Lily Adams, even reading her email on the air in a mocking little-girl voice. Lily was unfazed; she couldn't believe he took the bait.

The best is when we all join forces for a cause. President Obama's historic campaign in 2008 was a family project. All three kids volunteered, even though the twins weren't old enough to vote. Like millions of other young people, they got a front-row seat to the power of grassroots organizing and the importance of elections. Kirk and I and the kids were scattered across the country in the last week of the campaign. On Election Day, Hannah and I were in Florida, Lily was door-knocking in New Hampshire, Kirk was in Virginia, and Daniel was back home in New York City. Every few hours Kirk managed to organize a family-wide check-in to compare notes. I'm not sure how many other families were getting on a recurring conference call. On our last call of the night, when we realized Obama had won, Daniel ran out into the streets of New York City with thousands of others to celebrate. Of all the marches and campaigns we've done as a family, nothing will ever match being at Obama's first inauguration together, watching history unfold.

We were back at it in 2012, each of us in a different state for the reelection campaign. Lily was working on Tim Kaine's senate race in Virginia, and I wound up in Richmond on Election Day, on leave from Planned Parenthood to help get out the vote. Along with my friend

Shamina Singh, I spent the day phone-banking as if my life depended on it. After we got through our call lists, we headed out to knock on doors in the suburbs, where women were getting their neighbors to watch their kids so they could run over and vote after work. As the polls closed, we stopped at campaign headquarters to check in on Lily.

"We finished our walk lists and phones calls—is there anything else we can do?" I asked.

Lily looked around. "Is there anything else?" she called over to the field team.

"Well, there are a few polling places where people are still outside, waiting to vote," someone answered. "The election officers have to keep the polls open if folks are in line."

Before they could finish, Shamina and I were getting our coats on. First we headed to the closest Krispy Kreme and bought ten dozen donuts and some boxes of coffee. Then we drove to the closest polling place, where we poured coffee and handed out donuts to the people who were standing out in the cold, waiting for their turn to vote. They were elderly folks, women with kids in their arms, students doing their homework as they held the line. We sent a picture back to Lily at the office. It was the perfect election night.

10. There are some basic life skills every kid needs, whether or not they're an activist

Kirk and I have been really lucky. Despite the fact that our kids grew up on picket lines, in campaign offices, and at day care—or, I like to believe, because of it—they're good people, and each is working in their own way to make a difference. They are funny and kind, and they are patient with their parents, who have often put organizing ahead of clean clothes or sitting down for dinner at regularly scheduled times.

At the end of the day all we can do is make sure that once our kids are launched, they have the basic life skills that are necessary for survival and joy.

Most of all, I hope my kids, and all kids, have the confidence and opportunity to follow their own path in life—to take risks and do what makes them happy. And if, in the meantime, they change the world along the way, so much the better.

On one of countless adventures with Daniel, Hannah, Lily, and Kirk. Cape of Good Hope, 2016.

Chapter 8

Say Yes

I almost didn't go to the interview for the job at Planned Parenthood. At the time, I was running America Votes in Washington, DC, and there was a lot on my plate. When you run an organization, everything stops at your desk: hiring, fundraising, interoffice politics. We were a shoestring start-up, so even considering another job came with enormous guilt. As a master worrier, I immediately went there: *Who else would take this on? What about all the organizers around the country who were counting on me to raise the money to keep it all going?*

I was sitting in my office downtown when the search firm called to see if I'd be interested in taking over as president of Planned Parenthood. My first thought was *Are you kidding?* Ellen Chesler, whom I had met while working on reproductive rights for Ted Turner and Jane Fonda, had put my name forward. Ellen is a writer, historian, and public policy expert known for her book, *Woman of Valor*, the definitive biography of Planned Parenthood's founder, Margaret Sanger. She and I had been co-conspirators and good friends, reminding me yet again that you never know who will change the course of your life. I also knew Gloria Feldt, the outgoing president, so I had an inkling of what an enormous undertaking this would be.

I called Kirk. "Okay," I said, "I know we just finally bought a house in Washington, and the kids are settled at school, but the folks from Planned Parenthood just called. They want to know if I might be interested in applying for the job as president."

Kirk has always been the most supportive, positive person in my life.

Sometimes I think that if I called and said we needed to pack up and go to Mars, he would just ask, "What do I need to bring?"

"That sounds great! I love New York!" was his response. He knew the job was huge and complicated, but he pushed me to go for it.

A couple of weeks later I was standing in front of my closet, trying to pick out the right outfit to wear for the biggest moment of my professional career. At every other job I'd had, I was creating something new—Planned Parenthood was a huge organization with a hundred-year legacy.

The interview was at an office building a few minutes away from America Votes, where I would meet with the national search committee—which in and of itself sounded overwhelming. I went to a nearby coffee shop to gather my thoughts, but instead I freaked out.

I started running through my list of "why nots": *This is the wrong time. My kids are still in school. We could never move.* Here I was, barely in the first round of interviews, already worrying about what would happen if I got the job. I was on the verge of calling the search firm and telling them I'd take a pass.

Instead I did what any grown woman would do: I called my mom.

I told her what I was about to do, then immediately launched into all the reasons I wasn't the person for the job: The political climate was brutal. I'd never run anything this big before, let alone an established organization that millions of people counted on for health care each year. Why on earth would they even consider me for the position?

Mom was just not having it. I'm sure she was thinking about all of the women she'd known who'd sabotaged themselves because of fear and self-doubt, and she wasn't about to let me off easily. "Cecile, you will never know unless you try. And let's face it: You only get one life, and this is it. Besides, Planned Parenthood is doing more for women's health than any organization in America! How exciting!"

Her voice still rings in my head, asking, "What's the worst thing that could happen?" She was right. I could try for it and not get the job; I could handle that. Or I could get the job and be a colossal failure, which would be pretty bad, but even then I'd eventually get over it and do something else.

Though I was sure I'd never get the job, I showed up for the interview and found ten people sitting around the conference table, ready to ask questions. I didn't know any of them personally, but Mom's advice had calmed me down. And besides, knowing deep down that this was a long shot actually helped—I felt like I had nothing to lose.

I loved the search committee right away. One of the members was a legend in the world of reproductive rights, Jill June. She ran Planned Parenthood in Iowa, and though she looked like a kindly grandmother, she was as fearless as they came. "We're the very best at what we do, providing reproductive health care for women," she explained. "But we keep losing ground in the political arena, and we can't count on another organization to fix it for us. We need to get back to our movement roots. Are you interested?"

It was clear to me that the job would have a steep learning curve. On the other hand, I could be a good partner in a lot of the things they wanted to do. I was more than interested.

Having worked with Planned Parenthood across the country at America Votes and in Leader Pelosi's office, I knew firsthand the incredible depth of commitment and relationships they had. One in five women in America has been to Planned Parenthood for health care, and that great alumni association of current and former patients was an enormous asset. During Gloria's tenure I had served on the national Planned Parenthood Action Fund board and seen the challenges of building up the advocacy arm of the organization. Planned Parenthood was busy providing excellent health care, and was overdue for some serious investments in the grassroots movement for women's health.

We had a great conversation, and when Patricio Gonzales, a Planned Parenthood leader serving women on the Rio Grande border in Texas, spoke of the struggles to provide services in an area of the country I knew so well, he touched my heart. So many women in the Rio Grande Valley depended on Planned Parenthood for health care, and if they lost it—which was definitely a possibility—Patricio was afraid they would go over the border to Mexico. (Those fears would become a reality years later, when politicians in Texas forced health centers across the state to close, giving some women no choice but to leave the state for birth control and abortions.)

I left the interview thinking, *This could be really exciting*. So you might think I was thrilled to get the call saying they wanted me back for a second interview. Oh no: I went through all the same anxieties, only this time they were worse. Now it seemed like I really might get the job—and *then* what? I was terrified.

Somehow I gutted up and showed up again. They were definitely interested. The search firm called me almost immediately after I left that interview and made me an offer. When I hesitated, the woman on the other end of the phone jumped right in. "How are you *not* going to do this?" she asked.

She was right. I took the leap and said yes, having only the slightest idea what I was stepping into.

I knew Kirk was ready to go to New York; we'd had plenty of Washington. But I still had to break it to the kids. Hannah and I were driving in the car when I decided to tell her. Why is it always in the car where the most difficult conversations happen with teenagers?

"Hannah, I know how happy you are here in Washington, but I decided to take the job with Planned Parenthood." Gulp. Silence.

"You and Daniel can finish out ninth grade, but I'll go on up to New York and find us a place to live. It will be great, though I know it's a big change."

In her younger years Hannah was the master of the silent treatment, and this was no exception. In contrast to her tears at age six when we left Texas, this time she sat there like a stone. I have a terrible habit of filling any silence, so I kept talking. "Just think—you can meet all kinds of new people and go to a new school. And your friends will definitely come and visit!"

Eventually she came around, but it wasn't easy. It would be years before we could look back on this move, like all our others, and agree it was the right thing for us as a family.

Besides being worried about the kids, I was also concerned about leaving my job and my staff. After all, I'd started the organization, and it felt like a betrayal to leave it and those good people behind. I took Beth Ganz, our chief of staff, out to coffee and said I had some tough news to tell her. She looked stricken. She had moved from Denver to Washington to take the job at America Votes. "Okay, go ahead," she said nervously.

"I'm taking the job at Planned Parenthood," I said.

She was silent for a minute. Then she burst out, "I thought you were about to fire me!"

What is it about us women?

Once I'd accepted the job and gotten the word out, several things started happening at once. I had to find a place for us to live and a place for the kids to go to school, neither of which is a small feat in a new town. I felt like Mrs. Mallard in *Make Way for Ducklings*, searching out a safe spot for the family in New York City. In the meantime I was also training for a marathon with my friend Maggie. I'd never run one in my life, but running so much during the transition helped keep my head together. Come race day, I was definitely not the best-prepared marathoner, but Maggie and I finished the race, with Daniel running the last mile alongside me.

Part of the routine for a new Planned Parenthood leader is to have a security team evaluate their physical safety, I'm sorry to say. Because we'd be staying in Washington for a while, our house there had to be inspected. Daniel, at least, was excited to have a security team around, looking for any sign of vulnerability, showing us maps of where we were vis-à-vis crime statistics in the District of Columbia. I'd never had a job where security was part of the daily routine but quickly realized this was standard practice for Planned Parenthood CEOs around the country. It didn't give me pause, but I realized that life with Planned Parenthood required a different level of awareness—for me, the kids, and Kirk. And I would come to learn that making sure your house is secure isn't a lot of help once you start getting recognized in public. More than once I've been accosted on the street or at an airport, like the time a man—and they are almost always men—walked up as I was sitting at the gate, told me he was praying for me, and handed me a completely nutty self-published religious book. He stood there for what felt like forever, and all I could think was *How can I possibly get myself out of here?*

Meanwhile, through a friend of Gloria Feldt, I had found something unheard-of in New York: a rental apartment big enough for the five of us. I brought Kirk and the kids up for the weekend to check it out. We were right in the middle of Manhattan, near a public school that the kids liked and I hoped they could get into. I was so excited when we got off the subway that I went up to the local coffee cart outside our building, ubiquitous in the city. I greeted the coffee vendor with a big smile and said, "Hi, we're moving in right here! I'm Cecile, and this is my family!" That's me. You can take the girl out of Texas, but you can't take Texas out of the girl! The guy looked at me like I had lost my mind. Though he didn't say the words, his expression clearly communicated, *Lady, I serve coffee to a few hundred folks every day. How about you just give me your orders? You take it black or with cream?* Welcome to New York City!

The kids and Kirk were back in Washington when I started my new job. I had asked if I could have a meeting with the entire Planned Parenthood staff right away. Our communications director, Elizabeth Toledo, was skeptical. "I'm not sure you want to do that," she counseled. "You just got here, and they probably have all kinds of questions you aren't ready for."

Elizabeth was right, of course. She was and is an incredible communications expert, but I didn't know it at the time. I insisted on the meeting.

I got there early Monday morning, ready to go. Staff started assembling on the top floor, probably a hundred or so. Most were people I'd yet to meet. I said hello, introduced myself, and told them how excited I was to work with them and for Planned Parenthood. Then I asked if there were any questions.

Right off the bat, Jon Knowles stood up. Jon was a veteran at Planned Parenthood—a sex educator, writer, and editor, with a long ponytail and a beard. His office, I later learned, was the repository of every phallic replica in the place—a penis gallery! He cut right to the chase: "I was wondering, what's your plan to make sexual pleasure a universal value in the United States?"

I'm sure my expression was like the squirrel in the movie *Ice Age*: huge eyes and utter shock. "Okay, well, you've got me there, Jon. I'm going to have a lot to learn from you!"

That was just the beginning. The minute I said yes to the job, I knew my life was about to change in a million ways. This was one: when you work for Planned Parenthood, you spend more time talking about sex than you could possibly imagine. It comes up in meetings and emails— like the day a note came around from the organization's librarian, who wrote, "Will whoever took our last copy of *Anal Pleasure and Health* by Jack Morin please return it to the 11th floor?" Almost immediately hilarious replies started flooding in: "I'm still trying to master Chapter 12, but will return it as soon as I do!" I was definitely not working at the Capitol anymore!

My whole life I've tried to take jobs where I could learn something, and I definitely had a lot to learn at Planned Parenthood. It was sink or swim, and my only hope of swimming was to know what I didn't know: running the business side of an organization with a presence in every state and navigating America's convoluted system of health care delivery, among other things. It was humbling to admit, but necessary. Whether in politics or organizing, the best leaders are the ones who are always searching out new talent and bringing people on board who challenge them to be better. It was clear from day one that this was what I needed to do.

Mom was always full of advice, and one of the most brilliant ideas she had as I was getting ready to work at Planned Parenthood was to introduce me to a young woman from Texas she had met years earlier, Maryana Iskander. Maryana was barely thirty, but she had already done more than most people accomplish in their lifetime. A Yale law graduate, Rhodes Scholar, and all-around genius, she was living in Houston and working for the president of Rice University. I called her on the phone and said that I was going to be taking this job and needed a partner.

Maryana is the polar opposite of me: she's calm, thoughtful, and logical. We agreed that she would come up to Washington and have dinner. "It will be clear after that whether or not this is a good idea," she said. (Years later we gave her a Yoda statue for her office. She was always the wise one.)

We met at the Bombay Club in Washington and talked about this improbable job I was about to start. Would she be interested in coming with me? I knew enough about taking on big jobs to know that having a partner was an absolute must, someone to jump off the high dive with me.

Thank goodness for whatever inner message she received that night, because next thing I knew, Maryana had packed up and moved to New York City to take the job of executive vice president. She became my most trusted partner for the next several years. We did everything together, from hiring a new leadership team to crafting a strategic plan for the organization. It was a lesson that would get me through so many moments when I felt in over my head: Never be afraid to hire people who are smarter than you.

• • •

Even with Maryana on board, getting started was overwhelming. Neither of us had ever worked for Planned Parenthood, so we had a lot to learn. The early days were brutal, and we had a lot of late nights. I was on a first-name basis with the building's cleaning staff, who came in after hours, when I was one of the last ones still sitting at the computer. There were a million tasks: roles to fill, financial decisions to make, relationships to establish in Washington, donors to meet from all over the country. It wasn't remotely glamorous; we were working seven days a week. One evening, when Maryana and I were sitting in my office going through a massive to-do list after everyone else had gone home, she turned to me and said, "You know, at my last job, it was the president who left, and everyone else stayed and worked." Not us—we had too much to do!

As soon as I took the job, my kids became the go-to sources of information about Planned Parenthood for their peers. Lily, who had left for college in Massachusetts, suddenly found that high school friends everywhere were reaching out to her, looking for a place to get birth control or a way to be in touch with Planned Parenthood. She called me in October that first year. "Mom, Sarah just called me because a friend needs to get birth control. Do you know where the closest place is in Indianapolis?" I went to look up our clinic information and it dawned on me: there had to be a better way for us to be there for young people. I couldn't call back every college student in the United States, nor did most of them know to call Lily.

At the time, Planned Parenthood had a national website, but it was exclusively focused on activism. If you were trying to find birth control in, say, Oklahoma City, it would have been a challenge. Being able to get first-rate health care information or find a health center 24/7 was at the core of our mission. I knew if we got it right, the internet and Planned Parenthood could be a match made in heaven. I just wasn't sure where to start.

A lot of hardworking people—especially women—fall into the trap of thinking, "If I just stay at the office all night, I can do it all myself." Those first months at Planned Parenthood quickly put any such thoughts to rest. There were jobs I just could not do, no matter how late I worked or how committed I was. To build the kind of organization I envisioned, I'd need to find people who had talent and expertise in areas I knew next to nothing about. Then I'd need to step back and let them do their thing.

Fortunately I had met a guy working as a consultant for Planned Parenthood in Boston who was as excited about the possibilities of the internet as I was. Tom Subak was happily living his life, but I told him he had a bigger job to do: we needed his skills and drive to build a website that could take Planned Parenthood into the twenty-first century.

Tom and I came from the same organizing background. He had spent years working for the Public Interest Research Group, those people who come up to you on the street and ask if you have a minute to answer a survey on the environment. Tom's training told him that our first step was to ask folks what they wanted from us, and then work to deliver it.

As we suspected, about 95 percent of the visitors to our website were looking for something we were not providing: a way to find the closest Planned Parenthood health center. But convincing the whole federation that we could do more together than apart, especially when it came to the online world, flew in the face of long-standing traditions. At that point we had 128 local affiliates of Planned Parenthood, and everyone did things their own way. For example, longtime Planned Parenthood CEO in Houston, Peter Durkin, was appalled that local leaders in San Francisco talked about sex in a way that could scandalize his supporters in Texas.

"Here's the thing, Peter," I told him. "The internet has changed everything. What we say in California has to be what we say in the South. We're going to have to come together and figure out how to be consistent." He looked unsure, but was willing to give it a try.

Convincing folks that the need to connect with millions more people online was an opportunity, not a threat, took some doing. Planned Parenthood was started by troublemaking, fiercely independent leaders all across the country, and the last thing they wanted was the national offices in New York and Washington telling them what to do. Plus, people who are born to challenge authority do it every chance they get—including in their own organization. But Tom, along with a dedicated group of Planned Parenthood CEOs, made it happen. Those early investments and painstaking efforts have allowed us to build the only national reproductive rights website that receives more than 72 million visits a year, lets patients make appointments on their mobile phones day or night, and provides health information twenty-four hours a day, seven days a week, in English and Spanish.

Meanwhile Planned Parenthood's most important work was happening at health centers across America. I was itching to get out of our office and get to know the organization from a different perspective. Dawn Laguens, a longtime friend and back then a strategy consultant for Planned Parenthood, helped me design a "thirty-day dialogue," so that I could spend a month hearing from staff and volunteers across the country. It was an early glimpse of life on the road, which would become my new normal for the next decade. The stories I heard and the people I met would inform some of the most important decisions I had to make in the early days—decisions about the investments we needed to make in the future of Planned Parenthood.

An energetic staff member named Amy Taylor was game to go with me. Together we saw a lot of the country that first month, from Minnesota to Florida. Local Planned Parenthood CEOs welcomed me, gave me the lay of the land, and arranged for me to spend a day at their health centers, listening to their staff and volunteers.

There was so much to learn and see for myself—most important, the kind of heroic work that was taking place in the states. As Jill June had mentioned back in my first job interview, Planned Parenthood leaders were not only providing health care but were also battling daily to protect access to all the services Planned Parenthood provides.

One important battle was the fight for safe, legal abortion in South Dakota, one of the most conservative states in the country. The local Planned Parenthood CEO, Sarah Stoesz, had an essential combination of skills: she knew a lot about political organizing from her early days with Senator Paul Wellstone of Minnesota, and she had experience delivering first-class health care in some of the most remote, and most politically challenging, areas of the country.

Just as I arrived, the South Dakota legislature passed a bill making all abortion illegal, full stop. It looked hopeless. Our folks on the ground were tirelessly working to keep the Planned Parenthood health center in Sioux Falls up and running. It was the only location in the state for access to safe and legal abortion, and folks wanted to know what Planned Parenthood was going to do.

"We have got to fight this on the ground," Sarah told me. "What they're trying to do is clearly unconstitutional, but rather than go to court, we have the right to take this unconscionable law straight to the voters in South Dakota and convince them to overturn it. That's what we need to do."

It sounded crazy to me. After all, if the law was unconstitutional, why not sue? But Sarah disagreed. "This is an opportunity to fundamentally challenge the belief that people in South Dakota—people anywhere, for that matter—want abortion to be illegal. I know it'll be hard to win, but we have to try. Litigation should be our last resort."

Sarah was persuasive and, as it turned out, completely right. She collected the signatures to get the law on the ballot and raised the money for a statewide repeal effort. She hired and trained organizers to go door to door in South Dakota, explaining to voters that this legislation would take the right away from women and their families to make important decisions about pregnancy. Sarah took me to visit the health center in Sioux Falls, where courageous staff continued to provide care for women. We also met some of the organizers on the campaign; these young women were undaunted. After talking to complete strangers about abortion in South Dakota, they could do anything.

Sarah was the first to show me that people are capable of holding two important ideas at the same time. "A person may have their own deeply felt opinion about abortion," she explained. "They may not believe it is a choice they would make. But they are also able to respect the decisions that each woman, or family, may make themselves." In fact a mother who ended up making a television ad for the campaign reflected just that. She and her husband had been overjoyed to learn that she was pregnant with twins. But after discovering a serious medical complication, they made the tough decision to terminate one of the pregnancies so the other twin could survive. She had never been an activist before, but she decided that if telling her story could help someone else, it was worth it.

When the voters in South Dakota went to the polls, they voted down the legislation overwhelmingly. What Sarah believed was proven true not only on that Election Day but subsequently on a second effort in South Dakota, another in Mississippi, two ballot measures in North Dakota, and yet again in defeating so-called personhood initiatives in Colorado. It just goes to show: people's ability to respect a woman's right to make her own decisions about a pregnancy, including abortion, just might surprise you.

• • •

I was learning so much about the work of the organization and the people at its heart. In one day I would visit with young teen sex educators in East Los Angeles in the morning, and sit next to a business leader at dinner, listening to her declare that Planned Parenthood was the reason she had been able to finish college and have a family and career.

One of the best-kept secrets about Planned Parenthood is that it is the largest provider of sex education in America. For so many young people, it is their only source of honest, nonjudgmental information about their bodies and their lives. Planned Parenthood educators are out on the front lines, where often no one else is.

One of the first educators I met was Irwin Royster, a young man who was running Planned Parenthood's Ophelia Egypt Health Clinic in Anacostia, Maryland, right across the river from DC. Irwin was like the pied piper of Anacostia. There, in the shadow of the nation's capital, with the

highest rate of HIV infection in the country, he ran an after-school program connected with the Planned Parenthood clinic. He had convinced
a small strip mall to give him an abandoned sporting goods storefront,
which he filled with secondhand furniture and cast-off computers. (I
would later donate our foosball table to the cause.)

Working twenty-hour days, with barely two nickels to rub together,
Irwin and his team helped high-risk teens in the area get testing, counseling, and health care. Most of all, he was providing young people in
Anacostia with a safe place to go after school. Some of these teens became educators themselves and were a lifeline for their fellow students.
I started getting excited about the opportunity to connect these young
people to others across the country.

It was in Kalamazoo, Michigan (home of Kellogg's), after the obligatory stop to get a photo with a life-size Tony the Tiger (part of a complete
breakfast—Daniel would be so happy!), that it all came together. I was
sitting with a group of local teens who were part of Project T.R.U.S.T.,
a Planned Parenthood–sponsored teen sex education program. They
told me about learning everything there was to know about birth control, consent, sexually transmitted infections and how to prevent them,
and more. They had testified before school board meetings and had
publicly spoken out in favor of comprehensive sex education. In small,
conservative-leaning Kalamazoo, that wasn't easy. I was captivated.

Lindsay Swisher, a high school senior about to graduate, told me,
"When I started as a teen peer educator four years ago, I was really shy."
But after being part of Planned Parenthood, she said, "I can talk to anyone about anything. It has changed my life." Another high school student,
Ricky Bicknell, had a sparkle in his eye; I knew our paths would cross
again. (Who could have predicted where we'd all end up ten years later?
Lindsay graduated from college and has just finished serving in the Peace
Corps in Senegal. Ricky became an LGBTQ campus leader at the University of Michigan. He later worked for Planned Parenthood, organizing
young people just as others had done for him. And in 2016 I wrote him a
recommendation for graduate school, where he's now getting his master's
degree in public health.)

These teens weren't simply sex educators; they were leaders, and they belonged at the center of everything we did. Every investment we could make in them would help build our organization, and more than that, our movement. We decided to invite a group of teens from across the country to present at our national meeting, where hundreds of the most important Planned Parenthood leaders came together.

That first time, I wasn't really sure how it was going to go. The great thing about bringing teens into the meeting was that they were going to shake things up—for better or worse! What happened that first year, and ever since, turned out to be magical. Leaders who had been asking me, "Why don't young people get involved and appreciate all we've done?" were now seeing them in action. These established figures were learning from the next generation of Planned Parenthood activists, who were without a doubt the most diverse group in our organization. Today I hardly ever hear those questions from longtime Planned Parenthood leaders. Where are the young people? *They're everywhere!*

But despite the world-class health care, the great organizing, and the young leaders at Planned Parenthood, there was no escaping the fact that our biggest threat was political.

Early on, we did focus groups on Capitol Hill with congressional chiefs of staff and other people who were influential in policy and politics. Almost everyone said the same thing: "We only hear from Planned Parenthood when they need us to take a tough vote. But we can't depend on them to support us back at home." Members of Congress who voted with us were flooded by calls from our opposition. It wasn't good.

To make matters worse, increasingly the Democratic Party was openly recruiting candidates who were against abortion rights. I felt it was critical to show that standing with us was both the right thing to do and the politically smart thing to do. We had to back up our principles with action. We needed to build our grassroots so that members of Congress heard from people back in their home district.

At that point the Planned Parenthood Action Fund had only ever endorsed one presidential candidate: John Kerry in 2004. The 2008 presidential election was wide open. George W. Bush had finished two terms, and we had survived. But now we had to get to work, and fast. I brought on Texas Freedom Network alum Samantha Smoot, who was tough, with a stubborn streak, and knew how to get things done. In 2007, for the first time in its history, the Planned Parenthood Action Fund held a presidential forum. There were no Republicans who were pro-choice or even pro–family planning, so we invited Senators Barack Obama, Hillary Clinton, and John Edwards. Obama and Clinton actually came, and Elizabeth Edwards participated in lieu of her husband.

On the day of the forum, hundreds of Planned Parenthood leaders packed into a ballroom in Washington, making history. We believed that we had a real chance to elect one of these leaders to be president, which would finally give us an opening to stop simply fighting back and actually expand rights and access to care. The best part of these forums was the fact that teen leaders from Anacostia and grassroots organizers from the states took the lead. It was incredible—our very own people questioning a potential future leader of the free world!

We didn't endorse in the primary—all the Democrats were good on our issues—but we were there in force in Denver when Obama accepted his party's nomination, rocking the house. The Planned Parenthood Action Fund event—named, what else, "Sex and Politics"—was standing room only, with folks lined up down the block to get in. That celebration helped put us on the national scene, with leaders like Governor Kathleen Sebelius and the wonderfully irreverent actor Alan Cumming making an appearance. Senator John McCain, the Republican nominee, wanted to outlaw abortion, so the general election would be a real contest of ideals. Our folks were pumped, and we signed up hundreds of volunteers before we left. The favorite giveaway of the night was a pink condom pack with the tag line "Protect Yourself from John McCain."

The next morning, on the plane flying home, everyone's cell phones lit up at the same time with the news that McCain had chosen Sarah Palin as his running mate. I turned to Kirk and asked, "Who is Sarah Palin?"

It was only over the next few days that her profile became clear. She was against everything Planned Parenthood was for: legal abortion, birth control, sex education for teens. When the news came out a few weeks later that her teenage daughter was pregnant, Palin became a poster child for the Far Right. What could have become a bipartisan, teachable moment instead became a rallying cry for the fringe of the Republican Party.

Planned Parenthood, on the other hand, was flooded with donations in Palin's honor. We had to send stacks of thank-you cards to her office.

Barack Obama's campaign was an unprecedented chance to engage our millions of supporters, and we made the most of it, training organizers and recruiting as many new volunteers as we could. From college campuses to rock concerts, anywhere two or more were gathered together, we signed them up. We dug into data and assigned every woman voter in the country a score on her likelihood to support abortion rights and to support Planned Parenthood. With this kind of information, our organizers and volunteers could target voters and districts no matter where they lived. It was an exciting time, but I was anxious. This was our first big test, and we had a lot to prove—to the country and to Planned Parenthood. On election night, when Obama won, I cried and celebrated with the rest of America—and I breathed an extra sigh of relief that our big bet had paid off.

Four years later Planned Parenthood had grown, as had our ability to impact policy and politics. This time President Obama was facing a tough opponent in Governor Mitt Romney from Massachusetts. Romney was known as a moderate—a successful Republican governor from a progressive state. It was hard to paint him with the extreme-right brush, unlike so many of his primary opponents. He and his wife had even come to Planned Parenthood events in support of women's issues.

But in March 2012 he made a crucial error. Boasting on television, as only an elite guy would do, he tossed off a fateful line: "Planned Parenthood? We're going to get rid of that." That piece of video footage became a television ad that we ran across the country. And as the race tightened, with women becoming perhaps the most critical swing voters, the president and the governor were at Hofstra University for their second, pivotal debate.

I was backstage, watching with a handful of others who had been asked to be available for the press afterward. I heard Obama say, "There are millions of women all across the country who rely on Planned Parenthood." I could hardly believe it. He proceeded to mention Planned Parenthood, and the work we do, three more times—not that I was counting!

In a short time we had gone from being a political pariah to one of the most important and effective groups to be associated with. It was the first time Planned Parenthood had been mentioned in a presidential debate, and Obama went on to win the election with the largest support from women of any presidential candidate to date. Best of all, we had cracked the code, making sure that when politicians and the public thought about us, they knew who we were and what we did.

This came home to me a couple of days after that debate, when a woman came into our health center on the Gulf Coast Freeway in Houston. She didn't have a doctor, but she had found a lump in her breast and needed to see someone. The clinician welcomed her and said, "We're so glad you're here. May I ask who referred you?" The woman answered, "Well, I heard President Obama say on TV that you do breast exams. And that's why I'm here."

Twelve years later I'm grateful every day that I went to that interview. Watching Planned Parenthood grow and adapt, and getting to be part of an organization that does such incredible work, has been the privilege of a lifetime. Today the number of Planned Parenthood supporters has tripled, reaching more than 11 million. Nearly half are young people. Planned Parenthood has been on the leading edge of getting birth control coverage for women in insurance plans. Millions of appointments have been scheduled on mobile phones. The organization has invested in thousands of young people who are changing the world, for reproductive justice as well as a number of other important causes. And those young people have shepherded us into the twenty-first century. Most of all, I've been so fortunate to meet doctors, medical staff, clinic escorts, and local leaders who, despite all the political attacks, continue to open the doors of Planned Parenthood health centers every single day, no matter what.

In my time at Planned Parenthood I've visited health centers from Brownsville, Texas, to Milwaukee, Wisconsin, and in every one the waiting rooms were full of women and young people who needed health care. I experienced so many unforgettable moments, like sitting across the desk from a health center manager in Mobile, Alabama, who had been a teen mom herself and was now counseling women on their options. With all the taboo subjects in the South, she explained, "Planned Parenthood is straight-up health care, the way it should be. This is a judgment-free zone." I've talked to clinicians in Hawaii about the challenges of delivering health care to people away from the mainland, and in Alaska, where we once delivered birth control by float plane to a remote village in the Arctic Circle. In December 2015 I finally checked off my fiftieth state with a visit to Fargo, North Dakota.

Along the way I've picked up a few tips. Warren Buffett told me he always travels with his own pillow. Good advice. A navy blue suit never shows dirt, even if you get mistaken for a flight attendant every now and then. When someone tells you they're praying for you, just say a polite "Thank you" and move on. After all, it can't hurt, right? Calling home every night, no matter where you are or how late it is, helps. Even when Kirk is already asleep and I just get his voice mail I feel better. Try to know where the best ice cream is in any given airport terminal. A portable clothes steamer can be a lifesaver, since you can use it anywhere and don't need an ironing board. (Believe me, it works—even in a public bathroom an hour before an event.) Sleep whenever you can, even if it's for fifteen minutes on a flight. And never shy away from telling people what you do. You dispel myths, for others and yourself.

Not long ago I got on a plane and took my seat next to a guy who looked like a stereotypical businessman. He asked what I did, so I told him that I worked for Planned Parenthood, then waited for the nervous silence. Instead his eyes lit up.

"Wow," he said, "I just read the *Esquire* story about that doctor in Mississippi who provides women abortions because he believes it's the Christian thing to do."

"Yes, that's Dr. Willie Parker," I replied, a little shocked to hear he'd read the article. "He's a good friend and a great man."

"Well, I have to say, I had never really thought about how hard it is for women down there. I'm a religious man myself, and it really opened my eyes. So good luck to you." He went on to tell me about his kids and his life. Who knew?

People ask me whether I am concerned for my safety when I'm on the road. The truth is, most of the people who stop me want to thank me or tell me why they love Planned Parenthood. There was the woman who chased me down on the airport tarmac in Texas to tell me she'd just been at the fundraiser where I spoke and was inspired to call her parents and tell them she'd had an abortion years ago. And the soundboard operator at a big women's conference in Los Angeles—one of a small handful of men present—who stopped me backstage to tell me his wife and daughters go to Planned Parenthood, and he just had to get a picture.

These days when someone asks me for career advice, some of the first words out of my mouth are the lessons I learned at Planned Parenthood: At every job, look for someone who can teach you something. Stay close to the ground, and remember that you're never too big of a deal to knock on doors. Find something outside your job that brings you joy—don't look up years later and realize you missed out on the things you love. Give your staff vacation days, play sports, travel. Doing this will make you a better person and a better organizer. Know that there's no road map for social change—so keep making it up, don't get stuck or tied down, and never turn down a new opportunity. And never ever hold yourself back from accepting a big job or a big chance. You can and will figure it out—take it from me.

Chapter 9

What Would Ann Richards Do?

One of the best things about moving to New York City was that our apartment had room enough for Mom to visit as much as she wanted. Mom loved New York, and I couldn't wait for her to join us. But shortly after we moved in, she called with news that would change everything. Something in her throat had been bothering her for a while, and the doctors confirmed her fears: she had esophageal cancer.

Mom was scared but stoic when she delivered the news. I was in a state of disbelief. This was not how I'd imagined the future. I had just started at Planned Parenthood and, selfishly, pictured us together in the city, with Mom fighting alongside me for women's rights. We had more adventures to take together. Plus, she was such a force in my children's lives. Things were always bigger, brighter, and funnier when she was around. How could she have cancer? It just didn't fit.

"We'll figure this out," she said.

We quickly discovered that hers was a really tough form of cancer, and she had to decide whether to fight or try to manage it for as long as she could.

My mother hated being sick. To her, it was a sign of personal failure. As much as she had battled her upbringing, there were some ways in which she was absolutely a product of her environment. In Texas the most hallowed attribute, far greater than intelligence or educational achievement, is toughness. In our football-obsessed culture straight out of *Friday Night Lights*, the greatest praise goes to someone who "plays hurt"—regardless of torn ligaments or broken fingers.

Mom subscribed to that school of thought. I cannot remember a time when any of us kids stayed home from school. It wasn't because she was a working mother and had to have us out of the house; it was because, no matter what, you were going to suck it up and go, even if you didn't feel good.

It was a lesson I internalized to a fault. My own kids never missed a day of school unless the teacher called and said I had to come get one of them. I couldn't shake my mother's conviction that any acknowledgment of being sick was a sign of weakness.

Of course that philosophy has its drawbacks. One Christmas I was dragging Lily from place to place, rushing to finish shopping for gifts, when she said, "Mom, I really feel sick."

"We just have this one last stop at the music store. You'll be fine," I told her, only to have her throw up all over a gigantic bin of CDs. We haven't been back to Waterloo Records since.

Mom's view of sickness as a weakness surely came from her mother, who was strong as an ox and worked as hard as anyone I've ever known. Mom used to tell the story of the time she got a call at the governor's office from one of Nona's neighbors. "Ann, you are going to have to come get your mother. She's up on the roof again, cleaning out the gutters. I don't think that's safe for an eighty-year-old-woman." Mom just laughed—there was no way her mother was coming down from that roof until she was good and ready.

My mother walked through fire many times, and, as she liked to say, "the fire lost." There was no doubt in my mind that she would beat cancer too. After the diagnosis she made the decision to move to Houston for experimental chemotherapy at M. D. Anderson Cancer Center, and in between trips for my new job, I visited her there. We spent the time watching *Project Runway*, which she found endlessly entertaining, and she laughed uncontrollably as we sat through *Blazing Saddles* one night.

She admitted during one of those visits that she had suspected she was sick before she went on a long-planned trip to India, but she'd decided not to tell anyone for fear the doctors wouldn't let her go. When she got home from what would end up being her last adventure, she told me about visiting Varanasi, where Hindus cremate their dead on the banks of the Ganges River. "It was so important, Cecile," she said. "I have never been anywhere so spiritual." Clearly the experience had touched her deeply. I realize now that she was thinking about her own mortality.

Getting cancer was the first time Mom acknowledged that there was such a thing as human frailty, and she understood that taking care of herself had to be her full-time job. She approached it with campaign-like determination, and became interested in *chi*, the life force particularly important in Eastern systems of medical treatment.

When Mom was governor, her friend and partner in everything she did, Jane Hickie, made her a note pad with "Ann Richards: The Problem Lady" emblazoned at the top. That was what Mom used to call herself, since she had an answer for every problem. There were a lot of opinions in the world, but only one correct one: Mom's. The hardest thing was, she was almost always right. When word spread that she was sick, she received desperate phone calls from people asking for advice, perhaps because subconsciously they realized it could be their last chance to get some Ann Richards wisdom. But after spending much of her life shaking hands with strangers, calling them "honey," she had finally learned to save her energy for herself. When someone called upon her for her time, she'd say, "Cecile, I'm just not going to do everything everyone wants me to—it's wasting my chi!" That was as close to self-care as she ever got.

．　．　．

After months of treatment Mom went home to Austin. In the exit interview, one of her doctors said, "Ann, you've been a perfect patient. We feel really good that through radiation we've gotten the cancer, and now you can start to recover." The radiation had made it impossible for her to eat anything for weeks, and she was relying on a feeding tube, which we were taking home. "I need you to get healthy, so we can do the final surgery," he said. Mom and I just looked at each other—it was impossible to imagine her recovering enough to have surgery.

As we were leaving, I saw Dr. Fan, Mom's oncologist, who really made an impression on her. Dr. Fan was brilliant, yet Mom was always in her cheese, giving her advice about her life, her decisions, and everything she needed to do. *Welcome to the family!*

"Thank you, Doctor," I told her. "You have been so good to Mom."

"Well, she's helped me too, given me a lot of advice. Just be sure to let her know I traded in the old car and got a new Prius, just like she told me to."

My mother died just a few weeks later, in September 2006, at her home, in her own bed, with all of us at her side. She had made her own decisions, right to the end. She knew her own mind and was counting on us kids to respect that, and of course we did.

She'd already picked out a plot in the Texas State Cemetery, under an oak tree. Her gravestone, designed by her friend Robert Smith, is a piece of white marble that looks a whole lot like her Texas bouffant. It's smooth and welcoming, and Mom always dreamed that people might visit it and leave stones or charms—which they do. (Even after she was gone, Mom had a surprise in store for us all. She had quietly arranged for Bud Shrake, her longtime companion, to be buried in the adjoining burial plot. When he died not long after, his equally unconventional gravestone was placed next to hers, reading, "So far, so bueno.")

All of Mom's friends came together to plan her funeral; it was like the old campaign operation sprang up all over again in her apartment. At a small ceremony with family and friends, Lily Tomlin and Anna Deavere Smith spoke, and Nanci Griffith, a favorite singer-songwriter from Austin, sang "Across the Great Divide." Then came the memorial at the Erwin Center, with well-wishers and presenters including Jessye Norman, Hillary Clinton, and Ron Kirk—people who had been an important part of her life and who would carry the torch going forward.

Mom left us way too early in that she had so much more to give to this world. She set many of us on our path and left us a lot of life lessons. My daughter Lily summed it up best in her speech at Mom's service: "Every time Mammy saw one of us grandkids, she would say, 'How's school?' And then she would ask, 'Are you the smartest one in the class?'

"And if we hedged in our reply, she would ask, 'Well, why not?'

"This might seem a little too demanding, but it wasn't. Because Mammy had learned the most important lesson of all, and she was teaching it to all of us. That lesson was simple: This is your life. It is the only one you get, so no excuses and no do-overs. If you make a mistake or fail at something, you learn from it, you get over it, and you move on. Your job is to be the very best person you can be, and to never settle for anything less.

"This message was not just given to her children and her grandchildren, but also in countless speeches and one-on-one conversations with thousands of people, many of them young women, across this country. She delivered this message as only she could—with wit, with intensity, but most importantly, by example. Mammy was the very best person she could be every single day."

The December after Mom died, for the first time in a long time, our family decided to go back to Texas at Christmas. It just felt like the right thing to do. For the previous fifteen years Christmas had been spent on some madcap adventure with Mom, eschewing the presents and eggnog in favor of climbing a pyramid in Guatemala or taking a midnight train from Amsterdam to Paris. We were adrift without her. But after a couple of days in Austin, the thought of sitting around the Christmas tree and wrapping and unwrapping stuff was too much to bear. We spontaneously saddled up and drove out to Big Bend National Park, where Kirk and I had taken our first camping trip many years ago, to raft the Santa Elena Canyon. It wasn't the best-planned trip, and several minor disasters occurred, not the least of which was locking our keys in the car that contained all our camping and rafting gear. Kirk broke a couple of fingers, and we slept in wool clothes that had been abandoned at the rafting put-in place. But we floated the canyon anyway, something Mom had done decades earlier. We still look at that as one of our more successful adventures—and Mom would have loved it.

To see Mom evolve and change, right up to her very last years, was a gift for me. Plenty of people get more conservative as they get older. She got more radical. During treatment she had a phalanx of doctors, all of whom were from other countries. She would say, "Can you believe these right-wing politicians who want to end immigration? Who in the hell do they think is going to keep them alive when they get old?"

The more years she spent in the fight for LGBTQ rights, civil rights, and so many other issues, the more outspoken she became. That was especially true of women's rights. Mom saw history repeating itself and was downright furious at the idea that her granddaughters' generation would have to refight the same battles she'd helped wage.

Once she left elected office, she was very much in demand as a speaker on the campaign trail, and candidates were constantly calling her and asking her to stump for them. After years of helping so many Democrats, she made it absolutely clear: unless you were 100 percent pro-choice, she wouldn't lift a finger. But if you supported women, she would travel to the ends of the earth for you.

•   •   •

Near the end of her life, Mom knew she only had a certain amount of time left, and she was determined to spend it fighting as fiercely as she could to leave behind a better world for us all. Before she was going to make a speech, she loved to call and read me parts that she had worked on and was really proud of. She had recently fallen in love with the irreverent words of the Irish American labor activist Mother Jones, and the more outrageous the quote, the better. "Listen to this: 'I'm not a humanitarian, I'm a hell-raiser!'" she read. "Don't you love that? And how about, 'Whatever your fight, don't be ladylike!'" Meanwhile I'm thinking, *How is that going to go over at the Waldorf-Astoria mental health luncheon?* But she didn't care. One of her mantras was "Ask for forgiveness, not permission." She firmly believed in the idea that if you aren't pissing off the powers that be, you aren't doing your job.

Before she died, Mom decided that one way she could make a lasting difference was to start a girls' school. She'd had friends who started girls' schools in New York and California, and she thought, *Why not Texas?* That's how, one year later, the Ann Richards School for Young Women Leaders came to be, a public school in Austin with one of the most diverse student bodies in the city. It has been a resounding success; there are now young women scattered all over the country who are graduates of the Ann Richards School. Many of them are the first person in their family to go to college. Every time I go back to visit, I feel it's the place where Mom's spirit truly lives.

Over the years I've gotten many calls from filmmakers and writers wanting to tell Mom's story, but one stood out from the rest. The actor

Holland Taylor told me she had met Mom years ago, with their mutual friend, the legendary columnist Liz Smith. Holland had become fascinated with Mom and now wanted to write a one-woman play about her life. For the next three years she researched and wrote, and in the process went from being a total stranger to becoming part of our family. Kirk, the kids, and I were in the audience at Lincoln Center to see the opening of *Ann*, and as one of the producers, Kate Hathaway, told me afterward, "It was like getting a couple of hours back with your mom." Seven years after her death, Mom's life story was taking Broadway by storm.

Even now, everywhere I go, I run into people who want to talk about Mom. Many recount how something she did or said changed their lives, how because of her, they decided to travel, run for office, or get involved in a cause they care about. Gruff-looking men will come up to me in airports to say, "I just loved your mother."

But perhaps the most fitting tribute happened at the Texas capitol, where Mom lay in state for two days before her funeral. Anyone who wanted could come. Bill Clinton was to deliver the eulogy, and while we expected a crowd, we didn't anticipate that thousands of people would travel from far and wide to say farewell, leaving behind handwritten notes, old campaign buttons, and, in more than one case, an AA chip from someone who had gotten sober because of her. It was a kind of pilgrimage for farmworkers and teachers, for mothers who brought their kids to pay their respects to this iconic woman governor. As I was standing there in the middle of the rotunda that day, a union truck driver from Tennessee walked up and introduced himself. He told me he had gotten his dispatcher to give him a twenty-four-hour leave to drive to Texas to be there. Activists from the disability rights community, who had barricaded themselves in her capitol office on her first night as governor to protest the conditions at the state schools, came to be part of it. They all wanted to share a story. But mainly they wanted me to know that they loved her. That is Mom's legacy.

Today her portrait hangs in the rotunda in Austin. I love seeing the pictures folks take with Mom, who watches over us. For all she accomplished, and all the people she inspired, she left a lot for the rest of us to do. I know that if she were here, she would be at the barricades with us, standing up for women, for DREAMers, for anyone who needs someone on their side. She'd tell us, *This is it—your only life—so whatever the question, the answer is yes. Don't look back. Don't hesitate.*

Not a day goes by when I don't miss Mom. Some days I miss her so much I can hardly stand it. It catches me off guard, like the time I came across a video clip from an old interview. "You may go somewhere else and you may make a lot of money," she said, "but you will never receive the kind of gratification that you receive from looking someone in the eye who says, 'Thank you for helping make my life better.' " She made all of our lives better—those of us who knew and loved her, and countless people she never met.

As activists and troublemakers, that may just be the finest compliment there is.

Chapter 10

Resilience

It was a Sunday morning, and I was sitting in my kitchen in New York drinking coffee with Kirk. I was two years into the job at Planned Parenthood, working harder than ever in my life. The twins were in high school, and I tried to be home on Sundays at least. The 24/7 nature of my work meant there wasn't a lot of extra time for parenting, and Kirk was, per usual, taking on way more than half of the responsibility—and doing it with total joy.

The phone rang, and I picked it up. As strange as it is, I can't remember who was on the other end. But I certainly remember what they told me.

"George Tiller has been shot," they said. "He was in his church, handing out programs for the service, when someone came right up and shot him. Reports are he died right there."

I was in shock. "Did they catch the shooter?" I asked.

"Yes, it seems so. He literally just walked up and shot him in front of everyone, in cold blood. This is a terrible, terrible day."

. . .

I have always been an expert worrier, but at Planned Parenthood I'd learned to prioritize the worrying. On any given day the list could begin with "Did we get the website up for the new birth control campaign?" or "What happened in court today in Texas?" But what every Planned Parenthood leader in every state in the country worries about the most is the safety of our staff and patients. On that day in May 2009 our worst fears were realized.

George Tiller was a beloved doctor and an abortion provider in Wichita, Kansas, and while he wasn't a Planned Parenthood doctor, he was an integral part of our community. We referred patients to him, and he to us. For several years he had provided abortions to women from all across the country, particularly women who needed to terminate late in their pregnancy. He dealt with some of the most medically complicated cases. The walls of his office were papered with thank-you notes from grateful women he'd treated with dignity and respect at one of the most difficult times of their lives. He had so many sayings, "Tillerisms," as people called them, that someone compiled a list: *It is never the wrong time to do the next right thing. It's nice to be important, but it's more important to be nice.* His motto, "Trust women," lives on in buttons and hashtags and is repeated every time politicians try to intervene in the personal medical decisions of women and their families (which is almost every day).

George was a hero in part because his path was so unlikely. His father was a well-respected women's doctor in Wichita. In the 1950s and '60s George served in the navy. His own plan was to become a dermatologist, until one tragic day, when his sister, brother-in-law, and parents were killed in a plane crash. George decided to go into women's health instead, and before long, women were coming to George to ask, "Can you help us like your father did?" That's when he realized his father had provided abortion care to women in Kansas—something he had never known while his father was alive—and his loss left a void in the community. And so, in the heart of Kansas, George became one of the few providers of safe and legal abortion.

In the years George and his family lived in Wichita, they faced unimaginable threats to their safety. He had been the target of some of the most hateful, violent extremists and had the bullet scars to prove it. Once his clinic was firebombed. Before he began rebuilding, he hung up a sign that said "Hell no, we won't go." The fact that he was in the line of fire every day only made his ability to keep a sense of humor that much more admirable.

He was a gentle man, devoted to his church and family. I had met him at medical conferences and, like others who knew him, appreciated his commitment to the work as well as his passion for politics. He was constantly thinking about the bigger picture and spent a lot of time contemplating how on earth we were going to change the awful political climate in Kansas. His own favorite Tillerism, and one I often think about to this day, was "Attitude is everything."

I couldn't believe he was dead. Almost immediately I started hearing from friends, staff, and volunteers. They all knew George, who had survived so many other attacks; the thought that a terrorist could shoot him in his own church, where he ushered each week, was too much to bear. As I sat there at the kitchen table, I thought of the spree of violent killings of abortion providers back in the 1990s. Until that Sunday morning I had thought—naïvely—that those days were behind us. It was the first time anything like that had happened in my time as president of Planned Parenthood.

I called Planned Parenthood's CEO in Kansas, Peter Brownlie. Like George, Peter was known across the country for standing up to the state to protect abortion access and the confidentiality of patient medical records. Peter was shaken to his core—George was a friend and hero, and they had been through so much together.

"Let me know what we can do to support you, Peter," I said. "As soon as you know anything about the service arrangements, can you tell me? So many of us from around the country will want to be there."

Once the funeral was set, I flew out to Kansas with Lynne Randall, who ran abortion services for Planned Parenthood. Peter and his wife, Deborah Jenkins, met us at the airport. Together, we headed for the hotel.

The outpouring of support for George's family—his wife, their four children, and many grandchildren—was overwhelming. "They had to move the service to the biggest church in Wichita," Peter said. "George's home church couldn't begin to handle the flood of people. Even as it is, they are going to set up overflow space for those who can't make it into the sanctuary."

"I think we need to leave really early tomorrow morning for the service," he went on. "The crowd is going to be enormous, and we have seats, but the protesters are going to be out in force. The local police are expecting Fred Phelps and his group." Phelps and his followers at Westboro Baptist Church in Topeka protested against Catholics, LGBTQ people, the Jewish community, and others. They were notorious for picketing the funerals of fallen soldiers, and the Southern Poverty Law Center had declared them a hate group.

"That sounds right," I replied. "Are you sure you have enough security?"

Peter lifted up his shirt. He was wearing a bulletproof vest. "It's what we have to do here in Kansas," he said. There was nothing I could say. That's the kind of courage Planned Parenthood leaders have in states across the country.

We drove to the hotel and met up with Pedro Irigonegaray, who had been George's lawyer over the years, and a few other folks who had flown in from out of state. Peter, Pedro, Lynne, and I sat in the hotel bar and talked about George, who had to have been in court more than any other doctor, constantly suing or being sued by the state's fanatical attorney general, Phill Kline.

"I remember the time George was shot in his car by that violent protester," Pedro said. "She hit his hands, which is the last thing any doctor wants. But George was amazed at her incompetence." It was a somber moment, since the latest attempt had succeeded. We shared George stories until it was time to call it a night.

The next morning a security car picked us up two hours early, in hopes we could get to the church before the protests got going. It was a clear, quiet morning in Wichita, but as we were cresting the hill near the church, I saw a phalanx of Harley motorcycles with huge American flags attached to poles off the back. There were dozens lined up, single file, and the riders held their helmets under their arms. I thought to myself, *Oh no, the place is already surrounded by protesters.*

"This doesn't look good," I said to Peter.

The road was open, so we continued on. As we approached, I realized that the motorcyclists weren't there to protest. They were, in fact, the Patriot Guard Riders, a volunteer group that ensures dignity and respect at memorial services honoring military heroes and veterans. As we got out of the car, it was hard not to cry. These burly motorcycle riders, with their American flags and attendant insignia, were honoring George and protecting his family and friends. In that moment, divisions of ideology and politics no longer mattered. We were all Americans, joined in sadness, paying tribute to a fallen hero.

"Thank you," I said as we passed the entourage. "You cannot know what it means to have you here."

"We honor our fellow veterans. It's our duty," one of them replied. Two imposing tattooed men in leather vests quietly escorted George's wife, Jeanne, from her car into the church.

As far as the eye could see, people had gathered to pay tribute to George. Some wore T-shirts with his most famous sayings and held white carnations. Others carried photos of him. The church was full. Out in the lobby, baskets contained Tillerisms written on slips of paper as keepsakes. George was eulogized by his fraternity brothers from the University of Kansas, and his children spoke. The pastor of the church he attended each week was there with an "Attitude is everything" button on his robe.

"Just last week," his daughter Jennifer said, "Dad and I and his grandkids were at Disney World, on every ride. Dad loved it, and I'm so glad we had that time with him. He loved his family."

Jeanne stood up and sang "The Lord's Prayer," which she dedicated "to my best buddy and the love of my life." She has a beautiful voice. I do not know how she was able to get through the song.

Many of our staff and community hadn't been able to go to the services in Kansas, so we planned to have our own memorial for George at our national offices in New York. The word had just gone out that we were holding a service, open to all, when I got a call from Luis Ubiñas, president of the Ford Foundation, one of the most important foundations to support social justice work, including women's rights. Luis and his wife, Deb Tolman, had become friends of mine, and in fact, Deb specialized as a feminist researcher and professor in gender and sexuality.

"Deb and I would like to talk at your memorial service for Dr. Tiller," he said.

"Well, that would be wonderful, Luis. We're expecting a lot of people from the community," I replied.

He hesitated for a moment, and I could hear him take a breath on the other end. "But you see," he said, "we especially want to be there, because Dr. Tiller was our doctor."

Deb and Luis have two extraordinary sons, whom I knew. But I hadn't known until that moment that years ago they'd had a much-wanted pregnancy that had come to a heartbreaking end. They had learned late in term that the fetus was not viable and that Deb's life was at risk, and one of only three doctors in the country who could help them was Dr. Tiller. They put their trust in him because he trusted women. As their experience unfolded, they learned that one of the reasons Dr. Tiller was so remarkable was that he loved and respected his patients; he listened to women.

The days surrounding George's death were painfully sad, but they were also a reminder of the incredible power of working with a group of people who can support each other through the most difficult tragedies. There was nothing good to come of all this. A brave man had been shot in cold blood—a man who had cared for so many women, especially women in the most terrible medical circumstances. But George's legacy and work inspired a renewed commitment among many of us. From that day forward, whenever one of us at Planned Parenthood was trying to make an important decision or dealing with the latest political attack, we would ask, *What would George do?* Not long after his death, the Planned Parenthood Federation voted to ensure that every affiliate across the country provided abortion in at least one health center. The years that followed brought an onslaught of laws introduced in states across the country to make it harder for women to access abortion—by forcing them to wait seventy-two hours, undergo biased counseling, or have medically unnecessary procedures. Through it all, we returned again and again to George's mantra: "Trust women."

Meanwhile the ground was starting to shift. One of the reasons everyone knew George's name was because he had been public about being an abortion provider. Back then, most were not—and for good reason. Back in the '90s, Dr. David Gunn, Dr. John Britton, and Dr. Barnett Slepian had been murdered, as well as staff at two health centers in Brookline, Massachusetts: Shannon Lowney and LeeAnn Nichols. The Right's Nuremberg Project printed "Wanted" posters that featured the names and faces of abortion providers and became the subject of much publicity as well as a lawsuit.

After George's death a wave of doctors began to change the pattern. They understood that we could never change attitudes toward abortion unless people started speaking openly—so that's just what they did. In 2010 the *New York Times Magazine* published a feature story about doctors who provide abortion services, including a brave and committed Planned Parenthood doctor named Rachael Phelps. I was impressed by her courage and knew such a story was breaking new ground. It generated a great deal of conversation and argument within the women's health community. There were plenty of people whose response was "Speaking out isn't safe. That's not what we do." But brave individuals like Dr. Phelps ushered in an entirely new era of abortion providers being open and public. Today many doctors are also increasingly advocates for their patients and for women everywhere. Now, no lobbying day on Capitol Hill is complete without Planned Parenthood doctors and clinicians, wearing their white coats and stethoscopes, walking through the halls of Congress to meet with elected officials about the care their patients need. I know George would be proud of these young doctors. Seeing how they're shattering stigma and refusing to hide in the shadows fills me with hope that we will one day be able to break out of this political back-and-forth and start recognizing abortion for what it is: health care, and a vital service that is part of so many people's lives.

• • •

Dealing with adversaries isn't easy, but when people on your own team turn on you, it's a tough pill to swallow. That was what happened in 2012 with Susan G. Komen for the Cure, the largest breast cancer advocacy organization in the United States.

For many years Planned Parenthood has partnered with community organizations to increase education and early detection for breast cancer. One in eight women in America will be diagnosed with breast cancer in her lifetime, yet many women do not have access to early screenings that can catch cancer when it's most treatable. Even worse, African American women are 40 percent more likely to die of breast cancer than white women. It's a national disgrace.

Komen, especially at the local level, knew that for many patients, especially those without insurance, their annual visit to Planned Parenthood was the only time they got a breast exam. Like other women's health care providers, Planned Parenthood refers women who need further care to radiology clinics, and Komen provided grants that helped ensure patients could get that care. Many clinicians are like ombudsmen, helping women with no insurance and no doctor navigate the health care system, which is no easy feat. Komen appreciated that we reached women who might otherwise go without care. So you could have blown me over when Dawn Laguens, at the time Planned Parenthood's vice president of policy, advocacy, and communications, called me and said, "I'm hearing a rumor that Komen is going to put out a statement saying they will no longer work with Planned Parenthood."

"Are you serious?" I responded. "We work together all across the country. They're the leading breast cancer organization, and we're the leading reproductive health organization. We're partners—that just doesn't make any sense."

"Well, they've been shaky ever since Congress tried to defund us earlier this year," Dawn said. "We do have tremendous working relationships at the local level—that's not where this is coming from. It seems like someone at the top is trying to get political points by dropping us."

This was awful news—not only for Planned Parenthood but for the thousands of women who counted on our partnership to get lifesaving care and education. I was furious. It was one thing to have our opponents coming after us every day; watching our friends turn their backs on us was a stinging betrayal.

"They want to get on the phone with us, off the record," Dawn reported. "Let's hear what they have to say."

Not long after, Dawn and I got on a conference call with the acting executive director for the Komen Foundation, who explained that from now on, there would be no more partnership with Planned Parenthood. "But we aren't going to announce anything publicly," she added, as though that would somehow reassure us.

"What do you mean, you aren't going to say anything in public?" I asked, incredulous. "You think, in this highly charged political environment, it's going to stay a secret?"

"We don't want to make a big deal of this," she said. "It would be better if it were just understood between us."

Dawn and I looked at each other. *Did they have any idea what the press would do with this story? How the opponents of Planned Parenthood would blast this all across America?*

"Well, I'm sure that's how you would like it to be," I said. "But I'm already seeing posts online by the most vocal antichoice groups about how Komen is ending this relationship. You may mean well, but I'm not sure you know what kind of groups you are dealing with."

Dawn added, "The organizations you're sidling up to aren't working with women who need breast cancer screenings. These are organizations whose sole purpose is to end access to Planned Parenthood, and frankly, they're using you to do it."

Having been the targets of the antichoice movement, Dawn and I knew what was coming. We had a few more conversations with Komen, asking them to reconsider. Their actions were going to be devastating for the very women who counted on them.

But Komen was undeterred. So Dawn and I talked it over. "We have to get ahead of this," she suggested, "and at least let our patients and the public know what's coming." She was rightly concerned that it would become a political story, when what we needed to emphasize was what it would mean for the thousands of women who depend on us for breast exams. "We need to get something out on Monday, because already the right-wing blogs are putting pink ribbons on their websites, ready to champion Komen for severing ties with Planned Parenthood."

So on Monday, January 31, 2012, without fanfare, we sent an email to more than a million supporters with the subject line "Disappointing news from a friend." The message explained that we had been notified by Komen that they would no longer work with Planned Parenthood. We were disappointed and hoped they would reconsider. In the meantime we promised to do everything possible to make sure our patients could get the care they needed, and we asked our supporters to stand with us. Boy, did they.

Within minutes the internet exploded.

Women began posting to the Komen website in droves. Komen frantically tried to take down the comments, which only served to enrage people. Women whose comments were erased turned to Twitter instead. We began to get calls from donors and people who wanted to make up whatever losses we had in breast cancer funding. One of those first calls was from New York's mayor Michael Bloomberg, who stepped up immediately with foundation support. Others followed suit: the actors Scarlett Johansson and America Ferrera, the author Judy Blume, and The Decemberists, an indie band from Oregon.

By Wednesday 1.3 million people had tweeted in support of Planned Parenthood. One supporter joked, "Will Planned Parenthood please give Twitter back?" The story made the front page of the *New York Times*, twice. It was on every network. Many women reporters who were breast cancer survivors were outraged, including Andrea Mitchell, who interviewed the head of Komen on her show, saying, "I have to tell you, this is shocking for a lot of your longtime supporters." More than two dozen members of Congress signed an open letter urging Komen to right their wrong.

Even many local Komen chapters reached out to our health centers, hoping the split could be repaired. But no matter how personal it felt, Planned Parenthood staff across the country refused to say anything negative about Komen publicly or to the press. As usual, the people closest to the patients knew the work we did together was irreplaceable.

Three days after we sent that email to supporters, Komen called to reverse course. They said they hoped we could work together again, and we have ever since. In addition, with the millions of dollars we raised that week, Planned Parenthood launched a new breast health initiative to provide more breast exams and support for women in need than ever before.

I was overcome with relief. It's hard to find a single family in America who hasn't been touched by breast cancer, and the screenings and early detection Planned Parenthood provides in partnership with Komen were at the heart of our mission. Not only had we managed to prevent our patients from losing access to this care, but a great diversity of people stood with us and refused to let women be used as a political bargaining chip.

Years ago Dutch Leonard, a Harvard professor who specializes in social enterprise and nonprofit management, said something I've never forgotten: "Nietzsche wrote that 'The most common form of human stupidity is forgetting what we were trying to accomplish.' In other words, always, always, always remember what you are trying to do." It seems so simple, and that is perhaps its elegance. Planned Parenthood is here for women who need health care, regardless of politics. In fact, if you're a woman who finds a lump in your breast, politics is the furthest thing from your mind.

When you're working for social change, there are new battles every day, and you never know if you're going to lose or win. But when I go home at night, if I can look in the mirror and say, *I did the right thing by women*, that's the only thing that matters. The Komen debacle crystallized that purpose in my mind like never before. And the truly incredible part was realizing that, maybe even more than anyone had imagined, the American people felt the same way.

• • •

People often ask, "Why do this? Why get up every day and do work that is so hard?" But the fact is, nobody ever asked the women I worked with in rural Texas, New Orleans, or East Los Angeles how they got out of bed every morning to do such tough jobs. Being able to choose to do work that makes a difference is a privilege.

When another awful bill is introduced in another state legislature, or I'm trying to rebut lies about Planned Parenthood on national television, or just dealing with the kind of internal politics that are part of life at any big organization, I often think of the health center manager I met in Des Moines, Iowa. One morning, before the center opened, we talked while she set up her procedure room for the day, organizing the cabinets the way she liked and getting the exam table ready for the first patient.

"You know," she confessed, "it gets hard, especially with the politics and the protesters. A few months ago I even started thinking about taking an easier job. But then I came to work, and I saw my patients. I held a woman's hand through her procedure and looked her in the eye. And I realized: they need me. They need me as much as any person has ever needed someone. How can I walk out on them?" She's right. At the end of the day, that's all that matters.

Of course that doesn't make it any more fun to listen to the things people yell at me when I walk into a health center, or to read my Twitter mentions (something I try to avoid at all costs). Worst of all are the attacks on my kids—those really hurt. I still think about the interview I did a few months ago with a male reporter who spent several minutes asking inappropriate, invasive questions about abortion; that was nothing new, and I could handle it. But when he started asking belittling questions about my daughter Lily and how she got her job on Capitol Hill, implying that she couldn't get there on her own—that was a bridge too far. It's hard enough for young women to succeed in politics or climb the career ladder *without* the casual sexism of a snarky podcast host. I clenched my teeth and got through it, but I didn't stop fuming until I finally finished the interview, walked out of the building, took a few deep breaths, and went on with my day.

I try never to be so immune to criticism that I just shut it all out—after all, sometimes there's a grain of truth to it. But I've learned from Mom's experiences and my own not to let it determine how I feel about myself. If I did, I simply would not be able to function some days—like the time, in the middle of an effort to defund Planned Parenthood, when my personal email address wound up on a right-wing blog. In a matter of hours my inbox was full of the same hateful message copied and pasted from thousands of people, telling me I was a baby killer, I was going to hell, and all the rest. More than anything else, it was profoundly annoying having to dig through all the junk in order to find the emails I actually needed to read.

But then, by accident or by chance, I opened one of the emails. It began, "I know you think this is just going to be another awful screed against you and against Planned Parenthood. Your email address was forwarded to me from my mother-in-law, who sent it to all of her anti-choice friends. I'm hoping somehow you find this note among all the hate mail because I think Planned Parenthood is great. You were there for me when I was in college, and I'll never forget it." Right there, in the middle of it all, was a diamond in the rough. That's true most of the time, if you're willing to look for it.

The hands-down best part of working for an organization like Planned Parenthood is that inspiration is everywhere, even at the slightly run-down health center I once visited in Albuquerque, New Mexico. It was an older building, badly in need of a new coat of paint. As we parked the car, I saw a young man and woman walking out the door together into the parking lot. It was in the spring, right about time for graduation. They couldn't have been more than seventeen or eighteen, and she was wearing a big varsity letter jacket with "Seniors 2008" written on it. I didn't know their backstory. Did they have parents they couldn't talk to? Were they worried they were pregnant? Were they trying to get birth control? But watching them made me think about how, for those teenagers, Planned Parenthood was the only thing standing between them and an uncertain future. It's not often that you get to see the immediate difference you're making in people's lives. But that day I did.

Every job has its own hurdles and challenges, and doing the right work means there will be some tough days. If there aren't, I figure I need to set my sights higher. Some of them have left me sad and resolute, while others have helped me reconnect to the core of why I do what I do. And knowing that there are people who get up every day, face down the picketers and protesters, and do everything they can to help a woman with a lump in her breast or a young couple in Albuquerque get the health care they deserve is what makes me want to stay in the fight.

Chapter 11

If It Was Easy, Someone Else Would Be Doing It

Molly Ivins said it best: "Since you don't always win, you got to learn to enjoy just fightin' the good fight."

In all my years as an organizer, I've learned that you lose a lot more than you win. If you can't celebrate the victories when they come along, and have a little fun the rest of the time, you just might be in the wrong line of work.

To put this in context: When Planned Parenthood was founded more than a hundred years ago, birth control was illegal. Back in 1916 a nurse named Margaret Sanger, along with her sister Ethel and a volunteer named Fania Mindell, opened the first birth control clinic in America. It was a tiny storefront in Brooklyn, where women could get a ten-cent pamphlet about preventing pregnancy. From day one women lined up around the block—women pushing baby buggies, holding babies in their arms. Ten days later an undercover police officer posing as a mother busted Margaret and threw her in jail—where she taught her fellow inmates about birth control.

Margaret began traveling the country, and a movement was born. She spoke to nurses in St. Paul, Minnesota, and women's clubs in Los Angeles; factory women in Racine, Wisconsin, and farmworkers in Tucson, Arizona. When the city council of Portland, Oregon, met behind closed doors to pass an ordinance banning Margaret's pamphlets, the women in town made pamphlets of their own, which read, "Shall five men legislate in secret against ten thousand women?" Suddenly Planned Parenthood centers started cropping up in towns across America. Once, on a visit to Dallas, the local Planned Parenthood CEO Ken Lambrecht and I stopped by the Ripley Shirt Factory. Years ago Katie Ripley, with the full knowledge of her husband, George, who owned the factory, would send empty shirt boxes to New York City. Organizers there would fill them with diaphragms, mark them "Returns," and ship them back to Dallas, where women would gratefully get one of the earliest methods of birth control.

It wasn't until the 1960s that a Planned Parenthood employee in Connecticut named Estelle Griswold decided to challenge the archaic laws outlawing birth control. With the help of her medical director, Dr. C. Lee Buxton, she started handing out birth control to women in hopes of getting arrested. The police obliged, and Estelle fought her case all the way to the US Supreme Court. In 1965, *Griswold v. Connecticut* legalized birth control for married couples.

Women have been searching for ways to prevent pregnancy for all of recorded history. In the United States we've been fighting about birth control for the better part of the past century, and there's no sign of that changing anytime soon.

For those of you who don't remember the long and arduous process of passing Obamacare, you might think that the most controversial topics were drug pricing or cracking down on insurance premiums. Nope. Nearly every knock-down, drag-out fight had to do with women's health.

Passing health reform had been one of President Obama's signature campaign promises, and he made it a top priority soon after taking office in 2009. Everyone, especially those of us working in health care, understood that finally fixing our broken health care system, as members of both parties had been trying to do for decades, would make a big difference for millions of Americans.

Back then, the uninsured rate in America was at its highest point in a generation. At Planned Parenthood we saw every day how the lack of health insurance affected our patients. This was an amazing opportunity to take a big leap forward.

In the early days of the fight for health care reform, I went to a press conference with Barbara Mikulski, a senator from Maryland and the longest serving woman in Congress, to announce Planned Parenthood's support for Obamacare. We were in the Capitol Visitor Center in a room overflowing with people. She always brought a step stool to public appearances, and this day was no exception. She jumped up to the microphone, highly distinctive with her vibrant yellow jacket and Spray Net hairdo, and pulled out her bright red lipstick. Smearing it on, she shouted, "Get ready, women, we are going to war!"

Of course she was right. During the many months it took to pass Obamacare, the debates over what to include in health care reform and what to leave out were often contentious. In one infamous hearing, Senator Jon Kyl from Arizona objected to covering maternity care, huffing, "I've never needed it." Senator Debbie Stabenow of Michigan shot back, "I think your mother probably did." I've been a huge fan of hers forever!

After many similar arguments had been waged and won, there was one last topic to resolve: the issue of abortion. A proposal had been introduced at the last minute—with support from the US Conference of Catholic Bishops—that would prevent insurance plans from covering abortion services under the new health care law. The amendment went against everything we stood for at Planned Parenthood.

For help, I turned to Laurie Rubiner. Laurie had come on to run our government relations office in Washington, and she was smart and savvy. She had worked on health care policy on both sides of the aisle, including for then Senator Hillary Clinton. Not only that, she had spent years trying to convince Washington to stop talking about women's health as merely a "social" issue, and start talking about it as a fundamental health care issue that affected half the country.

We used every tool in our toolbox to try to beat back the proposal, known as the Stupak Amendment, but we didn't have the votes, and it was included in the bill passed by the US House of Representatives. If it passed the Senate and became law, it would be a done deal: we'd lose abortion coverage for women and never get it back. I was devastated. That was my lowest point in a long time.

Early the next morning I was in a hotel room, getting ready for a day on the road, when my cell phone rang. My old boss, Nancy Pelosi, was calling. "I know this is terrible, and I'm as mad as you are," she said. "This was a last-minute attack and just know this: I am committed to getting the Stupak Amendment out of the final bill. I don't know how, but that's my word."

I thanked her and told her we would help however we could. But I wasn't hopeful. Having worked on the Hill, I knew that the likelihood of our changing the legislation was slim. And deep down I knew that the White House would sign whatever bill came out of Congress. There was no way we could count on the president to veto the bill everyone in his administration had fought so hard for. I felt awful and, frankly, totally discouraged.

A few days later Planned Parenthood leaders from across the country were scheduled to be in Washington for a meeting of the national board. Everyone was expecting an update from the front lines of the health care fight. Our organization had poured all of our energy into supporting Obamacare, and there was so much good in the bill. But I knew we could not support it the way it was. I just hoped the board would agree.

"This is it," I told them, bracing for a tough conversation. "I am asking you to give me the authority to tell the White House and our congressional leaders that if the bill bans abortion coverage, as it does in its current version, we will lobby against final passage."

There was an uneasy silence. For months, our volunteers had rallied, made phone calls, and come to Washington to speak to their members of Congress—all in the interest of getting the Affordable Care Act passed. To see those efforts derailed would be awful. I could sense the board members thinking, *All this work, for nothing?*

The board went back and forth, recognizing that if Planned Parenthood opposed Obamacare over abortion, the entire bill might go down, hurting the millions of Americans in desperate need of affordable health care. I listened as they played out the same internal debate I'd been having for days.

In the middle of their deliberations Reverend Kelvin Sauls, a board member and preacher from California, cleared his throat. He had a forceful voice and was imposing in stature. Everyone in the boardroom stopped their conversations and leaned forward to listen. "The Bible says, 'And I sought for a man among them, that should stand in the breach before me.' The question we must answer is, Who will stand in the breach? Who will stand for the women we care for, at a moment of need for moral leadership? I believe this is one of those times when we are called to be in solidarity with women who may have no one else to stand in the breach."

When he finished speaking, the room erupted with applause. Reverend Sauls had put into words what everyone was feeling. The board voted unanimously that Planned Parenthood would not support legislation that banned abortion coverage—even if that meant the defeat of the very bill we had worked so hard for.

It was my job to deliver the message. First I had to call the White House, knowing that they would be furious. It wasn't the first time I'd had a big disagreement with the administration, and it wouldn't be the last, but I had to remember what the president told me and other progressives after he was first elected: "It's your job to make me do the right thing." That sounded good as a slogan, but the reality was that no one liked being pressured by us.

Our only real hope was Speaker Pelosi, and though I remembered her pledge to me weeks earlier, her opposing this bill, here at the final hour, seemed nearly impossible. I knew how important health care reform was to her, and to millions of Americans. Our position wasn't popular enough to upend the entire bill. But I needed to tell her where Planned Parenthood stood, and I needed to tell her directly.

Waiting at the Capitol for my appointment with Nancy, I saw everyone I had ever worked with on the Hill—it was like a slightly awkward family reunion. I was wearing my best blue suit, with Mom's sheriff badge pin. She was going to have to help me from on high that day.

Being ushered into the conference room was a good reminder of how very different it was to be on the other side of the table from my former boss. This wasn't a negotiating meeting; I knew I had to be crystal clear on our position, take it or leave it.

"Thanks for coming in today," Nancy began. "I know you understand we are within only a handful of votes to get this bill passed, and I'm not sure we can get it done. But we are working hard."

That wasn't surprising to me, since everyone was hustling votes and it was down to the wire. But before I could reply, she floored me by saying,

"You know how much this bill means to me. I've worked for health care reform my entire career. But I want you to know: if there is an abortion ban in the Affordable Care Act, there won't be an Affordable Care Act. I won't pass it."

I opened my mouth to thank her, but once again Nancy was a step ahead of me, already strategizing on how to get the caucus in line. Her members were hard at work whipping the votes, and soon we would know whether the abortion ban had made it into the final bill—not to mention whether the bill could even pass.

That whole week was an endless vote-counting effort, and time on the congressional calendar was running out. Soon the voting would be over, for better or worse. We had Planned Parenthood supporters calling every member of Congress, either to buck them up or urge them to support only a bill that protected abortion rights. I was in Washington all week with the Planned Parenthood leadership, holed up in a conference room where we were getting reports from organizers out in the states. Late Friday night the phone rang in my hotel room. It was Congresswoman Rosa DeLauro from Connecticut, a key lieutenant to Speaker Pelosi and one of my favorite members of Congress. We'd been in the trenches together many times, and Rosa had never shied away from a fight.

"Cecile, we did it! We backed them down. They threatened us over and over," Rosa said. "And it won't surprise you—several of the Democratic men were ready to sell us out. But Nancy didn't blink. None of the women blinked. The Stupak abortion ban is out of the bill!"

Joy and relief washed over me, along with an overwhelming feeling of gratitude for the women who had stood with us. It was amazing. Had we really done this?

Yes, we had. Two days later the Affordable Care Act passed, and we made history. Without the women in the House and the Senate, it would have been a different story. Starting with Senator Mikulski, who announced that we were going to war, women in Congress were key to every victory for women under Obamacare. Thanks to their persistence and vision, not only did millions more Americans get health care coverage, but we took on deep injustices that have been part of our health care system for far too long. And of course, they were aided in their efforts by women who spoke out and told their stories, as well as courageous organizers like Sister Simone Campbell and the "Nuns on the Bus," who helped counter the narrative that supporting women's health meant going against the Catholic church.

For the first time, insurance companies could no longer charge women more than men for the same health care coverage—something that routinely happened before Obamacare. The many reasons women could be denied insurance coverage, from surviving sexual assault or domestic violence to having had a cesarean section, were no longer valid. And those pesky maternity benefits Senator Kyl objected to became part of the essential benefits all insurance companies have to cover. As Nancy likes to say, thanks to the Affordable Care Act, being a woman is no longer a preexisting condition in America.

Protecting coverage for abortion was a major victory, but certainly not our last battle in the fight for women's health care. Part of the promise of Obamacare was that under the new law, preventive care would be covered for everyone with no out-of-pocket cost. We thought if we could make a case for contraception as preventive care, maybe women could actually have their birth control covered by insurance, like every other prescription medication in America. After all, Viagra was fully covered, so why not birth control? Planned Parenthood saw more than 2 million patients for birth control each year, but what we were talking about could be life-changing for tens of millions of women. The stakes went far beyond just our clinics, and the potential impact was huge.

There are three things to know about birth control. First, it's incredibly popular; more than 90 percent of women will use it at some point. There's a statistic I use all the time from Guttmacher, which does excellent research on reproductive health: the average woman in America who wants kids spends five years pregnant or trying to conceive, and thirty years trying not to. In other words, this is a lifetime of medical care that people need, and that's a lot of birth control. Second, too often women don't use the birth control method that's best for them because they can't afford it—think about an IUD, which is really cost-effective over the long term but comes with an up-front cost. Third, a lot of people (58 percent of women using birth control, to be precise) rely on it at least in part for reasons other than preventing pregnancy, such as treating endometriosis, acne, or cramps. Others use it because they want to be able to have sex and not get pregnant—also a compelling reason! The bottom line? Birth control is basic health care for millions of people.

That might seem logical enough, but we knew from experience that getting a majority of legislators on our side was going to be a massive battle. We were fresh off a fight against laws that would let pharmacists refuse to fill a woman's birth control prescription, and we weren't about to take anything for granted. We needed both the medical and scientific community *and* the general public to stand with us like never before.

Unsurprisingly, the public debate over birth control was Exhibit A in how little many of the men making decisions about health care legislation know about women's health. It was a revelation to them that birth control could be anything other than a pack of pills or a condom. Men, including supporters of Planned Parenthood, had no idea how many women use birth control. That shouldn't have come as a surprise. A Fox newscaster once said that women didn't need Planned Parenthood because they could go to Walgreens for their pap smears. That kerfuffle caused Walgreens to put out a statement telling women *not* to come to their stores expecting a pap smear. God bless Stephen Colbert, who was on it instantly, saying that women should go to Walgreens and look for the stirrups, right between the cat food and Swiffer refills. Clearly this was a teachable moment.

One of our more successful lobbying visits at that time was with Senator Harry Reid, the Democratic majority leader from Nevada. We brought a group of women athletes from the University of Nevada–Las Vegas to see the senator, who had been a competitive boxer. They explained that they use birth control to regulate their menstrual cycle during the season, which improved their performance—a story he was eager to repeat the next time he saw me. "I met these incredible women athletes from UNLV," he said. "Did you know they need birth control to compete?"

"Well, yes, I did know that, Senator Reid, and thank you for meeting with them," I answered. Meanwhile I was thinking, *It was really worth it to bring these young women to Washington. They're more effective than any paid lobbyist in town.*

We had the public on our side, the optics on our side, and the science on our side. But as with so many other women's health issues, the decision was ultimately a political one. Despite the shenanigans in Congress, it was the administration that would make the call. We had supporters in the White House, but we also had some very high-ranking opponents.

The most organized force against us was, again, the Conference of Catholic Bishops, who understood that offering no-copay birth control for the first time would be a really big deal. While most of our organizing was highly public, theirs was primarily behind the scenes. We would show up at the White House, only to realize that the Bishops had been there before us, arguing that birth control was immoral—though the fact is that a huge majority of Catholic women use it.

So we turned up the heat. Members of the US Senate, led by Patty Murray and Richard Blumenthal, demanded to talk to the White House. Activists flooded the administration with letters in support of the birth control benefit. The mother of a Planned Parenthood staff member came up with the idea of sewing a human-size, wearable birth control pill pack. We named the costume "Pillamena," and it made the rounds on college campuses. We were throwing in everything but the kitchen sink.

One morning in February 2012, I was sitting in our office in Washington, wondering if all our efforts would be enough. I got a text message from a friend in the administration, saying, "Don't be surprised if you get a call from the White House today." That meant good news or bad news, but I didn't know which.

A few hours later, sure enough, my phone rang. The woman on the other end said, "Would you please hold for the president of the United States?"

"I can definitely do that," I said, thinking, *This is the first time in my life I've gotten a call from the president of the United States. Whatever he says, at least I'll always have that!*

A minute later President Obama—who is notorious for being on time—came to the phone. "Hey, Cecile, how's it going?" he asked in a cheerful voice.

"Well, hello, Mr. President. It's going just fine, thanks."

"Cecile, I wanted to call you because I'm making three phone calls today: the Catholic Bishops, the Catholic Hospital Association, and you. Suffice it to say, I think yours is going to be the happiest phone call I'm going to make."

At that point I started feeling hopeful.

"I'm going to tell them the same thing I'm telling you: later today, I'm going to announce at the White House that, from here on out, birth control is going to be covered for all women under their insurance plans with no copay. I know you've worked hard for this, and I think it's going to be a huge advance for women."

I took a deep breath. "Well, Mr. President, thank you for calling me yourself, and for understanding what a difference this is going to make. We're going to be busy making sure women know about this benefit and can get it."

Later, the entire staff gathered around a television in a conference room to watch as the president took the podium in the White House press briefing room. "As part of the health care reform law that I signed last year," he announced, "all insurance plans are required to cover preventive care at no cost. That means free checkups, free mammograms, immunizations, and other basic services. We fought for this because it saves lives and it saves money. . . . We also accepted a recommendation from the experts at the Institute of Medicine that when it comes to women, preventive care should include coverage of contraceptive services such as birth control."

We let out a cheer as he went on: "Whether you're a teacher, or a small businesswoman, or a nurse, or a janitor, no woman's health should depend on who she is or where she works or how much money she makes. Every woman should be in control of the decisions that affect her own health. Period."

It was a phenomenal moment, surrounded by Planned Parenthood staff that had spent months organizing, tweeting, writing reports, and gathering the stories of women across the country. We hugged, high-fived, and took it all in for a few minutes. Then we started strategizing about what we needed to do to make sure no-copay birth control was a rousing success.

And it was. As soon as the birth control benefit took effect, women started walking into pharmacies to refill their prescriptions, walking out with another month's supply of birth control with no out-of-pocket cost. They'd go to check out at the doctor's office after a well-woman exam, ask what they owed, and hear the receptionist say, "The total for your visit is zero dollars." Women started sending Planned Parenthood thank-you notes written on the back of a Walgreens receipt, with the copay circled: $0.00.

Here's the headline: In the first year alone, women saved $1.4 billion on birth control pills. Today we're at a thirty-year low for unintended pregnancy, a historic low in teen pregnancy, and the lowest abortion rate since *Roe v. Wade*. These facts are too often overlooked, even though this is one of the biggest public health success stories of the last century. It didn't happen on its own—it happened in large part due to better and more affordable access to birth control.

But of course elections have consequences. Since President Obama left office, women's health has come under fire by the Trump administration, which believes insurance companies shouldn't have to cover birth control. While the Obama administration was full of people—including the president himself—who were aware of how many women rely on affordable contraceptives, the current administration is home to high-ranking officials who claim birth control doesn't work and don't think it should have to be covered by insurance.

• • •

At a time when so many people's opinions on issues of reproductive health seem to be set in stone, it can seem nearly impossible to change someone's mind. By refusing to back down on birth control coverage in the Affordable Care Act, we certainly changed the way a lot of people understood birth control. Many of the men who once rolled their eyes when they talked about it were persuaded by the many women from all walks of life who felt so strongly about making their own health care choices.

There is a takeaway here for aspiring hell-raisers: We get only what we're willing to fight for—nothing more and, I hope, nothing less. That's a lesson I learned growing up in Texas. During the summer of 2013 the rest of the country learned a little something about it too.

It started when Governor Rick Perry and the legislature shut down the state women's health program in an effort to get rid of Planned Parenthood in Texas. More than eighty health centers shuttered or stopped providing family planning services, the vast majority of which were not even Planned Parenthood. All were health care providers that delivered basic health care to the most underserved Texans.

Then, after slashing family planning, Governor Perry and the legislature called a special session and tried to force through the most restrictive abortion laws in the country. The measures they were trying to pass would force all but five of the remaining abortion clinics left in the state to close their doors. In a state the size of Texas, that's a really big deal—thousands of women would not have a single abortion provider within hundreds of miles. The politicians' goal was clear: to end access to safe and legal abortion altogether.

By that point, women in Texas had been so beat down that the governor and his friends must have thought they would be too exhausted to fight back. Instead it was like a match on dry kindling. Suddenly Texans from every corner of the state were showing up to testify against the bill. Parents left kids with neighbors and headed to the capitol. Students from Texas A&M in College Station, Texas Tech in Lubbock, and every college in between drove to Austin to stand in line for the chance to get their three minutes before the Texas Senate. Hundreds of activists waited for hours, some until 2:00 or 3:00 in the morning. People in California and Wisconsin watching on social media ordered pizza and coffee to be delivered to protesters at the capitol.

Legislation terrible for women was being debated in states across the country, but Texas was clearly in a class all its own. I told Dawn Laguens, "We really ought to figure out how to provide more support down there. I've been doing this work a long time, but I've never seen spontaneous organizing like this."

I was on a train on my way back to New York from a Planned Parenthood event when I got a call from Kirk Watson, the former mayor of Austin, a longtime friend, and now a state senator and head of the Democratic caucus. "Look, this bill's happening," he told me. "I know we don't have the votes to block it. We can't win. But I think we can filibuster the bill. This is our chance to say something."

To filibuster, a state senator would have to talk until they ran out the clock. And the Democrats had someone lined up to do it: Senator Wendy Davis from Fort Worth. I had met Wendy and knew she was tough and fearless. I'd heard her speak, and she had real star power.

"Wow," I said. "Okay. I'll see how quickly I can get there."

When I landed in Austin I headed to Steve and Amber Mostyn's apartment to meet up with Wendy. Steve and Amber were progressive warriors. They knew everything about the workings of the state legislature and were always up for a good social justice fight. Yvonne Gutierrez, a brilliant and tireless Planned Parenthood leader from San Antonio, was there too, helping to compile facts about Planned Parenthood and stories of patients from across the state. The fact that Wendy was willing to filibuster and speak openly about abortion, and that her senate colleagues were committed to supporting her, was momentous.

The next morning I headed to the capitol with Yvonne to wish Wendy good luck. She was lacing up her now famous pink running shoes, and I could see it in her eyes: she was definitely ready. On the front door of her office she'd hung a sign reading *Stand with Planned Parenthood*. "I want to make sure every senator has to walk by this sign on their way to the floor," she explained.

The energy in Austin that day was like nothing I'd ever experienced. Normally the capitol is pretty empty except for the people who work there and the occasional tour group of schoolkids. But on this day the line to get into the senate to watch Wendy's filibuster snaked up three stories of the capitol rotunda, and every overflow room was full to capacity. The "Stand with Texas Women" coalition had ordered hundreds of T-shirts in the only color you can get in such huge quantities in Texas at a moment's notice: burnt orange, the color of nearby University of Texas. As a result, the entire place was a sea of orange, and the marching orders for our side became: "Come early, stay late, wear orange."

As I walked around, taking it all in, I met a seven-year-old activist named Scarlett who had set up shop in a corner of the capitol, where she was decorating and distributing homemade pins that said, "Stand with Wendy." I still have mine. Everywhere I went, I ran into activists, members of the state legislature, and people who had worked on Mom's campaign, along with brand-new activists who had never set foot in the capitol. And everyone had brought their kids.

At 11:18 a.m. the filibuster started. Wendy stood up, her posture strong and defiant, and said, "I intend to speak for an extended length of time." She read facts about abortion, testimony from Planned Parenthood doctors and patients. Every time I started to worry she might be losing steam, she launched into another powerful personal account from yet another woman in Texas. In order to defeat the bill, she would have to filibuster until midnight—no breaks, no rest.

As she continued into the afternoon and then the night, we knew the eyes of Texas were upon us; we didn't know that hundreds of thousands of people outside the state and around the world were also watching it all unfold.

I was getting texts from people all over the country who were glued to their computer screens. A young social studies teacher named Christopher Dido was streaming the chanting and cheering in the rotunda from his cell phone. Every now and then he would hold the phone in front of his face, selfie-style, and ask, "Do you guys want me to keep streaming, or have you had enough?" Thousands of comments would roll in from around the world: "Keep going!"

At one point even Barack Obama tweeted to a cool 41 million followers, "Something special is happening in Austin tonight." Someone read the tweet out loud in the rotunda; it was a real morale boost, and possibly the one time in recorded history a president's late-night tweet actually did some good.

While we were trying to manage the chaos outside the senate gallery, senate staffers were sending us text messages and emails about what was happening inside. Wendy could have only three procedural strikes before senate Republicans could call the filibuster off and pass the bill. She already had two strikes for completely ridiculous matters, and it was clear that Lieutenant Governor David Dewhurst, who was also president of the senate, intended to stop the filibuster by any means necessary before midnight—even if it meant breaking every rule in the book to do it.

I realized that if they called a third strike on Wendy, the capitol was going to erupt. That's when I turned to Earl Jordan, the head of security for Planned Parenthood of Greater Texas. He was our go-between with the Texas Department of Public Safety, and an ex-DPS officer himself. Earl has a head of silver hair and would sooner be caught dead than without a tie. He's a wonderfully mild-mannered guy—the person you'd want by your side in a crisis.

"Earl," I said, "if they declare the filibuster dead, we're going to jail tonight. So I need you to get ready."

Earl didn't miss a beat. "No, ma'am. No, ma'am, we're not," he said in his calm drawl. Translation: *Don't even think about trying something*.

I just looked at him. There were thousands of people in the capitol, and it was clear to me that we were going to have massive civil disobedience if they tried to cut Wendy off. And I was convinced that was what we needed. No one was going to be able to change my mind, not even Earl.

I began to look around the rotunda for lawyers I knew, quickly spying the veteran civil rights attorney Malcolm Greenstein. I also texted Rick Levy, a friend from our Tyler days, and asked if he could be on call in case we all went to jail. Then I turned to the women on either side of me. "Now might be a good time to put your ID in your bra. That way you'll have it if we get arrested later." I'd learned a few things since my first arrest back in California.

Meanwhile, inside the chambers, Republicans had not only stopped Wendy's filibuster and tried to call a vote, they had cut off the microphones on the Democratic side. It was complete chaos when Senator Leticia Van de Putte, who had hastily come back from her father's funeral in San Antonio earlier that day to be part of the fight, stood up and declared, "At what point must a female senator raise her hand or raise her voice to be recognized by her male colleagues?" She was speaking to the frustrations of women across Texas whose voices had been shut out for far too long.

I was standing out in the rotunda, surrounded by people chanting, by cameras clicking, and by Planned Parenthood staff juggling phones. Yvonne and I were trading information back and forth, along with Planned Parenthood of Greater Texas CEO Ken Lambrecht, when I got a text message from someone on the senate floor. It just said, "Make noise."

And so we did. We shook the capitol to its foundation. We knew that our last hope of stopping the bill before midnight was to create so much raucous noise and chaos that they couldn't continue with business as usual. The lieutenant governor called us an "unruly mob." Funny—in some parts of the world, they call that democracy in action.

We continued to rally well past midnight. The Department of Public Safety threw everyone out of the senate gallery, but nobody left the capitol. At one point they even tried to change the clock on the senate floor to make it look like they had passed the bill in time. The Republicans were trying to claim the filibuster had failed.

Finally, around 3:00 a.m., Ken got a text message from Wendy. As he read it, his eyes widened. Grinning, he handed me his phone so I could read it for myself—and then shout it at the top of my lungs to the crowd. It said: "First, I love you guys. The lieutenant governor has agreed that SB 5 is dead."

In the midst of the deafening applause, Ken grabbed my hand, leaned in, and said, "This is why we do what we do." Someone started to sing "The Eyes of Texas," and everyone joined in. I kept looking up at Mom's portrait in the rotunda. She ran for governor to open up the doors of gov-

ernment and let the people in, and here we were. She would have been so proud. There was nothing she loved better than making good trouble.

I had to make a plane back to New York at daybreak, but it was 4:00 a.m. and I was starving, so Earl and I drove to the only place open for breakfast at that hour. As we walked into the Magnolia Café on South Congress, the booths were filled with fellow protesters wearing Planned Parenthood pins and T-shirts reading "What Would Tami Taylor do?," in reference to Connie Britton's legendary *Friday Night Lights* character. Earl and I wedged in with the rest of the protesters and celebrated with a stack of pancakes.

· · ·

It didn't take long before we got the news that Governor Perry had called a second special session to pass the bill. We knew it was coming, and we knew we had to keep people organized and our fight in the news. So we got to work, planning a statewide bus tour. We wanted to make sure this wasn't just an Austin story, but a story about what was happening to women across the state. On my way back to Texas from New York, I passed a store window displaying a burnt orange dress—the color everyone was wearing at the capitol. I ran in and bought it. That orange dress would be my uniform for the next several days.

We kicked off with a rally on the steps of the capitol, the likes of which no one had seen since Mom's days as governor. Natalie Maines of the Dixie Chicks came from Lubbock with her father, Lloyd, who was a singer-songwriter and one of the first people to be inducted into the Austin City Limits Hall of Fame. We all had goose bumps when she sang "Not Ready to Make Nice."

The next day we headed out on orange buses emblazoned with "Stand with Texas Women." The two buses (nicknamed "Ann" after Mom and "Maggie" after Margaret Sanger) crisscrossed the state, greeted by crowds in Houston, Dallas, San Antonio, and even in smaller, more conservative towns like Midland in West Texas. Everywhere she went, Wendy Davis got a hero's welcome. Women would walk up to me with tears in their eyes and share deeply personal stories about ending a pregnancy while struggling to comply with medically unnecessary laws intended to shame them. No matter the outcome of our fight, they were determined to stand up and be counted.

Days later, when the bill came up for a vote, we didn't have the votes to block it, nor could we filibuster again. Even so, people were still showing up in droves.

Walking up the steps to the capitol that morning, feeling somber but determined, I passed a mother and her young son. The mom elbowed him, saying, "Show her your sign." He held up a piece of orange tagboard on which he had written in Magic Marker, "I still have my mom thanks to cancer screenings at Planned Parenthood." His mother started to cry and said simply, "Thank you." I gave them both a hug and went into the capitol.

As usual everyone had to go through security. But this time there was a rumor floating around that the Department of Public Safety was confiscating women's tampons and sanitary napkins, apparently worried that the women would throw them from the gallery onto the senate floor. Senator Kirk Watson quipped, "I'm really confused—I thought sanitary napkins were kind of soft, fluffy things." It was irony at its finest: you could bring a gun into the state capitol, but not a tampon.

Things did feel different that night, as though everyone were saying goodbye. I ran into Jessica Farrar, a member of the Texas House of Representatives who had been an organizing powerhouse since the beginning of this legislative fight. She was walking around in her shorts and a tie-dyed T-shirt. When I saw her coming, I started clapping, and so did everybody else.

That night, after the bill passed, hundreds of people were waiting outside the capitol, including my husband, who had flown in to help. We requisitioned a bullhorn and held an impromptu rally, with Wendy, Kirk Watson, and many other senators who had led the fight. But the evening wasn't complete until we marched past the governor's mansion carrying a sign that read, "In it for the long run!"

That night I couldn't sleep. All I could think of were the people we'd met and the makeshift family we had built. There were activists of all ages who had been part of this—including one of my favorites, Beau Guidry. At nine years old, Beau had not only watched every minute of Wendy

Davis's filibuster, but he had live-tweeted it. Later that fall he would run for president of his third grade class—and win.

On my flight home the next morning I met two young women, one in a bachelorette tiara. They had flown into Austin on Friday night for a party with the bridesmaids, but ended up moving the festivities to the capitol on Saturday to be part of the protests. I was sure that they and Beau and all the others would be in it for the long run as well.

And of course, it was the filibuster and all the organizing that went into it that led to Wendy's race for governor. She became a national leader for reproductive rights, and that never would have happened if not for everything that summer. We'd woken up a sleeping giant in Texas.

· · ·

The best and worst part about being a professional troublemaker is that the trouble never ends. Once the law we'd been protesting took effect, we had to continue fighting back while making sure women could still get abortions in Texas, despite the unbelievable barriers they faced. And we had to make damn sure we told these women's stories—with the help of health care researchers, women's magazines, the *Texas Tribune* and *Texas Observer*, and many others.

While health care providers had been racing to get ready for the laws, women were whipsawed when the changes took effect. Women who were scheduled to have an abortion on Friday morning showed up and found out it had been canceled. One woman who came to Planned Parenthood was stricken. "What do you mean, I have to come back? I can't. I've left my kids with my neighbor and can't miss another day of work." She left, sobbing, and never returned.

One of the many heroines from those awful days is Melaney Linton, a Planned Parenthood CEO who oversees parts of Texas and Louisiana. The day after the laws took effect, and other abortion providers were forced to close their doors, Melaney reported that her staff was working around the clock to be there for the flood of patients who filled their waiting room, lobby, patio, hallway, and parking lot. "We are still providing services," she said. "We will never, ever go down without a fight."

We knew the case would eventually make its way to the Supreme

Court, and with the help of Whole Woman's Health and the Center for Reproductive Rights, it did. But we also knew our chances of winning were uncertain. The day of the argument, the gathering in front of the Supreme Court was massive. Reproductive rights and justice leaders, allies from the labor movement, and more gathered to cheer on the Center for Reproductive Rights attorneys and plaintiffs.

I was honored to be in the courtroom to watch oral arguments before a Court with three women on the bench. In these situations women are always fewer in number but bigger in impact, and it was certainly true that day. Justices Samuel Alito and John Roberts couldn't get a word in edgewise between Justices Ruth Bader Ginsburg, Elena Kagan, and Sonia Sotomayor.

The irony of that day's argument? The lawyer for the state of Texas couldn't give a single reason why enacting these restrictions was for the benefit of women. His only justification was that it was the state's right to do it. Minutes into the lawyer's oral argument, Justice Ginsburg set the tone for the hearing by asking how many women lived one hundred miles or more from a clinic under the new law. When he answered that it would be about 25 percent, but that didn't include women in El Paso, who could go to the clinic just over the border in New Mexico, Justice Ginsburg sat up straighter.

"That's odd that you point to the New Mexico facility," she asserted, referring to the fact that New Mexico doesn't require clinics to meet the onerous and unnecessary requirements Texas claimed were so important to protect women's health and safety. "If that's all right for the women in the El Paso area, why isn't it right for the rest of the women in Texas?" It was a knockout punch.

It wasn't simply that the women justices dominated the argument and had read every page of the material. They were able to bring something that had seldom been heard before in the Supreme Court: women's lives and experiences. It was proof that elections matter. Those three women on the Court, twenty-two others in the US Senate, and many more in the US House of Representatives are carrying an entire gender on their shoulders.

Months later, on the day of the verdict, everyone at Planned Parenthood was refreshing ScotusBlog, nervously waiting for the Court to rule. Just after 10:00 a.m. they did. You could hear shouts and cheers making their way around the office as people realized the Supreme Court had ruled 5–3 against the Texas law. Best of all was Justice Ginsburg's concurring opinion: "It is beyond rational belief that HB 2 could genuinely protect the health of women." I couldn't have put it better!

Of course the fight is far from over, and women in Texas are still living with enormous barriers. But not long ago Planned Parenthood started providing abortions again in my hometown of Waco, an important sign of hope and progress.

• • •

Mom used to quote Edna St. Vincent Millay, who said, "It's not true that life is one damn thing after another; it's one damn thing over and over."

Abortion was legalized by the Supreme Court more than four decades ago, and extreme politicians have been chipping away at a woman's right to make her own health decisions ever since. In fact we've seen more attempts in the past five years than ever before to make it harder to access safe and legal abortion. Making matters worse is the appointment of Justice Neil Gorsuch to the Supreme Court, who was one of the first judges to rule on the side of the arts and crafts store Hobby Lobby in a case that allowed employers to deny women access to birth control based on their own personal beliefs. I often think of the signs I see at protests for reproductive rights, typically held by women of a certain age, reading, "My arms are tired from carrying this sign for 40 years."

But while the fight to keep abortion safe and legal can feel like it's two steps forward, one step back, there is one area where we've made progress no one can take away.

It's hard to think of a medical procedure in this country that carries the stigma and judgment abortion does. Too often women's experiences are seen through the lens of cultural and political battles instead of lived experiences. A woman who says she's relieved after having an abortion is often criticized—though, based on thousands of postabortion interviews, this is overwhelmingly how patients feel. If she says she feels regret, anti-abortion activists may use her words to push for laws that restrict abortion access or treat women as though we are incapable of making our own decisions.

For far too long, intense public debates about abortion had hardly any firsthand experiences at the center of the discussion. That's changed in recent years, inspired in no small part by women in the reproductive justice movement who refused to be shamed or silenced. More and more, people have come forward to share their experiences.

Four years ago I started speaking more publicly about my own abortion. Before becoming president of Planned Parenthood, I hadn't talked about it except to family and close friends. The truth is, it wasn't an agonizing decision for me. It wasn't tragic or dramatic—it was just my story.

Kirk and I were working more than full time and had three kids in school when I realized I was pregnant again. Like millions of other women, I was using birth control, but no method is foolproof. We were doing the best job we could raising our kids, and I couldn't imagine we could do justice to a fourth. Having another child just was not an option for us. I already felt like I wasn't doing enough for Lily, Hannah, and Daniel as it was. I was fortunate in that, at the time, accessing abortion in Texas was not the nightmare it now is for so many women.

Being able to terminate a pregnancy early—it had hardly even begun—was a relief. I realize women have many different feelings about abortion, and I respect that. But the thought that the government could force me or any other woman to carry out a pregnancy that was unplanned or unwanted was and is absolutely unconscionable. Many women have echoed how I feel; nothing makes you firmer in your belief in the right to abortion than being a mother yourself. I look forward to the day when men can empathize with an experience they will never have.

After my public declaration, women came up to me from Arizona to Maine to tell me that they had decided to share their stories, too. I met young women who, inspired by the people and organizations that were addressing abortion stigma, were starting their own campaigns online and in their communities to encourage others to talk about their experiences.

Since then I've seen things I never expected: a major party's presidential nominee talking openly about abortion in a national debate. The actor Kerry Washington as Olivia Pope having an abortion in prime time on the television show *Scandal*. (Thank you, Shonda Rhimes, for telling women's stories.) Hundreds of women lawyers even submitted briefs to the Supreme Court in the Texas case telling their own abortion stories.

In 2016 I was at a conference celebrating 125 years of women students at Brown University, my alma mater. I was sitting in the audience, making last-minute edits to my speech, when a middle-aged woman took the stage to introduce me. Something in her voice made me sit up and pay attention.

She thanked Brown and gave a shout-out to her daughter, who was in the audience. Then she started to tell her own story. Days before her graduation in 1968, she traveled to Philadelphia for an illegal abortion. A few days later, barely able to stand, she got out of bed and welcomed her parents to campus. She managed to walk through the Van Wickle Gates to get her diploma, hiding how much pain she was in.

Looking back, she said, she was lucky to be alive. She choked up as she said she would not be where she is today had she not been able to get an abortion. "We can't ever go back," she insisted. It was the first time she had ever told her story in public.

We're still waging the fight for abortion access in America every day. But along the way we're also transforming the culture, and that change can't be reversed.

Taking on controversial issues is hard. Since my first weeks at Planned Parenthood, there have been people who have said, "Why don't you just change the name, or split the organization in two, so people don't associate you with abortion?" Sometimes these are well-intentioned people; they just want the controversy to go away. But what is important is that we quit apologizing for abortion and do everything we can to support people who need one.

Any time you're trying to change the way things are or challenge the powers that be, it's going to be controversial. That's been true in every organizing job I've ever had. Often the work that's most worthwhile seems the most intractable and impossible. But just because someone else hasn't figured it out yet doesn't mean you can't. After all, if it was easy, someone else would be doing it. And in the meantime, at least I'm enjoying fighting the good fight.

CHAPTER 12

All In

I could almost see Mom again, standing on the floor of the 1984 Democratic National Convention in San Francisco, waiting for Geraldine Ferraro to take the stage. That night Ferraro would become the first woman ever nominated as vice president on a major party ticket. Susan Stamberg from NPR, with her wonderfully curly hair and an enormous grin, walked up to Mom carrying her ubiquitous microphone. "How does this feel, Ann?" she shouted above the screaming delegates. Mom was not a sentimental person; life hadn't afforded her that luxury. But at that moment she was overcome, teary-eyed, as Ferraro's name was announced over the speakers. "I wasn't sure I would ever live to see this day," she said. "Finally, one of us."

Thirty-two years later, as Americans waited for Hillary Clinton to announce whether she would run for president in 2016, I remembered the look on Mom's face back then: full of hope, expectations, and wonder at how far we'd come.

The first inkling I had that Hillary was in was a call from my daughter Lily. She was working at the Democratic National Committee as deputy communications director, and like a lot of young people in politics in 2015, she was waiting to see how the presidential race shaped up.

"Mom, Joel called me and said he wants me to start thinking about the campaign," she said. Joel Benenson was a friend of our family and a pollster for President Obama. Rumor had it he was looking around for talent in case Hillary ran. "Do you think that means she's going to do it?"

"You tell me!" I answered. Up until then, everything was speculation. Even though Bill Clinton had been close to my mom, and Hillary
had spoken at Mom's memorial service, I was not in the "Friends of Bill
and Hillary" circle. I figured Lily was going to be my best inside source.

"I'd do anything to work on the race, so I'll let you know," Lily said,
and hung up.

I knew Lily was ready for a new job, and after all, in her heart she's a
campaign rat, so I was almost positive it was only a matter of time before
she got involved. Sure enough, a few weeks later Jen Palmieri, who everyone was guessing would be Hillary's communications director, called Lily
and asked if she would consider moving to the Midwest to head up communications for the Iowa caucuses "should she decide to run." Jen made
her case, explaining that being in Iowa would put Lily at the heart of it
all, with the responsibility and action that came with being in a must-win
state on a national campaign. Next thing I knew, Lily had quit her job and
was packing to move to Des Moines.

When Lily called to tell me the news, I cheered, and then got down to
business. "Okay, if you're going to work for Hillary, you have to get some
new clothes. She dresses really nice, and Huma—my God!—so why don't
you come to New York before you head out, and we'll get you ready." *Who
did I sound like now?*

Lily came up for the day, and we bought her two perfect navy blue
suits and a kind of embroidered brown dress that she pushed for. Of
course the dress was the only thing from that shopping trip that she ever
wound up wearing. Just like my mother's fantasies about what women
wore in the Ivy League, I had some nutty thoughts about a presidential
campaign wardrobe.

Right as Lily was packing up to leave, I went to an event in New York
where Hillary was speaking. Before the program I made my way over to
her table to say hello and tell her I hoped she would run. As I leaned in
to shake her hand, my proud mother instincts kicked in. "Lily's moving
to Iowa," I told her. "She is my firstborn, so I'm doing my part to help you
get started!" She burst out in her infectious laugh. "Well, having Ann's
granddaughter on the campaign couldn't be better," she said.

It was March 2015, and Hillary still hadn't announced. Lily was headed off as a volunteer, without an official job, uprooting herself for the fourth time in five years for yet another campaign. I suppose some mothers might have been hesitant, but I was ecstatic, and I knew Mom would have been too.

• • •

It would be almost a year between Hillary's much-awaited announcement in April 2015 and the Planned Parenthood Action Fund's official primary endorsement in January 2016. Before the endorsement we held meetings across the country with our staff and supporters. Just as in 2008, patients and leaders interviewed all the Democratic candidates in the race. Yet again none of the Republicans running responded to our invitation to meet.

The Democratic primary was heated, and supporters of Senator Bernie Sanders were active on social media. There was a lot of ugly trolling on Twitter and Facebook—and of course, knowing what we do now, it could have been Russian bots as well. Senator Sanders had been a consistent vote for women's rights, but Hillary had been leading the fight her entire career. After we watched her listen to the stories of patients and activists at the endorsement meeting, it was clear she would bring compassion, bold ideas, and a deep understanding of Planned Parenthood's work to the White House.

The endorsement itself was a production, since we'd never endorsed in a primary before. We were breaking with precedent because we knew this election would have enormous consequences for Planned Parenthood patients and women everywhere, so we did it up right. Waiting backstage at Southern New Hampshire University in Manchester with dozens of our staff and patients, I saw Hillary come in through the back of the kitchen. Wouldn't you know, we were in matching navy blue pantsuits. The second we saw each other, we both burst out laughing.

The audience was packed with Planned Parenthood supporters in pink T-shirts, and they were roaring to make history. Kicking off the event was a Planned Parenthood patient, Natarsha McQueen, who had been on the endorsement screening committee. Hillary stood close to the monitor backstage, listening intently. When Natarsha told her story of how a screening at Planned Parenthood detected breast cancer when she was just thirty-three years old and may have saved her life, Hillary put her hand over her heart. "Wow," she said.

When she took the stage, Hillary got straight to the point. "I have stood with you throughout my career, and I promise you this: as president, I will always have your back. I've been fighting for women and families my entire life. I'll go anywhere, meet with anyone, and work my heart out to find common ground. But I'll also stand my ground. I'm not going to let anyone rip away the progress we've made."

Listening to her, I felt a sense of wonder. When Planned Parenthood was founded, women didn't even have the right to vote. Yet after a hundred years we were endorsing a woman for president, and she was standing there thanking us. After her speech she stuck around, shaking hands and giving hugs. As young women stood patiently waiting, cell phones in hand, Hillary grabbed them right up and took selfies with them like the pro she is.

Afterward Hillary headed backstage and graciously took a group photo with the team that pulled the event together. (That photo is one of my favorites; several of the young women in it would spend the rest of the year working day and night to help elect her.) I introduced her to everyone as fast as I could, certain she would have to run. But she wasn't in any rush to get out of there. Rather she made a point of thanking everyone, one by one. This wasn't her first election, and more than anyone she knew that these women—and millions like them—were going to be the heart and soul of her campaign.

• • •

By the time the Planned Parenthood Action Fund endorsed Hillary, the Iowa caucuses were only weeks away. Iowa is psychologically important in the Democratic primary. It's the first state contest, and the way it's organized is so complicated, people spend their entire life mastering the process. Which is why, when Lily made a quick trip home for Thanksgiving, so many of us asked her to explain how it works that she finally cleared a space on the dining room table and set up a demonstration. "Imagine these salt shakers are Hillary Clinton supporters. These pepper grinders are Bernie Sanders supporters. And these candles are Martin O'Malley supporters."

I was excited about the caucuses, but I was even more excited at the prospect of traveling to Iowa to see Lily. I had enough vacation time saved up and had managed to organize my life so that every spare weekend or day off could be used to campaign for Hillary. After our last-minute shopping trip, when I walked into campaign central in Des Moines all those months later, Lily was in ripped blue jeans, Converse All-Stars, and a shirt I swear we bought her in junior high. The campaign office was a joyful wreck. My first thought was, *Can't we invent a more easily disposable pizza box?* There must have been a hundred of them scattered over the floor.

One of the things I loved about the Hillary campaign, much like Obama's earlier, was the creativity of the volunteers, who had hung up yard signs and posters on every wall, in the shape of Iowa. I took a picture of Lily's desk; aside from press releases, it was littered with various treasures I'd gotten her over a series of campaigns: the sushi stapler, a small statue of Ganesha for good luck, desk monkeys, a photo of Lyle Lovett, and a bottle of generic ibuprofen.

Eventually we left the office and made our way to Lily's home-away-from-home in downtown Des Moines. Her apartment was a first-class disaster. I swung into action.

First, I washed all the dishes, then tried my best to gather up all the dirty clothes. (*There's that skirt I've been looking for!*) I did the laundry and threw out the dead flowers along with, yes, more pizza boxes. Just for laughs, I made the bed, knowing it would make not the slightest difference. But like all the other times when life feels out of control, doing the little things was enormously satisfying. I looked at her leather boots, which she wore daily—it was Iowa after all—and I just had to do something.

"I'm taking your boots to get polished," I announced.

"Ah, okay, Mom," Lily answered, sounding like, *Do you seriously think anyone cares how my boots look?* I went online and found Stan's Shoeshine Stand, right down the street from the campaign office. It was buried in an indoor mall in a bank building, like much of Des Moines. The next day I walked in and set the boots on the counter. "Do you think you can rescue these boots?" I asked the elderly gentleman in the one-man shop, presumably Stan.

"Ma'am, I've polished the shoes of every presidential candidate since you were knee-high to a grasshopper, so I imagine I can get these in good shape! Just give me twenty minutes." I decided to go get coffee, and asked if he'd like some. "Black with two sugars, if you would," he answered. Like the rest of Iowa, he was "midwest nice."

When I got back to headquarters, Lily had a phone in each hand and someone waiting to talk to her. Her sneakers up on the desk, she was in her element. I waited my turn.

"I'm finishing an event for Hillary late this afternoon, and then I'll get back to Des Moines by nine. Want to get dinner?" I asked.

She looked doubtful. "No way I'll be done by then, but maybe we can get coffee in the morning?"

I had forgotten the insanity of a campaign: eating whatever you could, whenever you could, and having no other life. I managed to keep my worries to myself—about how little sleep she must be getting, the constant stress I knew all too well. But her boots looked great!

The key to the Iowa caucuses is that every county matters, which means you get to see a lot of places that are really out there. Suzanna de Baca, the leader of Planned Parenthood Voters of Iowa, agreed to go on the road with me, and I'm forever grateful. I'm the kind of campaigner who will go anywhere—there's no meeting too small, no location too remote. It comes from my labor organizing days, knowing that around every corner there were amazing people you had yet to meet, and the farther from the center they were, usually the more grateful they were for the visit. That's how, just seven days before the caucuses, Suzanna and I found ourselves searching for a campaign headquarters in Conroy, Iowa, where the only landmark was an abandoned grain silo. Even the GPS couldn't help. Driving in circles, we finally saw a truck coming the other way, so I jumped out of the car.

"Hey there, hold on! Do you know where the Machinist Hall is?" I yelled.

The driver rolled down the window. "Yep, sure do," he replied. "Aren't you Cecile, Ann's daughter?"

How in the world? "Sure am! I'm out here campaigning for Hillary, and we're supposed to be meeting up with some folks."

"Well, me and the wife used to live down in Austin, and we retired up here a few years ago. I'm real glad for what you do—she's not gonna believe I saw you. Maybe we'll head over there, too."

We got the directions, and sure enough, there was a tiny union hall just a few miles away, with a couple of pickup trucks with Hillary signs and "Proud to Be Union" stickers parked outside. We gingerly tiptoed through the ice. Though there didn't seem to be any heat inside the hall, there were a couple of dozen people of all ages and walks of life, sitting on folding chairs, waiting expectantly. Like every other campaign stop I made over the next many months, I was struck by all the young women running around, getting folks coffee, handing out phone lists for the area, and making sure everyone left with something to do.

Within an hour we were back in the rental car, speeding down snowy country roads in Iowa. I was scheduled to introduce Hillary at a rally in New Liberty later that afternoon, where I would get to see Lily and Kirk. Kirk was working with the labor unions and Lily was working the press, so this was going to be a rare mini family reunion in a suburban Iowa elementary school.

For the next eight months I would do hundreds of events, from phone banks in Colorado to house parties in Nevada, some with a handful of volunteers and some with hundreds. But that day, with Hillary there in person, was something truly special. It looked like every red-blooded citizen in New Liberty had shown up. There were lines of folks trying to get into the school gym, as though the biggest playoff game of the season were about to begin. And backstage, as always, was the photo line. I'd never seen so many children, especially little girls, waiting to get their picture taken with the candidate.

After the rally in New Liberty, Lily, Kirk, and I made plans to meet up that night in Cedar Rapids. But first I was going to North Grinnell and then to a student rally at the University of Northern Iowa in Cedar Falls, where Tony Goldwyn, the charming actor from *Scandal*, was meeting up with us. As you can imagine, fans of his were waiting. There are a lot of celebrities who campaign for their candidate of choice, but I'd put Tony up against any of them for knowing every single policy position and issue, as well as Hillary's entire biography. Finally, he and I headed to Cedar Rapids for the last stop of the night, a phone bank packed to the gills, and then over to the hotel where the campaign was staying.

Lily was waiting in the lobby, as Hillary and her team had already arrived. "Hillary wants to know if you and Dad want to get something to eat?" she asked. There was no way I was saying no to that. Before I knew what had happened, we were sitting down to a family dinner with Hillary; Huma Abedin; Tony Goldwyn; Matt Paul, the Iowa state director; and Nick Merrill, her traveling press secretary—a great group of people with whom to dissect Iowa politics. The best part was seeing Hillary with Lily, especially since Lily had just learned that Hillary had gotten the endorsement of the *Des Moines Register*. In a state where every little bit helped, that was a big deal. Lily added, "And we just heard we got the Cedar Rapids paper too—the two biggest papers in the state."

"We did?" Hillary said, shocked. "I didn't even go to that editorial board!"

Kirk and I sat there beaming with pride. Suddenly my mind shifted gears: *With fifty states and hundreds of towns, how in the world can Hillary Clinton remember she didn't go to the Cedar Rapids paper? The woman astounds.*

What made that dinner especially fun, besides the awesome company, is that it was in a teaching hotel, where they prepare students for careers in the hospitality industry, including culinary arts. Our waiter looked to be maybe nineteen, and here he was serving possibly the next leader of the free world. He was so nervous, we must have all gotten five forks and extra appetizers, but he did a wonderful job. If you ever get out to Cedar Rapids, I highly recommend the Hotel at Kirkwood Center.

Our dinner conversation covered everything from the Iowa caucuses to how much my mom would have loved being there. Kirk talked with Hillary about the labor unions and their plans for turnout. There was no detail too small—she wanted to hear everything. When dinner ended, I was beat. I couldn't imagine how Hillary did it, especially since it was only January. My years of doing the same kind of schedule with Mom came rushing back, as did the protective daughter in me.

"Lily, you have to get her to bed," I said. "She cannot stay up like this and go campaigning again all day tomorrow!"

"Oh, that's nothing. She has to get up early for an interview with Stephanopoulos in the morning." I was exhausted just thinking about it.

Though Kirk had to drive back to Des Moines, Lily and I stayed at the hotel overnight. As I was curling up in bed, completely spent, lights out, I saw the telltale glow of her cell phone under the covers. "What are you doing?" I asked.

"I have to check any breaking news so she's prepped for the morning," Lily mumbled. The next morning her alarm went off at five, and she spent the next half hour scanning all the national and local news, trying to stay a step ahead.

The race was incredibly tight heading into the caucuses. I remember being at the state headquarters, looking at the stacks of hundreds of packets ready for caucus night. The team had planned what looked like a statewide invasion. They had caucus leaders in every polling place, and they'd even done a dry run, basically a dress rehearsal for the big day. There was no room for error. And the planning paid off: later that week Hillary won the Iowa caucuses by a nose.

"It was so close, but we won," Lily said first thing the next morning. "Turns out every single thing we did mattered. And listen—I've already packed up my apartment and should be getting to New York by next weekend." After nearly a year in Des Moines, my older daughter was going to work out of the Brooklyn campaign headquarters and live with us. The primaries were going to be a hard-fought battle, and Lily would be running press for the rest of the state contests, which were coming fast and furious.

• • •

By that point, I had a go-bag packed and ready at all times. For campaign travel, you need solid-color clothes (best for TV), whatever doesn't wrinkle, the aforementioned hand steamer, and sensible shoes. Voters are not looking for you or the candidate to make a fashion statement, and you can easily wind up doing five events in a day. Marisa Feehan, a feisty, funny young woman from Colorado who manages my schedule and keeps me sane, joined me on the road whenever she could. And my trusty aide, a New Hampshire native and real political talent, Matt Burgess, became my traveling buddy for the next several months. He'd managed campaigns for governors and senators and knew the state of New Hampshire inside and out. Before our first trip together, I gave him a quick rundown.

"Okay, Matt, here are the rules. We never, never check a bag. Got that? And I'm always hungry, so your job is to make sure no matter what random town we end up at for dinnertime, we're gonna have something decent to eat. Tacos are a five-star when you can pull that off, though north of Virginia it might be hard." He nodded, a little dazed. And he went out and bought his own steamer that night.

We ended up eating fish and chips more than a few nights, since it seemed like the Hampton Inn specialty, but Matt is a foodie. As we drove through Nevada and Florida, we would fantasize about what we were going to cook when we finally got back home. His favorite was roast chicken, and he liked complicated recipes requiring hours of prep. I am more of a baker, so we had lots of discussions about the perfect pie and crust: lard or butter? Food processor or by hand? I'm a butter gal and swear by the recipe from my favorite bakery, Tartine—something we discussed at length during our many hours in the car.

Volunteering and traveling the country, I saw up close what a completely insane primary system we have and how challenging it is for voters in many states to participate. The states where voters go to the polls for the primary election have complicated enough rules, and to top it off, in states like Iowa that have a caucus system, people actually have to show up and literally stand and be counted for their candidate. That's tough to do for anyone who works a night shift or needs someone to watch the kids—namely, women.

A crucial state for Hillary, despite having relatively few electoral votes, was Maine. I jumped at the chance to go, since it is almost an adopted home state for me. I'd gone to work in Maine as a nanny when I was a teenager, and I've been returning every summer. The kids were raised going to an island off the coast of Portland, and it is a place after my own heart. Give me a Maine woman any day. With so many cold months, they are scrappers, like my friend Sarah Meacham. They quilt, they crochet, they split wood. They can fix a tractor and know how to take wild apples and make thirty jars of sauce. Sarah taught me to make jam from wild raspberries and blackberries to last the year. Hillary reminds me of the Mainers I know, hardworking survivors who don't complain.

One afternoon Matt and I drove up to Kennebunk, Maine, for a house party, right ahead of the caucuses. The host and hostess must have been baking all week; there were muffins and cheese sticks and stuffed mushrooms. After I gave my spiel about Hillary, the local organizer explained how the caucus would work. "You are going to need to be at the school by seven," he said. "If you get there late, you can't participate. Then you should plan to be there for at least a couple of hours. And you are going to need to be ready to publicly state that you are caucusing for Hillary."

There was an uncomfortable silence. Finally, an older woman spoke up. "We have a lot of Bernie supporters in this area, and they are really adamant," she said, sounding apprehensive. "I'm so excited about Hillary, but I don't want to fight with my neighbors. We all have to get along here, it's a small town."

And so it went. A lot of our supporters didn't want to fight—they just wanted to be for Hillary. The attacks were coming from all sides, and many women felt they just could not speak up. I had volunteered and campaigned for many less-than-perfect men running for president, and found it overwhelming to witness the double standard. Just like with Mom, the attacks felt personal because they *were* personal. I tried my best to give pep talks to the women I met, encouraging them to talk to their friends and neighbors about why they were for Hillary.

If I had to do one interview, I had to do twenty where the reporter asked, "Why aren't young people for Hillary?" It was a narrative that was not supported by facts, but that didn't stop it from becoming a trope of the media.

I was on enough college campuses during the primary to see how hard it was for a lot of the organizers and volunteers on Hillary's campaign. I also saw it firsthand with my daughter Hannah. We went out for coffee on a trip through Denver, where she was running canvasses for Change Corps, a progressive organizing group based out of Colorado. Per usual, she had her laptop in tow. But now it had an enormous "I'm with Her" sticker plastered to the front.

"I just figured I'm getting it out there," she said. Hannah was working with other young progressive organizers on environmental issues. "I get all these comments from the dudes in my office who are Bernie supporters, and I want to make a statement every time I flip open my computer. They aren't going to intimidate me." That's Hannah. She had done her homework, and she knew Hillary was her candidate, with no encouragement from her sister or me. As it turned out, Daniel felt the same way. I was glad they were able to support each other through a primary that got pretty unpleasant at times.

The primaries were hard-fought, and in the end it all came down to California. If Hillary won the state, it would give her a decisive victory as the Democratic nominee—not to mention a critical boost heading into the general election. In the final week Lily had gone to Los Angeles to help for the home stretch. She flew back on a red-eye the night of the primary to get to New York in time for the California results. A Hillary event was planned that night to celebrate if she secured the nomination, and by that time Hannah was running a canvass office in New York City. I was in DC, in the middle of the Planned Parenthood national conference. That night, when it was announced that Hillary had won, Lily and Hannah were together at the Navy Yard in downtown Brooklyn, along with thousands of others, celebrating the victory. They snapped a photo and texted it to me, and I burst into tears. They looked completely worn out and ebullient at the same time. Kirk was in New York as well, so they found each other and we got on the phone, patched in Daniel, and celebrated.

Even then there was no time to waste. My thoughts immediately turned to the next day. Hillary had long been scheduled to speak to the Planned Parenthood Action Fund in Washington at a national meeting. We hadn't expected then that the primary would go on for so long— which meant that now a routine campaign stop had taken on new meaning.

I was in touch with Lauren Peterson, who had written speeches for me at Planned Parenthood and was now working for Hillary. She was on deck to write that day's speech and had called a few days earlier to check in. "It's looking like she might clinch the nomination on Tuesday, which could make this her first public appearance as the presumptive nominee," she said. "Everyone will be watching."

That morning I'd asked for something completely out of hand: Would Hillary take a photo with every single Planned Parenthood CEO from across the country—fifty-eight and counting—before her speech? She would. I can't remember a prouder moment, seeing everyone dressed and pressed and ready for success. I felt like the ultimate wedding planner, making sure we had a Planned Parenthood pink backdrop for the photos, watching as Hillary took her time with each and every one. The night before, the singer Kesha, who also happened to be a former Planned Parenthood patient, had performed. I never in a million years would have imagined I'd find myself introducing Kesha and her mother to Hillary Clinton, but there I was.

Soon we were at the main stage of the Washington Hilton before a thousand cheering members of the Planned Parenthood Action Fund. I introduced her, and Hillary took the stage.

"Today I want to say something you don't hear enough: Thank you. Thank you for being there for women, no matter their race, sexual orientation, or immigration status," she began. "Thank you for being there for every woman in every state who has to miss work; drive hundreds of miles; endure cruel, medically unnecessary waiting periods; walk past angry protesters to exercise her constitutional right to safe, legal abortion. I've been proud to stand with Planned Parenthood for a long time. . . . Because I know for a century, Planned Parenthood has worked to make sure that the women, men, and young people who count on you can lead their best lives—healthy, safe, and free to follow their dreams."

There were many firsts in the campaign, but one of them was that afternoon. It was the first time a nominee for the presidency had spoken without hesitation and without qualifiers about her support for women's fundamental reproductive rights. By the time she finished, many people in the audience had tears in their eyes. National board member and lifelong Planned Parenthood volunteer Naomi Aberly turned to me and said, "I never thought I'd live to see a presidential candidate stand with us." And they stood with her—a standing ovation to beat the world. For the next six months the women and men in that room worked their hearts out for Hillary—people who had devoted their lives to reproductive rights and young activists who had just begun. The one thing that united them was Planned Parenthood and, in that moment, the opportunity to elect the first woman president.

• • •

The rest of the summer went much as everyone had planned, organizing phone banks and canvasses and training volunteers. Except for one thoroughly unexpected development: it became clear that despite all their best efforts, the Republican Party could not stop the momentum of Donald Trump. He was about to win the nomination at the Republican National Convention in Cleveland, setting the stage for the most unpredictable presidential election in memory.

As we had with President Obama's campaign, we made the Democratic National Convention a family affair. Kirk and Hannah and I drove to Philadelphia, passing car after car with Hillary stickers and people waving and honking. Hannah had never been to a convention and had agreed to travel with me for the next few days. I had to prepare my convention speech, which was stressful, and I was still trading drafts with Lily and Lauren Peterson back in Brooklyn. I also had to find an outfit that would be suitable for television, my mother's voice ringing in my ears: "Is *that* what you are planning on wearing?" Since, as has already been established, I'm not a fashionista, it was an enormous relief to find a navy blue suit that would do. Plus, as always, I had Mom's gold sheriff's badge pin with me, and it was going right on the lapel.

Even though Hillary clearly had the votes for the nomination, there were more than a few delegates who were not having it. When Hannah and I left the hotel for my first appearance, we walked by a gentleman who was covered with buttons saying "US Out of North America" and "Democrats Are Fat Cats." Hannah turned to me as if to say, *What is going on?* I simply said, "Welcome to the Democratic Party!"

It seemed like the entire world was in Philadelphia, and we saw them all, including many of the volunteers I had met during the primaries. The Planned Parenthood Action Fund had organized hundreds of folks to help out, so every street corner had a pink-shirted canvasser signing people up to work on the campaign when they got back home. The excitement of young women was over the top, and they were there for Hillary.

On the day of my speech Hannah and I went backstage to do a run-through with the teleprompter and make sure we knew where to go. Meryl Streep was there with her three daughters; it turned out she was speaking right after me. We talked about my mom. "I can't get her out of my mind," I told her. "This is what she lived for, and believe me, her spirit is in this city this week."

That night Hannah went with me backstage to the makeshift hair and makeup studio where speakers were getting ready. There were about a dozen raised canvas chairs, makeup lights, hair dryers, and women everywhere. And there, seated in a row, were the Mothers of the Movement. They were about to go onstage and testify about the loss of their children to gun violence and police brutality: Sybrina Fulton, the mother of Trayvon Martin; Lucy McBath, the mother of Jordan Davis; Gwen Carr, the mother of Eric Garner; Geneva Reed-Veal, the mother of Sandra Bland; and Maria Hamilton, the mother of Dontre Hamilton. These women could have been at home, silently grieving, but instead they had traveled to Philadelphia. I had heard them speak before, but to see them all gathered together was overwhelming. They were some of the most powerful storytellers in the nation.

"Thank you," I said, not knowing how else to convey how in awe I was of them. We joined hands, quietly acknowledging the importance of the reason we were there.

Once I'd been blushed and brushed, I went back to the greenroom, where all the speakers were cooling their heels, and who should I run into but Tony Goldwyn and his wife. "I can't believe it," I said. "Did you think we'd be here, all those months ago in Cedar Rapids?" It was like old home week.

There is nothing quite like speaking to thousands of people in a convention hall. It was impossible not to remember sitting on the stage, watching Mom deliver the keynote address in Atlanta to the same convention all those years ago. Unlike the convention floor in San Francisco when the women were cheering for Geraldine Ferraro, tonight *everyone* was cheering for the woman we hoped would become president.

As I was about to go out to speak, Jim Margolis, who had the thankless task of running the entire four nights of the convention, grabbed me. You could tell he was sweating bullets. "Oh my God, Cecile," he said, "we are running so far behind! Don't wait for the applause, don't wait for anything, just barrel through!" I felt for him, even though that's not exactly what you want to hear before your three minutes. But it didn't matter. As I walked out onstage there was a lot of Planned Parenthood love in the room, and even though the red warning light telling a speaker "You are over time" was blinking the minute I started, I had fun. "When my great-grandmother was growing up, women couldn't vote under Texas law," I said. "Two generations later her granddaughter, Ann Richards, was elected governor. Tonight we are closer than ever to putting a woman in the White House. And I can almost hear Mom saying, 'Well, it sure took y'all long enough!'"

The night Hillary made her acceptance speech you could not have fit another body into that hall. Every young woman I knew was there. We were all proud of her, and proud to be part of history.

• • •

That entire fall was a blur of crisscrossing the country, going to phone banks to encourage volunteers, and speaking at college campuses to get out the vote. Everywhere I went, I met women I will never forget. On the way from Silver City to Reno, a young woman from Chicago named Angelica Alfaro took us to a convenience store she swore had the best breakfast tacos in Nevada. She told me, "I ran for office last year, but the old boys network rallied behind the guy in the race. I'm proud that I did it, and I'm not giving up." She had picked up stakes and moved to Nevada just to work for Hillary and get more political experience under her belt. I expect to see her in Congress someday. In Traverse City, Michigan, I met a young woman who ran a volunteer phone bank. She introduced me to the crowd, which is how I learned her story. "I was homeless in high school," she stated. "Planned Parenthood was where I went for my health care, and with their help, I made it through school. And today I have a job working for Hillary. I'm on my way." No matter how tiring the road was, these women made me want to work that much harder.

Despite all the good energy, no matter how well Hillary did, it seemed impossible to break away from Trump. Everything he'd done would have been the end of any other candidate. Like women (and men) across America, I felt sickened and disgusted by the *Access Hollywood* tapes—this was a presidential candidate bragging about sexual assault. But nothing seemed to dissuade his supporters. Many young women at Planned Parenthood had never known any president other than Barack Obama, and they were horrified that anyone would support Trump. I agreed that it was hard to imagine someone backing a man with such disregard for women, but after all, my mom had nearly been beat by Clayton Williams, so anything was possible.

My job was to remind women how strong Hillary was for them, and we knew that the Planned Parenthood Action Fund was the very best messenger for women voters. Which may be why the campaign asked if I could go to Las Vegas for the third and final debate, ready to work the press afterward. Both campaigns would have ten designated spokespeople to do interviews and rebuttals in what's known as "the spin room."

Since I was going to do press afterward, I sat right up front, with a perfect view of the candidates, so it would be easy to get to the press room right after the debate. I wound up sitting next to a longtime Hillary supporter and creator of the Power Rangers, Haim Saban, and his wife, Cheryl. We watched as the Trump family filed in. They were like automatons walking in a perfect line, no human contact, nothing.

Then Hillary and Trump took the stage, so close to our seats I could practically touch them. Until that night I'd never seen Trump in person. For the next hour and a half, my anxiety rose steadily. Haim and I looked at each other in horror. Hillary was brilliant. But Trump was a disaster! As he talked about foreign policy, it was obvious that if they pulled out a map and asked him to point to Syria, he would have been clueless. When he called Hillary a "nasty woman," I thought, *He is stark raving nuts.*

When it ended, Hillary had clearly wiped the floor with him. I hustled past all the campaign folks, who felt the same way: she had performed spectacularly. I began my first interview and realized that I was flanked by two Trump "spinners," his over-the-top former Republican primary opponent, Ben Carson, and Omarosa, from *The Apprentice.* You cannot make this up. It was another indication that his entire campaign was one big reality television show, which is how I felt minutes later when Katie Couric asked me about an unsettling moment in the debate. A question arose concerning abortion, and as always, Hillary had stood for every woman's right to make her own personal decisions about her pregnancy. Trump had gone off on a rant about ripping babies from the womb and sounded completely unhinged. Katie was clearly disturbed, and I was worried she and other reporters were getting used to that level of discourse.

That was the night that Hillary really broke away. Trump was clearly not fit to be president, and voters had seen it on the debate stage. Poll after poll showed she was in the lead. But I knew from my own experience how unpredictable campaigns can be. So even though I felt good, I never felt sure. That creeping dread was reinforced when, back in New York, I went to Brooklyn to talk with Marlon Marshall, Hillary's field director, about how best to spend the last two weeks of the campaign.

"We'd like you to go to Michigan and Wisconsin," he said, which was worrisome, since those were two must-win states and ones I had assumed we had locked up. "Folks just need shoring up. Oh, and we are going to get the final women's rally that Mini Timmaraju, head of women's outreach, has been pushing. We'll do it with Hillary ten days out, in Cedar Rapids."

"Great," I said. "We really have been needing to do something to energize women, and that sounds perfect." I figured there was no better high note to end on.

The Cedar Rapids rally was going to be fun. My friends Ilyse Hogue, from NARAL Pro-Choice America, and Stephanie Schriock, leader of EMILY's List, were coming. I had been campaigning all by my lonesome for months, so it was awesome to finally be with a crew. The three of us went to Raygun, my favorite Iowa T-shirt shop, and I bought all kinds of "Nasty Woman" and "Bad Hombre" gear, especially for Hannah and Daniel. We got into our best Hillary T-shirts and struck an obligatory Charlie's Angels pose for a photo. Our spirits were so high I could actually imagine winning. It had never felt more tangible.

The whole town of Cedar Rapids turned out. There were vendors selling Hillary T-shirts, folks who'd made Hillary jewelry and pins, and young girls wearing pantsuits. As we got onstage, I spied Annie Leibovitz, with her trademark Hasselblad, in her olive green jumpsuit, shooting photos from every angle. There were hundreds of Planned Parenthood folks in pink—girls, women, boys, and men. There wasn't a cloud in the sky—it was a perfect campaign day.

Each of the speakers had her turn; then Hillary gave it her all. I couldn't figure out how she was still standing, with just ten days to go. After she began to say her trademark line, "If fighting for equality for women means I'm playing the woman card," the entire crowd yelled along with her, "then DEAL ME IN!" The music played, everyone waved and cheered, and we went backstage to the holding area.

But while the mood onstage was energetic and upbeat, behind the scenes was another thing entirely. Lily was texting me, but by then everyone on the detail knew: the FBI director James Comey had just announced he was reopening the investigation into Hillary's emails. We were in disbelief: ten days away from a national election, he was jumping in, raising concerns about "new" emails that would later turn out not to be new after all. We had no idea that this story would manage to dominate the news for the crucial days to come, but that's what happened. It was like watching all the helium leak out of a balloon. (A few weeks after the campaign ended, when I had a chance to catch up with John Podesta, Hillary's campaign chair, he confirmed what I had sensed at the time: "Before the Comey letter, we had finally gotten the momentum we needed to push through in the key states. Folks had decided that Trump was unpresidential, and she had been masterful in the final debate. But the Comey blast just sucked the energy out, and there simply wasn't the time to make it up.")

During the next ten days we simply soldiered on. There was nothing to do but fight it out on the ground, while the national media was having a heyday. My traveling buddy Matt Burgess and I went to Michigan, as Marlon had asked. We may have felt down, but the volunteers remained full of energy and hope. At that point it was all about turnout and executing the plans that had been put in place months ago. We knew our voters; we just had to get them to show up on Election Day. Everywhere we went there were young women determined to leave it all on the field. Back at the Planned Parenthood offices, I knew everyone was trying to stay focused and calm.

At a staff meeting a few weeks before the election, a member of Planned Parenthood's finance team named Julie Reyburn poignantly asked what everyone could do to feel better about "the world, the election, and humanity." I sent out an email listing all the things that were helping me keep it together: my favorite Instagram accounts, consisting mostly of adorable animals like "Harlow and Sage" and "Chipmunks for Choice"; fiction—Elena Ferrante, Michael Connelly, Harlan Coben, and Haruki Murakami were all on my reading list; meditation, which I had appreciated ever since my congressional testimony; learning a new language (I was using the Duolingo app to learn Italian and fantasizing about a postelection trip to Rome); reading the inspiring stories Planned Parenthood patients posted every day on Instagram, Facebook, and Tumblr; knocking on doors, which feels much better than worrying; and best of all, visualizing being on the Mall in Washington with hundreds of thousands of people to witness the inauguration of the first woman president of the United States.

On Election Day, Matt, Marisa from my office, and I headed to New Hampshire, where we needed to win not only the presidential race but Governor Maggie Hassan's race for the US Senate. We had been to New Hampshire so many times during the campaign that ending up there just felt right. The day started out with James Taylor and his wife, Caroline, dedicated Planned Parenthood supporters who had been traveling all over for Hillary. He is a delightful man, and he had just the right air of serenity for a day that would turn out to be so tense. Matt and I worked polling places in Manchester, thanking volunteers and doing a bit of media. Late that afternoon I hopped a plane back to New York in order to be there when the voting returns started coming in. My sister, Ellen, had been volunteering in Philadelphia for the past week, so I was excited to see her and compare notes. Plus, Lily was at the Brooklyn office, and I hoped I'd get to celebrate with her before the night was over.

After I landed I ran home and dressed in suffragette white—a sleeveless dress with a gold buckle that had also been a staple on the campaign. I figured if anything had good karma, it might be that dress. I phoned Kirk, who was still working the polls in Tampa. Yet another thing to love about Kirk: he never leaves the field until every vote is cast.

"I think we've done it. We hit the turnout numbers we needed in Broward County," he said. "And today's votes seem to be solid. If we win Florida, this is done."

Kirk is a crazy combination of realist and optimist. He's the one who believes until there is absolutely no hope left. He sounded pretty confident on the phone, but we'd both been through a lot of close campaigns and knew it could be a long night.

"Okay," I said, "I'm headed downtown to find Ellen, and then we'll be at the Javits Center. Let's stay in touch, since I know you can't get a flight out tonight." I ran for the subway and got to Penn Station in time to see hundreds of people in the streets, headed to the convention center. Polls hadn't closed yet, so I texted Ellen and we met at a New York institution, the Tick Tock Diner on Thirty-fourth.

Ellen told me she had been on her own in Philadelphia, but, as is her custom, she had quickly made friends. Though she'd gone there just to work the phone banks, within two days the local organizers put her in charge of coordinating attorneys who had volunteered to protect the polls. "I'm not sure how they figured out that it wasn't my first campaign," she laughed. "But I was working twenty-four/seven. It was great!"

Ellen had left her husband, Greg, and daughter, Kate, back in Austin for the duration, because like so many women, she felt she had to run through the tape with Hillary. I was so glad to see her. Even though I was never alone out on the road, it could get lonesome. I was happy to see the last of the Hampton Inns for a while and excited to sleep in my own bed.

We met up with our friend Shamina, who had been volunteering as well, and her wife, Ashley, who had been doing advance work on the campaign. It was mayhem at the Javits Center, but fortunately one of the staffers recognized me and helped us get in. At this point the polls were beginning to close around the country, and the mood was excited but anxious. I hadn't talked to Kirk again and didn't tell anyone what he'd said about Florida. I didn't want to jinx the numbers.

That night was like one big family gathering. I recognized phone bank coordinators from Iowa and folks who drove me around Colorado. Shuttling over to where all the media was set up, I ran into John Heilemann from NBC. "You must be feeling pretty good, Cecile," he said. "This is a big night."

Deep down inside, though, I wasn't feeling all that good. And he obviously sensed it. "Yes, eager to see some returns," I replied. "There are lots of big states out."

There were microphones and cameras everywhere, and after a couple of warm-up interviews, I was scheduled to do *Rachel Maddow* live. Over at the MSNBC booth they wired me up and got me on the stool, and from my vantage point I was watching the reporting. I heard in my earpiece, "Cecile, thanks for being on," from the control room. "We'll be with you in about four minutes."

"Got it," I said, as I watched the map of the country, where more than a few states looked uncertain, including Florida. Even Wisconsin.

A couple of minutes later the control room was back on. "Listen, we are getting returns so fast, can you hold on a bit longer? There is a lot breaking."

"Sure," I said as I felt my heart sinking into my stomach.

I sat, wired into MSNBC, and watched the worst train wreck of my life, as states we needed to win, including Pennsylvania and Michigan, were now too close to call. After another five minutes or so, I knew this interview wasn't going to happen anytime soon, and if it did, it was going to be miserable.

"Hey," I called to the producer, "you have my cell. How about you all just call me if you want me to come back? There doesn't seem to be much point in sitting here."

"Yep, you got it. Thanks, and sorry about that."

I'm not sure if he meant sorry about the interview, or sorry that the world we were expecting had just slipped away. In any case, I hopped off the stool and turned to Devon Kearns, Planned Parenthood's media assistant, who was standing by.

"Devon, I just pulled down MSNBC—they were getting too many reports to stop and talk to me," I explained. "And honestly, if this night is going the way it looks, no one is going to want to talk to me about the women's vote."

Devon, like thousands of young women, had busted her ass for Hillary. I couldn't believe I was having to say this to her. "I'm going to go see if I can find my sister. So just text me if you need me."

Devon held it together. "Got it. I think I'll just hang around here a bit longer."

By this point the ripples were going through the Javits Center. Politician after politician came to the mic to speak to the assembled volunteers. But it was not looking good. My sister had left, but I looked over and saw my friend Lisa Benenson, whose husband, Joel, had asked Lily to work on the campaign a year and a half earlier. Lisa looked pale.

"I just can't stay around," I told her. "Any chance you want to head uptown?"

"I've talked to Joel," she replied. "He's over in the boiler room. They are feeling like this is not going to break our way. Let's go." So Lisa, her son, Will, and I slipped out of the Javits Center, weaving through blocks of barricades, and finally hailed a cab uptown.

"I just can't believe this," Will said. Like every young person I knew, he was in a state of shock. I didn't know what to say.

"I'm sorry Joel is having to go through this tonight," I told Lisa as the cab neared our block. "Thank you for getting me out of there. I have to call the girls."

They dropped me at my apartment, and I immediately called Lily. Her job that night was to be the main point of contact with networks that were getting ready to call states for one candidate or the other.

"It looks like we lost Pennsylvania," she said. She was keeping her emotions in check—she had to, talking to every reporter in the country. "Hannah called me from Denver. She is in really bad shape. Can you call her?"

"Yes, of course—but are you okay? Can I do anything for you?"

"No, just have to get through these next few hours."

I phoned Hannah, who was in fact sobbing. "Oh, honey, I am so sorry," I said, now weeping myself. Nothing is more heartbreaking than trying to console your child, even if she is twenty-five.

"Mom, you have to call Lily!" she cried. "She's so upset." Each of my daughters was trying to figure out how to take care of the other.

The rest of the night we stayed on text, until finally it was clear it was over. I was emotionally and physically exhausted. Lily arrived at the apartment at 4:00 a.m. and got into bed with me, and we lay there and wept.

Kirk was on an early flight out of Miami, so he got home a few hours later. We had faced devastating defeats before, and knew the only thing to do was to get up and keep going. Running on a few hours sleep, I headed into the office. The night before, I had made a few phone calls to Planned Parenthood leaders out in the states. Today, there would be more calls to make, meetings to pull together, and intense planning to do. But most of all, I needed to make sure the staff were holding up.

When I got there, I walked by every desk on all three floors, checking in on people one by one. So many of the staff had worked their hearts out during the election, with some spending months out on the road. They were understandably distraught. I couldn't promise anyone that it was going to be okay—it wasn't. But I wanted them to know how much everything they had done mattered, to tell them we were going to get through this together.

To a person, they each said how relieved they had been that morning to have a place to go where they could be with others who believed in the same things they did. We talked about people's partners and family members who had to go to work that day at a "straight" job and try to pretend the world had not just fallen apart. I was overwhelmed with gratitude that everyone had managed to get out of bed and come in. The work ahead of us was going to be as important as anything we'd ever done.

CHAPTER 13

The Resistance Is Female

The flight from Miami Friday night was packed, despite the fact that we were leaving a balmy 85 degrees and headed straight to the cold. It was January 20, 2017, and we were flying to Washington, DC—not to celebrate the inauguration of the first woman president of the United States, as we'd hoped, but to protest the inauguration of a president who had bragged about sexual assault. The Women's March on Washington was scheduled for the day after the inauguration. The mood on the plane was not at all what I'd expected: everyone was laughing, trading knitting tips, complimenting each other's "Nasty Woman" shirts, offering a spare room or a couch to itinerant marchers. We weren't dejected. We were determined.

I had finally finished knitting my pink pussy hat after the third try, hell-bent on making my own since my visit to *The Daily Show* the week before. After I taped a segment, the producer brought me backstage, where all the women producers and writers were knitting away. When they saw me, they yelled, "See you in Washington!" In between work trips I ran down to my local knitting store, a hole in the wall on Seventy-ninth Street, in Manhattan, that was overflowing with women of every age.

As I arrived, the proprietress was yelling, "Make way for another shipment!" A delivery had arrived, carrying pink yarn in every possible hue and thickness.

"I just don't know what to do!" I told a young woman in a beautiful pink hat. "This is taking forever, and I have to have my hat by next Saturday for the march."

"Let me help you," she said, finding me bigger needles and thicker yarn. "That will do the trick." I sat down and knitted a few rows to get the hang of it. Everywhere I looked, there were women knitting. Some brought in hats they'd made at home to give away to folks who couldn't make their own. Mothers were teaching their daughters to knit, and everyone was in a joyful, revolutionary spirit. Xeroxed copies of the "Pussy Hat Instructions" were piled up on the counter, and everyone was leaving with a hat—one way or another. After some photos with my comrades, I headed out, confident that my hat was going to Washington along with thousands of others.

On the plane, the flight attendant was desperately hoping for the elusive "on-time departure," but one very tall man toward the front was working up a sweat, struggling to fit an oversize poster into the overhead bin. A couple of us shouted, "Show us your sign!" He unrolled it and held it up for the entire plane to see. Elegantly written in Magic Marker were the words "I am very upset." The passengers burst into applause, and he smiled sheepishly back at us. We were on a pilgrimage together.

I pulled out my pink pussy hat, and so did everyone else. My seatmate was a man from Los Angeles; the only flight to Washington he could find had been routed through Miami. "There are a bunch of us on the plane," he said. "We simply had to be there!"

The flight attendant, a middle-aged Latina wearing a pin commemorating her twenty years of service for the airline, stopped to talk to me. "Do you think this march will make any difference?" she asked.

"I hope so," I answered, not really sure what we would find when we got to DC. Though I was beginning to get the feeling that the march might just be really big.

· · ·

National Airport was buzzing when we arrived that night. Women wearing pussy hats and Hillary T-shirts were everywhere, greeting each other like long-lost sisters. I met Kirk at the hotel and unpacked my outfit for the march—black pants, black T-shirt, marching boots, and the pièce de résistance, so to speak: my bright pink blazer, on brand for Planned Parenthood. The next morning the streets were already packed as I made my way to an early breakfast we'd organized for elected officials and other leaders. Governor Terry McAuliffe of Virginia, along with Lieutenant Governor Ralph Northam and Attorney General Mark Herring, were there wearing matching bright pink Planned Parenthood winter scarves—the first of thousands I'd see that day.

After grabbing coffee, I gave a quick rallying cry to the breakfast crowd. I was preparing to head out when I spotted Karen Pearl, a predecessor of mine at Planned Parenthood. She was with a beautiful little girl in a knitted pink hat. "This is my granddaughter, who came all the way from California," Karen said. The little girl beamed up at me with the most exquisite smile; she could not have been much more than seven. "Show her your sign," Karen urged. And she held up her multicolored handmade sign that simply said, "I am a girl. What's your superpower?" *Out of the mouth of babes*, I thought. *She is why we march today.*

Then off we went, with a crew of Planned Parenthood staff and others who needed a ride. Getting to the mall was nearly impossible, but we piled everyone into a van and drove as far as we could before hopping out and joining the streams of people heading down Capitol Hill.

We made it to the main rally stage and found a who's who of women. Cookbook author and social media rock star Chrissy Teigen was there, and so was Gloria Steinem. Janelle Monáe would soon provide one of the day's most powerful moments, singing onstage alongside the Mothers of the Movement, whom I'd met back in Philadelphia, and filling us all with an even greater sense of purpose. Lily was with her new boss, Senator Kamala Harris, one of so many women in the Senate and House who were marching. I ran into the veteran progressive publicist Ken Sunshine, whose eyes were starry. "I've been at everything, including the March on Washington," he said. "And I've never seen anything to match this."

As I was getting ready to go onstage, I ran into Callie Khouri, the movie producer who made *Thelma and Louise*. "I have a line I want you to use in your speech," she said. I quickly scribbled it on a scrap of paper: "We're not going to take this lying down!"

From my place onstage I looked out over a sea of pink. "I'm honored to be here on behalf of the one in five women who has been to Planned Parenthood for health care," I shouted into the microphone.

A roar rose up from the crowd. The sound system was no match for the enormous group of people, but nobody cared. The stage was constructed near the National Mall, but no matter which direction you looked, you could see only marchers—all the way up to Capitol Hill and down to the Washington monument. It was so packed that a lot of people couldn't even make it over to the actual march; they just plopped down on the grass to listen from wherever they were. And people just kept coming.

Later we would learn that the Women's March was the biggest demonstration in American history. But right then I knew only that it was one of the most beautiful sights I'd ever seen: people from all walks of life coming together for the right of working women to earn a living wage; the right of immigrant women to live without fear; the right of mothers everywhere to raise families in safe communities with clean air and clean drinking water; the right to live openly no matter who you are or whom you love; and, yes, the right of every woman to get the health care she needs, including safe, legal abortion.

After I spoke, I pulled my pussy hat out of my pocket and got ready to join the march. I spotted Katy Perry in a pink faux-fur coat complete with sparkly pink boots and a pink "Stand with Planned Parenthood" button. One of her traveling assistants said Katy wanted to get out in the crowd, so she and I and dozens of others took off for the Planned Parenthood gathering point with the irrepressible actor Ashley Judd, who threw her arms over our shoulders and beamed.

There were so many people that the original plan to march to the Washington Monument just never happened. It was more like a virtual city, with spontaneous actions, singing, chanting, and celebrating. We kept stopping to point out our favorite signs and take photos: "This Texan does not regret her abortion." "Girls just wanna have fun(damental human rights)." "Tweet women with respect." "My undocumented father paid more taxes than Trump." It was an intergenerational march, from the woman carrying a sign asserting "Ninety, nasty, and not giving up!" to the two little girls holding matching signs warning "Watch out, Trump, my generation votes next!" Everyone seemed to have their own hand-knit pussy hat. The entire city was pink!

And it wasn't just women—men marched too, including Kirk and Daniel. There were fathers marching hand in hand with their daughters, grandfathers who lifted their granddaughters onto their shoulders to see the crowd, and a whole lot of guys who were there simply because they want to live in a world where women are valued and treated fairly.

Best of all, people didn't march just in Washington. In every corner of our country people came together, grabbed homemade signs, and marched: in Fargo, North Dakota; Salt Lake City, Utah; and Des Moines, Iowa. They braved a blizzard in Fairbanks, Alaska, and marched in the rain in Tallahassee, Florida. Hannah texted me a photo from the march in Denver, where she was rocking a vintage Obama '08 inauguration hat and carrying a hand-lettered sign reading "Forward together, not one step back!" In Boston even the *Make Way for Ducklings* statues were wearing tiny, carefully knitted pink pussy hats. And Austin saw the biggest crowd gathered at the state capitol since Mom was inaugurated. People marched in every state in the United States and on every continent, including Antarctica, where women scientists at the South Pole held their own demonstration. The photos from across the globe that day have been collected in a book that gives me chills when I look at it.

We each had our own reasons for marching that day. I marched for my mom and all the women of her generation who fought so hard to get us to this point; we won't let them down. And I marched for Lily, Hannah, and Daniel, and the future I so desperately want for them, one where everyone has the opportunity and the freedom to live life on their own terms.

All weekend long the streets of Washington were full of the makings of the resistance, with people from all over the country who had come to the biggest counterinauguration ever—one that dwarfed the inauguration festivities the day before. Friends from Texas, Elena and Kenneth Marks, had a hotel room they'd reserved months before, in hopes they would be there for Hillary, and they kindly let Kirk and me stay there since they'd decided to stay home. Because it was "the" inauguration hotel, there was nothing better than running around in my bright pink Planned Parenthood jacket. It was an incredible mashup of people in tuxedoes and gowns heading to inaugural balls, and women in pink hats unrolling banners and making "Resist" signs in the lobby.

Planned Parenthood had always intended to put on a big event during inauguration weekend, even before we knew what the election results would be. Months earlier we had rented the 9:30 Club, a super-hip music venue, and had a whole show lined up with celebrities, musicians, comedians, and activists—the Planned Parenthood party was always the place to be. We decided after the election that the party would go on, figuring we were going to need a place to gather in solidarity and help launch the resistance.

And so we did. The line to get in was insanely long, but folks were joyful. Everyone was riding high from the march that day. Kirk and I, along with Marisa, who had traveled with me for so many months of the campaign, went around back to get in through the talent door. We made our way backstage to say thank you to all the performers crammed in the holding area. I was thrilled to see that Daniel and Lily were there, and even they were impressed with the lineup of bands.

I could hear Brandon Minow, Planned Parenthood's master show-runner, yell, "Get excited, Sleater-Kinney is about to play with The National, and they're going to close with 'Fortunate Son.'" I could barely contain myself. "Oh my God," I said, "I can't believe it. 'Fortunate Son' is my favorite anthem! What a perfect night to sing it. I even know all the words."

Matt Berninger from The National heard me, and he didn't miss a beat. "Well then, you've got to sing backup with us."

I gave him a look that said, *Are you kidding?* "Listen, I'd love to, but I could throw the whole room off key. That's a skill I learned from my mother."

He shook his head. "No, you have to. Trust me, it won't matter."

A few minutes later I found myself onstage, living out every girl's fantasy of singing backup for a great band. It was one of the most fun things I'd ever done in my life, belting out the ultimate antiwar anthem: "It ain't me, it ain't me, I ain't no fortunate son!" Sure enough, while we were singing in unison along with hundreds of Planned Parenthood activists in the audience, nobody cared whether I was in tune or not.

Going to bed that night, I thought of what Tony Kushner wrote in *Angels in America*: "The world only spins forward." Even though it still felt like our country was in free fall, those words rang true. No matter what else happens, nothing and no one can stop the future from coming.

• • •

November 8, 2016, was a tough day (to put it mildly). But the days right after the new administration and new Congress got to Washington were worse. It seemed like every morning there was some headline or tweet that made just getting out of bed feel like a radical act of defiance.

The day Speaker of the House Paul Ryan announced that he was going to do everything he could to repeal the Affordable Care Act and defund Planned Parenthood, it was the bat signal people had been waiting for. Right away, the phone lines were so busy you couldn't get a call into his office. The congressional switchboard was jammed with calls. We could barely hold organizer trainings fast enough for the people who wanted to do something to help.

Meanwhile Planned Parenthood staff across the country were planning for different scenarios while working overtime to be there for a huge influx of patients. In the weeks after the election, our text/chat helpline was bombarded with urgent questions. We saw a 900 percent increase in requests for appointments to get IUDs, a form of birth control that lasts for several years; women wanted to make sure their birth control would outlast the Trump administration. We were doing everything we could to keep our doors open for the approximately 8,118 people who count on Planned Parenthood each day, and trying to figure out what would happen if we couldn't.

In other words, everyone at Planned Parenthood was hoping for the best but preparing for the worst. We brainstormed, planned, and made lists of anyone who might be a potential ally in the administration. After a few false starts, one day I got a call from a friendly acquaintance in the fashion industry. She was a strong Planned Parenthood supporter and suggested that the president's daughter Ivanka Trump might be inclined to help. The caller offered to help facilitate a connection.

I called Dawn, Planned Parenthood's executive vice president, and told her about the conversation. I had never met Ivanka Trump but wasn't feeling optimistic that we could convince her to be a champion for Planned Parenthood. Besides, the way the transition was conducted, it was hard to imagine having an honest, off-the-record conversation with anyone in the administration. America had witnessed what happened to former vice president Al Gore, who accepted the invitation to meet with the president-elect about climate change. Not only was the meeting leaked to the press, but Gore became a public spectacle when Trump completely dismissed everything he said and maintained that the jury was still out on climate change. Still, in the end Dawn and I agreed that even if there was only a sliver of a chance of changing anyone's mind, I owed it to Planned Parenthood patients to at least take the meeting.

That's how, one Sunday in February, I found myself climbing into a Lyft with Kirk to make the trip out to the Trump golf course in New Jersey to meet with Ivanka Trump and Jared Kushner. When I learned that she was bringing her husband, I begged Kirk to come with me; if nothing else, I felt I needed a witness. As usual, we were early, so we stopped at a nearby Panera to kill some time. I was terrified that one of our New Jersey supporters or a staffer would recognize me and ask me what I was doing there, so we sat in the car drinking our coffee, looking at each other and wondering how our lives had come to this.

What do you wear to a golf course to meet the daughter and son-in-law of the president? That seems like a trivial question, but suffice it to say, my closet isn't full of resort wear, let alone anything you might wear to a golf course. *In fact,* I had wondered while getting dressed, *how is "resort wear" even a category of clothing?* For me, it's either blue jeans or work clothes, so I opted for a navy blue dress that I hoped telegraphed "This is serious business for me and the 2.4 million patients I'm representing." Kirk went for his standard uniform of a button-down shirt and khaki pants. If nothing else was certain, we looked like upstanding citizens.

After getting lost in rural New Jersey, we finally found the entrance to the golf course. As we drove up to the main clubhouse, security waved us through. My worries that someone would recognize me were immediately put to rest—there wasn't a soul anywhere. The day was bleak and cold, and the grounds were completely empty.

Inside the clubhouse Jared and Ivanka were waiting for us, looking relaxed and totally at home. They kindly invited us to sit down and order breakfast. To say I didn't have an appetite was an understatement. Kirk and I ordered coffee, and they ordered something to eat. After some quick pleasantries about our families and kids, we got down to the task at hand.

"I know you may know some of this," I started, "but I wanted to give you a quick overview of Planned Parenthood's work: the health care we provide, our role as the largest sex educator in America, and the fact that many of our patients have no other doctor. We're it."

Jared nodded and said that, yes, he had read up on Planned Parenthood and knew a lot about our "business."

I forced a smile. "Great. So then you know what a devastating impact it would have on thousands of people every day if they couldn't come to Planned Parenthood anymore. And I don't want this to get overlooked: right now, teen pregnancy is at a historic low in America. Unintended pregnancy is at a thirty-year low. We are actually making enormous progress for women's health. And if we could just take politics out of the equation, we could keep making progress."

Jared leaned forward. It almost seemed as if he thought Kirk worked for Planned Parenthood too, like we were some kind of husband-and-wife company. He complimented us on everything we had built but said we had made a big mistake by becoming "political." He pointed out—as though I didn't know—that the Republicans were in control of Congress, the administration, and soon the courts. We had no bargaining power.

The main issue, he explained, was abortion. If Planned Parenthood wanted to keep our federal funding, we would have to stop providing abortions. He described the ideal outcome: a national headline reading "Planned Parenthood Discontinues Abortion Services." If we would agree to that, funding for Planned Parenthood might just increase. He told us he could even talk to House Speaker Paul Ryan for us. But, he added, any agreement on health care would be "baked" in three weeks. So if we were going to make a deal, we needed to do it quickly.

If it wasn't crystal clear before, it was now. Jared and Ivanka were there for one reason: to deliver a political win. In their eyes, if they could stop Planned Parenthood from providing abortions, it would confirm their reputation as savvy dealmakers. It was surreal, essentially being asked to barter away women's rights for more money. It takes a lot to get Kirk mad, but it looked like his head was about to explode. I was grateful he was there but glad he didn't speak up.

"Look," I said, "women don't come to Planned Parenthood to make a political statement. They come for health care. We are going to keep fighting to protect Planned Parenthood's federal funding, and I believe you know that except in very few circumstances, that funding is not used for abortion. But there is no way what you are describing is going to happen. Our mission is to care for women who need us, and that means caring for all their reproductive needs—including safe and legal abortion."

At that point Ivanka broke in to point out that during the Republican primary, her father was the only candidate who said anything nice about Planned Parenthood, but I had never reciprocated.

"Well," I said, "I did acknowledge those statements. But he also said he was going to defund Planned Parenthood, so that's not going to be much help."

"You have to understand, my father is pro-life," Ivanka said, without even blinking.

"That may be," I countered, "but that doesn't mean he should be taking away the right of all women to make their own personal decision about their pregnancy. I just fundamentally disagree with that. And by the way, Planned Parenthood does more to prevent unintended pregnancy and the need for abortion than any health care provider in America."

Eventually I sensed that the conversation was over; we had said everything that needed to be said. As Kirk and I stood up to go, Jared reminded us that things were moving "really fast." If we wanted to make a deal, it had better be soon.

As we were leaving, a television above the doorway showed coverage of the protests that had erupted in response to Trump's travel ban targeting Muslims who were trying to come to America. The discriminatory policy had been halted by the courts, and the administration was outraged. The topic of discussion on all the Sunday shows that morning was Trump's tweet attacking the "so-called judge" who had blocked his order. Jared turned to Kirk and said with a smirk, "Our folks just love it when we go after judges!" The total lack of regard for the Constitution, and the pandering to Trump's extreme base, would become themes for the year ahead.

We thanked them for the coffee and got back in the car to head into town for a birthday brunch with friends from Austin. "It will be good to see Annette and Jim," I told Kirk. "I felt like we were just in some kind of parallel universe."

On the way back to New York I called Dawn and told her about the conversation and the suggestion that if we stopped providing abortions our funding would continue. "Honestly, it felt almost like a bribe," I said. "I know there are people who will disagree with me, and maybe I shouldn't have just shut down the conversation, but I did what I thought was best."

Dawn was firm. "You did the right thing. Our patients are not a bargaining chip."

Kirk and I were quiet the rest of the ride home. Since the election it had been slowly sinking in who was in charge of our country. The idea that the two people I just met were as influential as anyone in our government was wildly unsettling. If this was the new administration's level of concern, and the depth of its engagement on reproductive health issues, I was deeply afraid for the future of women in America. And I wasn't reassured when I learned that Ivanka Trump would become the highest-ranking woman in the White House in charge of women's affairs.

• • •

We were heading into the battle of a lifetime at Planned Parenthood. With our issues in the headlines, we wanted to make it clear that any member of Congress who voted to defund Planned Parenthood would be voting to take away health care from women who lived in their district. It seemed like the best organizing idea was to get those women into the fight—and nowhere better than in Speaker Paul Ryan's backyard.

Planned Parenthood has been providing health care in Wisconsin for decades, including at three health centers in Speaker Ryan's legislative district. So on a snowy day in February, I flew to Milwaukee, picked up a car, and drove to Planned Parenthood in Kenosha, just three miles from Ryan's office. It's a typical, no-frills health center, and Katie Kordsmeier, the center manager, was there to meet us. Planned Parenthood of Wisconsin CEO Tanya Atkinson, a salt-of-the-earth leader from Milwaukee, was on hand as well. Planned Parenthood health centers are always covered with photos of everyone's kids and pets, and this was no exception. They'd even put up a handmade sign out front reading, "Welcome, Cecile!"

We gathered together in the small waiting room. As the cameras rolled, three of our patients, Sophie Schaut, Gina Walkington, and Lori Hawkins told their moving stories. Lori explained that she had turned to Planned Parenthood as an underinsured Catholic schoolteacher. One day she woke up with severe pain in her lower abdomen. Since she had a family history of cancer, she called Planned Parenthood. They got her in that day and found a large cyst and benign tumors on her ovaries. She was alone and scared that she'd never be able to have children. The clinician invited her to sit down, take her time, and use the health center phone to make the calls she needed to make. Now she was happy and healthy and had two great kids. "Planned Parenthood made it possible for me to be a mother," she said, her voice filled with emotion.

Near the end of the press conference, Sophie said something that has stuck with me ever since: "I used to be a silent supporter of Planned Parenthood. But I can't stay silent anymore." Her words captured a theme that has been repeated over and over since the election: women who had never been involved were now becoming the fiercest, most passionate activists.

Back in Washington, we were waiting anxiously for details of a new health care bill we were sure would end access to Planned Parenthood for millions of our patients. As the debate heated up, members of Congress were doing everything they could to avoid voters back home, so we decided to bring activists and patients to the Capitol.

In March hundreds of people from all across the country converged on Washington, including Lori Hawkins from Wisconsin. This time she brought her thirteen-year-old daughter, Delaney, who told me she had insisted on coming with her mother. "I want to look Speaker Ryan right in the eye," she said, "and tell him that I would not be here if not for the health care my mom got at Planned Parenthood." I loved seeing these courageous leaders meet each other, and get to know their champions in Congress. The energy and solidarity of that day set the tone for what we would need going forward.

Two days later the Republican leadership released their health care plan, deceptively named "The American Health Care Act." Sure enough, it would defund Planned Parenthood, deny many women their health insurance, let states decide whether to cover maternity care, and end Medicaid access for millions of people. Buried deep in the bill was even a provision that would force new moms on Medicaid to return to work within sixty days of giving birth or risk losing their insurance. It reflected total disdain for the struggles of working women. It reminded me of something Mom used to say: "You can put lipstick and earrings on a hog and call it Monique, but it's still a pig."

One of the hardest organizing challenges with something as massive as a national health care bill, especially one that was being jammed through in a matter of days without hearings or analysis, was breaking it down in a way everyone could understand. I talked it over with Geoff Garin, a good friend and pollster who has worked on the issue of health care for a long time. I wanted to know what would help our supporters understand just how bad it was, and motivate people to call Congress.

"Honestly," he said, "the biggest knock on this bill is that it would mean women could no longer go to Planned Parenthood. That's the easiest way for people to understand that they would lose affordable health care, because that is what Planned Parenthood represents."

We went all-out with our message. Every chance I got I went on television, or Dawn did. And we ran ads with our patients telling their stories.

Every time members of Congress traveled back home for recess, Planned Parenthood supporters were waiting for them. Women always managed to track down Senator Lisa Murkowski at the farmer's market in Anchorage and thank her for standing up for Planned Parenthood.

In contrast, Congressman Mike Coffman from Colorado was caught on tape running out a side door after a town hall meeting to try to evade angry constituents. We had helped make the health care bill, or Trumpcare, as it became known, incredibly unpopular, and not a single member of Congress wanted to talk about it, unless it was to say they were voting against it.

On one of the crucial last days of negotiations for the new bill, I was in the Capitol doing an interview with the *New York Times* when the news broke that the House "Freedom Caucus" had just been summoned to the White House to negotiate the final details. The Freedom Caucus is the Tea Party wing on the Hill; it looked like the president had given up on the moderate members and instead was trying to make a deal with the extremists.

I turned to Erica Sackin, Planned Parenthood's director of political communications, and said, "Somehow we have to get a photo of that meeting. That is going to be a room full of old white men deciding the details of a bill that is taking away health care from women."

Sometimes fighting the good fight is all about strategy, and sometimes it comes down to luck. As fate would have it, Vice President Mike Pence tweeted his own photo just a few minutes later, which showed that exact group of men sitting around a table in the White House, proudly negotiating the final details of the bill. Their signature accomplishment? Taking away maternity benefits from women.

It was such a great photo we shot it around Twitter, showing women who was deciding our health care. And then one of my favorite memes appeared: a group of Labrador retrievers sitting around the same table, with the tag line "Meanwhile, at today's meeting on feline health care . . ." At that point I would rather have had canines deciding our health care than that group of men.

The photo, the television ads, and our ongoing organizing effort resulted in thousands of phone calls flooding congressional offices. We constantly had to send out new phone numbers and new ways for our supporters to get in touch with Congress because the switchboard could not handle the volume.

According to a survey by *Daily Action*, a popular tool used to contact Congress, 86 percent of those calls were coming from women. They didn't need to be told why this bill mattered; they knew firsthand. They had been to Planned Parenthood, used birth control, or were worried about health insurance for their kids.

Eventually, Trumpcare passed in the House, and the leadership celebrated with a keg party outside the White House, complete with selfies. It looked like a fraternity party after voting to take health care away from women.

We didn't have a moment to waste as the bill moved to the Senate. I'd been invited to speak about health care at a conference in Aspen, Colorado. By some twist of fate, my interview was scheduled to immediately follow Tom Price, Trump's secretary of health and human services, the main flack for Trumpcare and a lifetime opponent of Planned Parenthood and women's rights. He had filled the Department of Health and Human Services with anti-abortion activists, and even appointed someone to lead the nation's family planning program who was on record stating, "Of course, contraception doesn't work." I had to hand it to him: it's not that easy to find a woman who is against birth control, but he'd managed.

Before my session I watched Secretary Price field questions about the Republican health care plan. He's a smooth operator and smiled as he promised that it wouldn't cost people their health coverage, but would actually cut through red tape and help people get the care they needed. Funny—the American Medical Association had come to a different conclusion. It was pretty clear the Aspen audience of journalists, business leaders, and health care experts weren't buying what he was selling, but I was frustrated that Jeff Goldberg, editor of *The Atlantic* and his interviewer, let him obfuscate on every single question.

I was up next. Pat Mitchell, the trailblazing media powerhouse who had opened doors for generations of women journalists, interviewed me onstage. She didn't mince words; she eviscerated the political attacks on abortion and birth control. And the crowd cheered when I promised, "Planned Parenthood has been here for a hundred years, and we'll be here for a hundred more." If getting the last word was any consolation, the crowd in Aspen was all ours.

Later that day I was sitting in the airport waiting for my flight home when the nonpartisan Congressional Budget Office released its estimate that Trumpcare would eliminate health care for 23 million people. Secretary Price wasn't there to hear the news, having flown home earlier that day on a private plane, but I'm sure someone told him eventually.

Meanwhile people were coming out of the woodwork to help us. Bands wanted to write songs for Planned Parenthood. *Vogue* editor Anna Wintour wore a giant "Fashion Stands with Planned Parenthood" button on her otherwise meticulous outfit at New York Fashion Week, and fashion designers Diane von Furstenberg, Tracy Reese, Gabriela Hearst, and Lela Rose organized on our behalf. We were working day and night trying to keep up with the offers of help—which is a great problem to have. When Emma Stone wore a Planned Parenthood pin on her couture gown to accept her Academy Award, the image flew around social media. Planned Parenthood board member and entrepreneur David Karp called me one day to say he wanted to start "Tech Stands with Planned Parenthood." "Do it!" I said. This was the moment everyone had been waiting for. People weren't looking to us for instructions; they were just getting to work.

In the midst of all the support, we got some hard news out of Iowa. Because of a law signed by Governor Terry Branstad before he left office, Planned Parenthood was going to have to close four health centers. It was heartbreaking, and a preview of what could happen if Planned Parenthood were defunded across the country.

I wanted to hear what was happening on the ground, so I picked up the phone and called Angela, the health center manager in Bettendorf, Iowa. "How are you doing?" I asked.

She took a deep breath. "It's really tough. Patients are scrambling to figure out where they're going to be seen once we close. They're in shock, and they're angry. Some of them have nowhere else to go. Meanwhile they're hearing politicians talk about them on TV, and the statements that are made about our patients—it's like facts don't even matter."

"What about the staff?"

"Oh, it's all the emotions you can imagine when you lose something you love. When the announcement was made that we would have to shut down, everyone was in tears. We had all lost our jobs. Someone said, 'Well, do you want to go home, and we can call the patients?' I said, 'No. I'm in this. I'm not going.' My staff said the same thing: 'Let's do this. Let's get ourselves together and see those patients.'"

By now I was barely holding it together. "Thank you for everything," I told her. "This is incredibly cruel, and the women of Iowa deserve better."

"You know, though, I wouldn't take it back for anything, my experience working for Planned Parenthood," she added. "I wouldn't give up a single day of being here. Even knowing what was going to happen, I wouldn't give it up for the world."

We said our goodbyes, and I crossed my fingers that I wouldn't be making hundreds of similar calls because this bill had passed Congress.

• • •

Trumpcare was so unpopular, it wasn't until July that the Senate scheduled it to come up for a vote. I went down to Washington, ready to do battle. We didn't know who was with us, but we were doing all we could to shore up the women of the Senate, especially Lisa Murkowski from Alaska and Susan Collins from Maine. They had been clear: they would not support a bill that defunded Planned Parenthood.

It was 6:15 p.m., and the Republicans were running out of time. I had spent the day on the Hill, talking with all our senators, finally sitting down with Senator Patty Murray, our lieutenant, nervous as ever. "I don't think we have the votes, Cecile," she said. "But never say never."

"We've got people calling their senators up until the very end," I said. "No way we are giving up." I texted Lily to see if she had any inside news. "Nothing you don't know," she responded. "Everyone here thinks I'm crazy, but I still think we can beat this."

I texted back, "That's because you lived to see us do the impossible and elect Ann Richards governor of Texas!"

As it got dark, I joined Ben Wikler at MoveOn and many members of Congress, including Leader Pelosi, to speak at an impromptu rally with hundreds outside the Capitol. The senators were on the floor and the vote was going to happen that night. There wasn't anything more to do on Capitol Hill, so I headed to the hotel to sit and worry and wait.

The debate over the bill was a major nail-biter and went on late into the night. I was texting with Kirk and Lily and watching TV as they did the roll call vote. Senator John McCain of Arizona, who had just been given a tough cancer diagnosis, had been flown back to Washington so the Republicans would have enough votes.

Lily texted, "Did John McCain just smile at Chuck Schumer?"

I replied, "Hmmm. Is McConnell frowning? Hard to tell, though, he's always frowning."

And Lily, "Everyone's waiting on John McCain. . . . He hasn't voted yet."

At that moment McCain stood and made his now infamous thumbs-down sign. We went crazy. Lily texted me: "I swear he's voting no!"

And in fact he had. The bill repealing Obamacare and defunding Planned Parenthood was officially dead. Chaos broke out on the floor of the Senate. All the Planned Parenthood CEOs, in California at a meeting, called, hysterical and cheering. Finally, around two in the morning, Leader McConnell stood up and said, "It's time to move on."

Once again we had done the unthinkable. We had beaten back the bill. "I know Ann is laughing her ass off, and so proud of these women senators," Kirk texted our group chain. "This day belongs to you and your folks. Here's to having many more like it."

In September of 2017, the Republicans made one more attempt to pass the bill, but it felt like their heart wasn't in it. CNN held a nationally televised town hall on health care—clearly, the debate over the issue wasn't going away. That night, a video clip came across my feed on Twitter. A familiar voice said, "My name is Lori. I'm a Planned Parenthood patient." It was Lori Hawkins from Kenosha, Wisconsin, on national TV! She looked the bill's sponsor in the eye and asked him why he would want to deprive anyone of the care she had gotten, which had made it possible for her to start a family. He answered in the most condescending way possible, even trying to mansplain childbirth—to a mother.

I texted her, "I'm so proud of you!" Yet again Lori made her very personal story public, because as hard as it was, she hoped it might make a difference for someone else. A few days later the vote failed before it even got to the floor. Right after that, Secretary Tom Price of the Department of Health and Human Services resigned his post after mounting controversy over his use of private planes. I knew that our work was far from over, but the tally was Women—3, Trumpcare—0.

· · ·

Women are leading the resistance. They're making organizing and activism part of their lives, bringing their kids along to town hall meetings, and signing up in record numbers to run for office themselves. In fact a few months ago I got an email from a candidate training program in Wisconsin, asking if I would recommend Lori Hawkins, who was thinking of running for office. Can you imagine how different our country would look if women like Lori, instead of men like Paul Ryan, were making decisions about the health care women need?

The fights we're facing—for affordable health care, equal rights, bodily autonomy, and more—are never fully won. But the lasting legacy of this moment will be the generations of women it has inspired and energized.

One of my favorite moments of 2017 happened on a trip to Arizona. I was there for the annual Planned Parenthood luncheon, and under the great leadership of CEO Bryan Howard, it was their best-attended event ever; in fact they sold out the Biltmore ballroom.

After the lunch, we headed to the Phoenix Planned Parenthood office to meet with the local organizers. The place was filled with signs made for a town hall meeting that was occurring later that night in Mesa, Arizona. Their senator, Republican Jeff Flake, was a huge proponent of defunding Planned Parenthood.

I hadn't gotten to eat at the luncheon, so the staff had kindly ordered in. We stood over a pile of tacos and I asked the young organizers if they were ready to give Senator Flake a piece of their mind. They answered loudly, and without a second's hesitation, "YES!" Everyone was giddy with excitement, but I couldn't help notice one young woman in particular with a sweet smile and a determined look in her eyes. Her name was Deja Foxx, and I had met her once before.

"Here's our plan," said another young organizer. "There are going to be hundreds of women there with pussy hats and Planned Parenthood pink on, so we are making sure a few of us are dressed in just regular clothes, to have a better chance of getting to ask a question at the microphone." Now that's an organizer for you! I wished them luck as I headed to the airport.

Later that night I got an email with the subject line "You have to see this." I opened the video inside and saw a determined-looking young woman standing up in front of a packed house calmly take the microphone at the town hall while her senator watched from the stage. "I just want to state some facts," she began. "I'm a young woman, and you're a middle-aged man. I'm a person of color, and you're white. I come from a background of poverty, and I didn't always have parents to guide me through life. You come from privilege. So I'm wondering why it's your right to take away my right to choose Planned Parenthood?" I leaned closer to the screen, and sure enough, it was Deja.

The crowd burst into applause that became a standing ovation. By the next morning more than 12 million people had watched the video of Deja schooling her US senator. Since then she's spearheaded an overhaul of her school's sex education curriculum, traveled to Capitol Hill to defend her right to affordable, compassionate health care, spoken out on national television, and been featured in *Teen Vogue*. If you want to see what's next for reproductive rights, go watch that video. Deja's generation is the largest, most diverse, most entrepreneurial and open-minded of any generation before them. More than 4 million young people turn eighteen every year in the United States. They are born troublemakers, naturals when it comes to questioning authority.

As I was finishing this book, I was in Sarasota, Florida, for a Planned Parenthood event and stopped by to visit with local staff and volunteers. Command central in Sarasota is a big, bright building that's home to the health center and a whole lot more, including the black box theater where their teen theater troupe, The Source, practices and performs sketches about birth control, consent, and staying healthy. I took the elevator up to the administrative offices and walked back to the break room, where volunteers of every age and background were gathered, drinking coffee and swapping stories.

We went around the room and introduced ourselves. There were college-age women who spent their Saturday mornings escorting patients past protesters and into the clinic. A high school volunteer was there, along with her mom, also a volunteer. Some older women were there, doing data entry. One by one they talked about what had drawn them to Planned Parenthood and how grateful they were, especially now, to be able to do something other than sit around feeling helpless about the state of the world. Some of the volunteers were old enough to remember the days before *Roe v. Wade* and safe, legal abortion. The younger members of the group had grown up in an era of no-copay birth control and information available at their fingertips whenever they needed it. As we talked, more volunteers kept trickling in.

The effort to stop the defunding of Planned Parenthood inspired organizers across America, including young women in Phoenix, Arizona, getting ready for a town hall meeting with US senator Jeff Flake.

Soon we were joined by staff from the rest of the office, mostly women in their twenties and thirties who manage the health center, work with the media, run sex education programs, and so much more. They talked and laughed with the volunteers, excitedly describing what was on the horizon for Planned Parenthood in Sarasota. It was a beautiful sight: volunteers of all ages who were so excited to help, and the young, vibrant, diverse staff leading them.

As I was leaving, a woman who must have been in her eighties said to me, "I just have to tell you that I've never done anything for Planned Parenthood, or anything like this, in my life. But after the election, I knew I couldn't *not* get involved. I just signed up, and now I'm volunteering every day. So it's never too late!" She was beaming.

Standing in that health center in Sarasota, I was witnessing something incredible: the extraordinary power of women reaching across generations to link arms and fight together. Women who never imagined becoming activists are standing alongside fiercely determined women young enough to be their granddaughters. In times like these, it's not enough to pass the torch. It's going to take all of us—the trailblazers, the leaders of tomorrow, and all the troublemakers in between—to light the way forward. The future is ours to shape, and that fills me with hope.

"Feminist" Is Not a Passive Label

"So now what do I do?"

It's a question I've been asked almost every day since the 2016 election, by everyone from corporate CEOs to a young woman on the C train last week. What they're really asking is *Now that we can no longer take for granted that America will slowly but surely make progress, our entire world seems to be spinning out of control, and we're fighting tooth and nail to protect our most fundamental rights—how do we make it all better?*

Great question.

Right now our country has some major soul-searching to do. We have to figure out how to address the fear and disruption that many people are feeling and continue to fight for the rights of women, immigrants, LGBTQ people, people of color, and anyone else who needs support. To do that, we're going to have to ask tough questions, speak clearly about what we believe, and maybe even let go of the political labels that have defined these kinds of debates for too long.

Here's the good news: there has never been a better time to become an activist, agitator, or troublemaker. I promise you, doing something—whether it's showing up at a town hall meeting, getting some friends together to start your own organization, or just refusing to keep quiet about what you believe—feels infinitely better than sitting on the sidelines. Looking back on my life so far, the moments I regret most are the ones when I was too scared to take a chance—the moments when I didn't know what to do, and so did nothing.

In some ways, being an activist in public is easy; standing up for yourself in your own life can be much harder. Even after years of loud and proud troublemaking, I've found myself in situations where I was too fearful to speak up for myself. There was the summer job in college when my employer groped me and tried more, yet I was terrified of losing the opportunity to learn from him, so I never said anything. Like so many women, I can remember every single detail forty years later. I don't want that to be the fate of my daughters or any other girl.

Then there was the conversation about a job in Washington where my future employer said, "I know you have three kids at home, so maybe you just want to work part-time?" "Nope," I replied, "I need this job, and my husband and I are both working full-time." It wasn't until later that I found out my "progressive" employer was paying my male colleague, working the same job, nearly twice what I was earning. Why didn't I think enough of myself to raise hell at the time?

Now the floodgates are open. Women are talking publicly about subjects that were once off-limits, and refusing to tolerate the sexual assault and harassment that have been accepted for far too long and there's no going back. As Mom used to say, "You can't unring a bell." It shouldn't be up to women to dismantle the patriarchy, but we can't sit around and hope someone else does it either. *Feminist* is not a passive label; it means speaking out and standing up for women everywhere, and also for yourself. One woman calling out an injustice is powerful enough; when we raise our voices together, we can shake the status quo to its foundation.

For activists and troublemakers, especially now, there's no shortage of fights to take on. I've been proud to be part of the movement for reproductive freedom for over a decade, and to have invested in bringing a whole new generation of leaders into the fold. I believe it's time for one of them to take over, which is why I decided to leave Planned Parenthood after twelve years and turn to the next chapter—in our movement and in my own life. It wasn't an easy decision to make—leaving a job you love never is—but I am confident it was the right one.

Now more than ever, women are the most important political force in America. We have enormous power to change the direction of this country, and it's time to use it. Marching, knitting, and protesting are great. But voting, and changing who is elected to office, is essential. The women who come through the doors of Planned Parenthood health centers every day have a lot on their minds, above and beyond getting affordable, nonjudgmental health care: they want a safe neighborhood for their kids and an excellent public school system. They want to earn a living wage, and work without facing harassment or abuse. They want family leave and affordable child care. They want to live in communities free from gun violence. They deserve all this and more, and that's what I'll be fighting for.

Sometimes I picture my thirteen-year-old self, getting on the school bus, wearing that black felt armband, preparing to embark on a lifetime of making trouble. There's so much I wish I could tell her: Stay strong even when people criticize or doubt you. Every meaningful relationship, every friendship, and the love of your life will come from standing up for what you believe. The world can be tough, unjust, and even cruel, but you have the power to do something about it—at any age. We all do. It's not about having it all, doing it all, or being perfect—it's about getting started.

There's a poem I always seem to find my way back to—"The Low Road," by Marge Piercy. Part of it goes like this:

> It starts when you care
> to act, it starts when you do
> it again after they said no,
> it starts when you say We
> and know who you mean, and each
> day you mean one more.

So here's to the troublemakers, the agitators, the organizers. This is our moment.

Afterword

"I'm trying to figure out what to do. There is so much going on in the world and I have to make a difference. What is your advice?"

The question was in a stack of cards from the audience in Vanderbilt Hall at the NYU School of Law campus in June 2018, at the tail end of the book tour following the publication of *Make Trouble* in April. The exact query, in so many words, had inspired me to write this book in the first place, and it had come up at every public event. A fourth grader had asked me the same thing in Nashville, Tennessee, where I was sharing the stage with author Ann Patchett. ("Run for class president!" we suggested.) College students in Chicago and moms in Houston echoed the same sentiment. Everywhere I went, the carefully planned and scheduled book events felt more like revival meetings, with women crowded into auditoriums to talk about this moment in our lives, and what each of us could do. One especially memorable Sunday out in rural North Carolina, in a driving rainstorm, we were all packed into a farmhouse like sardines. In any town, as if someone simply put up the Bat-Signal, women would appear.

Along the way, I covered everything: *How can I talk my sister-in-law into voting? What can I do at my job, where I know women are earning less than men? How do we raise our kids when our government is doing so many things we don't believe in?* And another familiar question: *When are you running for office?* Over the course of the book tour, my answer had shifted from the flat-out denial "I'm an activist" to the honest "I don't know what will happen in the future." It seemed hypocritical, I figured, to urge other women to consider running for office while writing it off as an option for myself. Never say never!

Best of all, I got to reconnect with many of the characters from my life, and hear about the new trouble they were making. There was my union organizing buddy, Jono, who came to a book event in Los Angeles, and brought his now college-graduate daughter—we had come a long way since the two of us were arrested together during our Justice for Janitors days! I was welcomed in Seattle, Washington, not only by Lindy West but also by the rowdiest crowd of abortion rights activists anywhere. In Phoenix, Arizona, high schooler Deja Foxx interviewed me in front of a packed room full of the other young women organizers who had mobilized for the town hall meeting a year before. I learned that Deja would be heading that fall to Columbia University, the first person in her family to attend college. Nothing, though, could match being back in Austin, with Senator Wendy Davis and more than a thousand of our friends at the historic Paramount Theatre. For many of us, it was the first time we had been together since we took over the state capitol—just a few blocks away—during Wendy's filibuster. The energy I saw on the road was contagious—it left me feeling reinvigorated and more confident than ever that we were living through a once-in-a-lifetime moment.

Back at NYU, the answer to the question of "What do I do?" actually seemed so clear. Nearly overcome with excitement, I answered without hesitation.

"I'm not sure who asked the question," I began, "but for anyone out there, if you want to change the world, quit your job and go work for Stacey Abrams in Georgia. She's the most exciting, inspiring candidate on the ballot this cycle, and she's already made history as the first African American woman to win her party's nomination for governor."

Two weeks later, I was boarding a flight when a message from a stranger popped up on my Instagram.

"Hi. I was in the audience the other night at NYU, and I listened to your advice. Just wanted you to know I went home, quit my job and I'm moving to Atlanta to start as Stacey Abrams's deputy digital director!"

I was overjoyed, but not surprised to encounter yet another courageous woman who had decided to, as Nora Ephron once urged, be the heroine of her own life. This is the theme of our times: women doing things they never could have imagined, being bold and audacious, and taking risks.

A few months before, as I was putting the finishing touches on this book, I was getting ready for a big change: stepping down as president of Planned Parenthood. It was hard even though I knew it was time. The staff, leaders, and patients at Planned Parenthood had been my family for the past twelve years, and we had been through so much together; I would walk through fire for them, and they had done as much for me so many times. It wasn't until I'd been gone a few weeks that I realized how much I missed my coworkers: Frank, who had gotten us through innumerable online hacking attempts. Chiko, our head of security, whom I literally trusted with my life. Travis, my fiercest competition in the annual office-wide pie-baking contest every Thanksgiving. And Oscar, who had worked the security desk since my very first day and whom I consider a friend to this day.

As I got ready to leave, I ignored all of the well-meaning advice to just "take time for yourself." We were in the middle of one of the most important, exciting moments in my lifetime when it came to women's organizing. There was no way I was going to kick back and contemplate my own personal or professional future (even if that would have been a good idea).

Instead, I hit the ground running, barreling into a national "listening tour" to hear directly from women so I could better understand what was fueling the wave of activism sweeping the country. Everywhere I'd been since the 2016 election, I had run into women who were organizing in their communities—all kinds of women, and in every state. In Charleston, South Carolina, I got to cut the ribbon on a new Planned Parenthood health center, one of my last official acts as the organization's president. There, I met three women in their eighties. "We'd never met before," one explained, "but we got together at the women's march and just kept on going!" On a trip through Ohio, you couldn't throw a rock without hitting a newly formed grassroots women's group—from the Matriots, a statewide group dedicated to electing progressive women, to the Nasty Women of Bay Village in Cuyahoga County, to a group in

Cincinnati started by a local woman to confront the epidemic of maternal mortality among black women. My daughter Hannah summed it up so perfectly when she said: "You know, out here in Colorado there are so many new women's groups . . . but you don't really see new *men's* organizations!" She had a point. Clearly, women everywhere were longing to come together, take action, and shake things up.

The organizer in me kept thinking: *What if all these women's groups from Florida to Wisconsin and everywhere in between could actually be linked together? What would it look like to finally build true, lasting political power for women? What if we had our own women's political party, so we could stand up and work for the issues that always seem to be pushed aside in the current environment?* Women were not satisfied to march and leave it at that. They were raising their hands to run for office, and voting in record numbers in political primaries. It seemed clear that the question in 2020 wouldn't be *whether* a woman would run for president of the United States, but how many would answer the call. Women were already taking our country by storm, and I was floored imagining what they could do with meaningful support, structure, and investment.

I felt strongly that we need a political movement of, by, and for women, dedicated to advocating for the issues that affect our lives—the same issues that are too often left out of discussions in Congress and state houses. I also knew that millions of women don't vote and aren't engaged in politics because they're too busy, or they don't know how to take that first step of getting involved. I knew we could be doing more to empower women and change the direction of the country.

I started talking to other women who have also spent years in the trenches organizing women. There was Ai-jen Poo, who leads the National Domestic Workers Alliance, advocating for millions of caregivers across the country who are watching over our children, the elderly, and other loved ones. There was Alicia Garza, a founder of Black Lives Matter and passionate advocate for building power for women of color. There were my friends and former colleagues at Planned Parenthood: Dawn Laguens, Deirdre Schifeling, and Kersha Deibel, whose experience building a smart and powerful political movement of women provided a great road map. Rounding out the group was Katherine Grainger, a law-yer, strategist, and feminist with a rare gift for diagnosing a problem, and offering an innovative solution in the next breath.

Together we set out to bring together women from every walk of life. In eighteen cities across the United States, we heard from women about their frustrations and their aspirations.

Women talked about everything from the rising cost of housing and the impossibility of finding affordable, quality child care to repro-ductive rights and education. The most remarkable part was hearing the way women spoke about their concerns for others in a way that indicated a new awareness that perhaps only the Trump White House could have created. "I cannot continue to watch young black boys being shot," said a young white mother in rural Wisconsin. "These are all of our children." One day, we sat with a hundred women in Phoenix, listening to a young woman talk about her daily fears of having her mother deported. I met countless women like the single mom in Mil-waukee, who broke down in tears describing working two jobs and barely making ends meet—but still showed up for two hours on her only day off with her daughter in tow to talk about what it's going to take to make things better for everyone. Women everywhere are awak-ening to a greater reality and connection, and recognizing that it's go-ing to take more than each of our individual efforts to create the change we so desperately need.

Just as important, at a time when our own government is caging children, incarcerating pregnant women, breaking up families, and ig-noring the experiences of women who are survivors of sexual assault and harassment, women are realizing more than ever that part of the solution has to be political. I was struck by a young woman in Austin who had fought for and won maternity coverage at the tech company where she works. "I realized it's not enough—I need to get involved in politics."

"No one was there to help me figure it out," said Dionna Langford, a young woman on the school board in Des Moines—and the only Afri-can American member. "I had to read up on how to even run." Down the road in Cedar Rapids, a longtime political activist looking ahead to the midterm elections said, "I'm going to volunteer to phone bank and knock on doors again this year like every year. But it's frustrating to know I'm working in a system built by men, for men."

The women we met on the road were immigrants, teachers, students, nurses, stay-at-home moms, and more. They were working-class women, black women, transgender women, and white women. They were grandmothers and teenagers. The one thing they had in common? They were relieved and energized to be together. They talked about what it had been like over these last two years to cheer each other on—from swelling with pride when the iconic Oprah Winfrey took the stage at the Golden Globes and voiced women's most desperate desire to live free of harassment to celebrating small everyday victories, like the young woman who described helping a family become US citizens, and then registering them to vote. A universal theme was the overwhelming desire to do more, and to do it together.

I believe we have reached a tipping point. Unlike in the 1960s, women are now almost half the workforce. We are more than half of college students, law students, and medical students. The amazing thing is we have made all this progress despite having to succeed in workplaces, societies, economies, and governments that were never meant for women to inhabit.

To continue and accelerate this slow progress toward equality, women will need to attain the one thing that has eluded us for more than a century: real political power. Because even though women are well more than half of voters in the United States, our political representation ranks 103rd—right below Indonesia. This imbalance is perhaps responsible for the fact that the United States is the only industrialized country in the world without nationally mandated paid family leave. And still, in 2019, women on average earn just 80 cents for every dollar a man earns. For black women, it's 61 cents. For Latinas, it's only 53 cents.

I truly believe if women had real, equitable political power, it would be a different story. Our health care system would quit treating pregnancy like a nuisance and rather as the basic reality it is for millions of workers. Maternity benefits and child care might actually be seen as—dare to dream—necessities for growing our economy. Public school teachers wouldn't have to strike to bring attention to the education needs of our children. We could have a government that supports families instead of tearing them apart. Issues that women care about could finally be understood not as distractions but as fundamental issues of fairness and dignity that are important to everyone.

The driving force behind nearly every inch of progress in America since the 2016 elections has been women at the grassroots. I was on the edge of my seat, cheering, as public school teachers, 75 percent of whom are women, led inspiring strikes across the country in states including Oklahoma, Arizona, Tennessee, West Virginia, and in Los Angeles to protect school funding. I am consistently in awe of groups like the Mothers of the Movement and Moms Demand Action that are taking on the powerful gun lobby alongside truly incredible young women like Emma González. When it comes to two of the most urgent challenges we faced in recent years—the fight to end family separation at the border and to preserve health care and access to Planned Parenthood—it's women who have led the charge. And in the 2018 midterm elections, a record number of women, including a record number of women of color, ran for office, and it mattered.

Unsurprisingly, women for the most part ran for office because they saw a problem that needed fixing, and they felt they could make a difference: Women like Lucy McBath in Georgia, a mother who lost her son to gun violence. She realized the criminal justice system is broken, and it is her passion to fix it. She's now a congresswoman. Or Angie Craig from Minnesota, whose congressman made such hateful statements about LGBTQ people that she decided to take him on. Now, she's the first lesbian mom in Congress. Or Lauren Underwood, a registered nurse in Illinois, who sees every day what it means when people don't have access to affordable health care. She challenged six men in her political primary, then went on to beat the incumbent, and is now the first African American woman in history to represent her district.

Across the country women challenged conventional wisdom and re-created politics the old-fashioned way: by knocking on doors, meeting their constituents, and often by outworking their opponents. I'll never forget the photo candidate Alexandria Ocasio-Cortez posted of her shoes, literally worn through the soles from walking neighborhoods. Now, she's the youngest woman elected to Congress. And Anna Eskamani, a former Planned Parenthood patient and staff member who was there that day in Sarasota, Florida (see chapter thirteen), ran for office in a swing district. She spent a year with a clipboard in her hand, knocking doors, talking to everyone she possibly could about why she was running. When I campaigned with her, she had been targeted by ugly attack ads and smears. But she shrugged it off and kept going. At twenty-eight years old, she won and was sworn in as the first Iranian American ever elected to the state legislature in Florida. Can you imagine how different our world will look when governments around the world are filled with women like Lucy, Angie, Lauren, Alexandria, and Anna?

Hundreds of women took on races with incredibly hard odds, and though they fell short on Election Day, they will be stronger candidates next time around—women like Lori Hawkins and Gina Walkington in Wisconsin, our Planned Parenthood friends who took a risk and ran for the statehouse. They didn't win this time. But they turned out and engaged new women, who changed the direction of the state and helped elect a governor who supports women's rights. In Georgia, Stacey Abrams made history by turning out record numbers of African American voters and fighting to ensure that everyone can vote and that every vote is counted. And her political career is far from finished.

Of course, the struggle for equality has never been easy, and those who have power are not going to give it up without a fight. The most heartbreaking moment for me since this book came out was the confirmation of Brett Kavanaugh to the Supreme Court, by the narrowest margin in 137 years. It brought back painful memories of the hearing, twenty-seven years earlier, when Anita Hill testified against (now a Supreme Court justice) Clarence Thomas. It wasn't lost on me that three of the same (male) senators who subjected her to tougher scrutiny than the man accused of sexual harassment are still on the Senate Judiciary Committee, and seem not to have learned a thing from their prior experience.

Having been through my own hostile congressional hearing, I had no illusion that this was an honest effort to get to the truth. But I was amazed at the courage and brutal honesty of Dr. Christine Blasey Ford, who, with absolutely nothing to gain and so much to lose, recounted before the world her experience of abuse by a man who now sits on the highest court in the land.

My immediate reaction was to call my daughter Lily. She was living through so much of this herself, working in the US Senate. Her boss, Senator Kamala Harris, played an important role on the Judiciary Committee. Even though Lily had a firsthand view of everything, I felt like I needed to apologize to her. How could I, as a mother, not have done more to change circumstances for women, including my own daughters? I felt like a failure. "This system is not fair," I told her. "I'm embarrassed and horrified for our country."

For me, it wasn't only Justice Kavanaugh's opposition to abortion rights and other basic civil liberties that unnerved me—that was awful, but not surprising. The worst of it all was the complete disregard that elected members of the Senate showed to Dr. Ford, treating her and other women as the suspects and the guilty ones. Their actions cast a harsh light on so many women's lived experience, where the risks of reporting harassment, or fighting back against men in power, feels futile. I can't bear the thought that this generation of young women will also live with and bury the shame of it all, choosing to just move on rather than subject themselves to the public humiliation of seeking justice. Every time I hear a man ask why women do not report sexual assault or harassment, I want to scream: "Because you won't believe us!" Some of the most bitter disappointment I felt was toward women who abandoned Dr. Ford and other survivors. And yet I prefer to lift up the women who, despite the politics, did the right thing—like Senator Heidi Heitkamp from North Dakota. In the middle of a very tough re-election campaign, which she later lost, she voted against Kavanaugh. She shared a deeply personal story about her mother's experience as a survivor of sexual assault, and stated that Kavanaugh lacked the "temperament, honesty, and impartiality" to serve. She made me proud. Others did not. Our gender is not a monolith, and even in my enthusiasm for organizing women as a political force, there is some hard reckoning to do.

This is a crucial moment to recognize and understand that sometimes our own sisters perpetuate oppression. I feel they have been oppressed so long they don't know what liberation might really be. I was recently invited—with some hesitation—to speak to a massive women's conference in Massachusetts. The organizers thought I was "too political," which, even at an event being organized by women, for women, seemed to be code for believing in reproductive rights. The printed program for the event prefaced a description of my session with the caveat: "Whether or not you agree with her mission . . ." In the end, perhaps it was a good thing they made me sound so controversial—we wound up drawing a huge crowd! And then there was the international women's conference I was invited to address—as long as I didn't talk about abortion because it was again "too political." I struggled with whether to speak, and ended up doing so, but I still feel uneasy with that decision. I am left wondering: *What are these women thinking?* No one ever won their rights by quietly waiting around. If there were ever a time to step outside our comfort zones and hold each other accountable, it's now.

To me, all of this underscores the fact that we cannot allow the current outpouring of activism to simply be a moment in time. We need to build a sustained, global political movement for women's equality—an intersectional, intergenerational movement that leaves no one behind. We need a women's political revolution that works for full equality—across race, class, sexual orientation, and political labels—because I believe there is so much more women share in common than what keeps us apart.

On this front, though it may not always seem like it, we are making progress. White women, to the despair of many, voted by a plurality to elect Donald Trump. And yet, in the 2018 midterms, for the first time in decades white women split their votes evenly between the parties. In fact, every single group of women, except Republican women, became more progressive. African American women, who have for decades been the most reliable progressive voters, delivered once again. But in many states, white women voted against candidates who supported women's rights. The issue of racial and economic privilege is as prevalent as ever. As white women, we must do more to work in solidarity with women of color. And while recognizing that is important, it's only the first step—we need to follow it with real, concrete action.

A student in Connecticut asked me recently how we move forward. "I feel like the parties have staked out their corners," she said. "It feels like a stalemate and that we are just stuck. What can we do?"

I have to say: I agree with her. The political party system in America is broken, and women are going to have to organize their own political power outside it. I believe it's women—not Democrats or Republicans—who are our best hope of rebuilding our democracy. We can start by reducing the barriers to voting, which hit women the hardest—women of color, working mothers, women of low income. We need to follow the lead of Stacey Abrams who stood up in Georgia and showed the world how our voting system routinely discriminates against certain voters. We need to make voting easier, and we can start by making Election Day a federal holiday. That's the work I'm committed to doing alongside others.

So what's next? Working with other women leaders, we are setting out to build a new movement for women's political equality. We want to begin giving the support women need to organize their friends and neighbors to be voters and activists; providing information about what other women are doing across the country, and how they are succeeding; connecting women to one another; and building political power.

It's time for a women's Declaration of Independence, dedicated to building a multiracial, multigenerational movement for women's equality and holding every politician, party, and elected official accountable to our agenda.

To me, it's pretty simple.

We believe that women's equality is essential to economic, political, and social progress for our country.

We believe in fighting for the basic human needs of all people, including universal health care, public education, a living wage, a clean environment, and affordable housing.

We believe in supporting families—the right of every person to decide whether and when to have children, to live in safe communities, and to provide and care for loved ones.

We believe in fairness and opportunity—that no matter your race, immigration status, sexual orientation, gender, or gender identity, you deserve a chance to thrive and succeed.

We believe we can only have true democracy when everyone has a chance to participate.

Therefore, we will fight for democratic reforms that enable women to take part in the political process—as voters, candidates, and advocates.

We will work to ensure that the stories of women's activism and participation in moving our country forward break through, particularly when it comes to lifting up women of color and women whose voices have gone unheard for too long.

We will bring women together across issues, communities, and levels of engagement to build an intersectional, intergenerational movement to transform this country.

We will hold candidates and officeholders accountable to not only vote for but also fight for women's equality.

It's not going to be easy. After all, if it was, someone would have already done it.

In the past, including in this book, I've cavalierly made light of work-life balance and self-care. These subjects struck me as self-indulgent and, yes, weak. But the past couple of years have humbled me. There are times I simply couldn't imagine going forward. And the day Brett Kavanaugh was confirmed was a day I, like so many others, hit rock bottom. But that day was also the moment I knew that for the rest of my life, this would be my work: fighting for women's political equality. Like Fannie Lou Hamer said, women are sick and tired of being sick and tired. And giving up isn't an option—because if we do, the bad guys win.

I've also come to realize that we have to look out for one another more. No one can take this moment on by themselves. We have to check in on others, especially people who are experiencing the ravages of this political time worse than you may be. LGBTQ people, immigrant communities, Muslim Americans—the list goes on.

And I'm committed to finding ways to bring joy to the work—that's my new mantra. If you need to, take time off and let someone else take your place on the field. There are enough of us now to do that for one another. There are no small challenges now; to make true, lasting change we have to be committed to the long haul.

And as I've thought about my own self-care, I realized that unconsciously, the need to see and be with young women is what feeds my hope and optimism.

Recently I was back in Austin, and I had the chance to visit the Ann Richards School for Young Women Leaders, and take a tour from a group of students. Crammed into a public school in South Austin, bursting at the seams, more than eight hundred young girls and women are doing their thing. We saw the Maker's Studio, where using a 3-D printer, girls were designing a habitat for outer space. I helped carry the wooden frames in the shop class where others were building pigpens for the local zoo. The drama troupe was on stage practicing the upcoming play. "It's not easy to find plays written by women, with parts for girls," the leader explained, "but we are doing it." As we walked through the halls, graduating seniors talked to me about where they were hoping to go to college, since this is an expectation of the school—and every girl does. One was determined to be an engineer, and others mathematicians. Most poignant were the questions. "Can you give me advice?" asked one bright-eyed girl. "What would you do if you just love EVERYTHING?"

Near the end of our tour, Sammie, a senior and the editor of the school newspaper, proudly showed off her latest editorial, describing the disappointment and anger she felt watching Justice Kavanaugh's confirmation hearings—and her determination that things should be better. She's headed to college next year and she is so much more ready to take on the world than I was at their age.

Standing in the hallway as we said our goodbyes, there was a cardboard cutout of my mom. We snapped a few photos together with this life-size Ann Richards, including one with my niece Kate, a sixth grader at the school. It was hard to match up the life my mother had, growing up in Waco when there were so few opportunities, with this school of hundreds of girls who were on their way to practically endless possibilities. I wish she were here to see it—but knowing her, she'd had them in her mind's eye long ago.

When the political world seems so backward, so mean-spirited, I look at young women and take heart knowing that it is only a matter of time before they are in charge. And I'm mindful that we need them to be not only brilliant scientists, writers, inventors, and students—but leaders and citizens of the world. We need to do everything we possibly can to be sure that young women, as my former boss (and now once again Speaker of the US House of Representatives!) Nancy Pelosi used to implore us, know their power. We owe it to girls today to think beyond the day-to-day fights, to let go of the idea that we can only dare hope for incremental progress and grudgingly granted policy gains. It takes audacity and vision to imagine a country and a world where women are true and equal partners—but just because we haven't yet lived it doesn't mean it's not within our reach. After all, so many of the earth-shattering changes women have made possible in the last two years alone would have been inconceivable to women of my mother's generation.

Building a women's political revolution is about building a future that lives up not to our wildest expectations, but to the expectations of the next generation. It requires reaching out to and engaging women around the country who have been left out of, or even deliberately excluded from, our politics in the past. It demands that we hold all candidates accountable to advancing women's equality. And it provides us the opportunity to build a truly intersectional, interracial, intergenerational women's movement.

I believe that's what we are now being called to do. There is no doubt in my mind that we are bold enough, brave enough, and powerful enough. Creating the kind of massive change we need is going to take every single one of us—whether you're a lifelong activist or you've been observing from the sideline until now. So ask yourself: What can I do right now to make my community, my workplace, or my school a better place for everyone? Then, put down this book, go out, and do it. Consider this your official invitation to make trouble—because we don't have a moment to waste.

Acknowledgments

Going through the last six decades has involved a lot of people, and I'm forever grateful to everyone who has helped reconstruct years of adventures in troublemaking. Thank you to my friends from the labor movement, the Planned Parenthood family, Capitol Hill, and elsewhere for your memories, editing, and guidance: Debra Alligood White, Peter Brownlie and Deborah Jenkins, Matt Burgess, George Crawford, Diane Dewhirst, Brendan Daly, Congresswoman Rosa DeLauro, Anna Eskamani, Roger Evans, Marisa Feehan, Eric Ferrero, Yvonne Gutierrez, Amanda Harrington, Lori Hawkins, Jane Hickie, Maryana Iskander, Rebecca Katz, Jennifer Kinon, George Kundanis, Ken Lambrecht, Dawn Laguens, Dutch Leonard, Chuck McDonald, Nick Merrill, Laura Olin, Selena Ortega, Democratic Leader Nancy Pelosi, Janis Pinelli, Lynne Randall, Callie Richmond, Steve Rosenthal, Laurie Rubiner, Jen Samawat, Dan Schwerin, Jono Shaffer, Dana Singiser, Evan Smith, Andy Stern, Emily Stewart, Sarah Stoesz, Tom Subak, Luis Ubiñas and Deb Tolman, Sarah Weddington, Brady Williamson, and Liz Zaretsky.

Thank you to the Ann Richards campaign family who raised my kids and taught us all what it means to dream big. To the hundreds of nursing home workers, janitors, hotel staff, and more whose courage to fight for justice continues to inspire me. In the words of Nelson Mandela, "It always seems impossible until it's done." And, of course, thank you to Hillary Clinton for giving me the honor of traveling the country to support your campaign. When we elect the first woman president of the United States, it will be because of you.

This book, and my life, are better because of the friends who have stuck by me and encouraged me every step of the way: Patti, Annette, Rebecca, Gina, Samantha Smoot, and many more.

Thanks to our tireless editor, Lauren Spiegel, and the team at Touchstone and Simon & Schuster: Carolyn Reidy, Susan Moldow, Tara Parsons, Brian Belfiglio, Emily Remes, Elisa Rivlin, Shida Carr, Meredith Vilarello, Cherlynne Li, Sydney Newman, Rebecca Strobel, Martha Schwartz, Lisa Healy, Judith Hoover, Nancy Inglis, Mike Kwan, Erich Hobbing, Amanda Mulholland, Julie Ficks, Paul O'Halloran, Cordia Leung, Tom Spain, Elisa Shokoff, Abhita Austin, Ryan Lysy, Noriko Okabe, Tara M. Thomas, Erica Weintraub; to Meg Thompson and Cindy Uh at Thompson Literary Agency, who helped us on our first book adventure; and to Robin Gaby Fisher for your infinite patience and for making this possible.

None of this would have happened without the partnership with Lauren Peterson, who believed we could write a book, and then we did. Her commitment to telling this story, and to doing it with me, is a gift I can never repay. Thanks for writing your first book with me—as Lin-Manuel Miranda would say, history has its eyes on you. Thank you also to the extended Collins-Peterson clan for copyediting, moral support, and for getting us across the finish line.

You are holding this book in your hands because of the generosity and support of my incredible family. Thank you to Dan for unearthing hilarious political cartoons and swapping stories; Ellen and Greg for discussing campaign life and child-rearing over breakfast tacos; Clark for being my attorney and adviser and great brother. And of course, thanks to Dad for your wisdom and recollections and for teaching us kids about justice and progressive values from an early age.

Hannah, Daniel, and Lily were invaluable collaborators with an uncanny knack for remembering some of our best (and funniest) moments as a family. I am so proud to be your mom. Thank you, Kirk—for your eagle-eyed copyediting, for walking Ollie, and for being my biggest cheerleader and partner in troublemaking all these years.

And to the thousands of organizers and activists without whom there would be no story: Thank you.

Index

Page numbers in *italics* refer to illustrations.

MAKE TROUBLE

CECILE RICHARDS

with LAUREN PETERSON

Introduction

Cecile Richards was raised to make trouble. The daughter of Ann Richards, who was the first woman elected governor of Texas in her own right, and David Richards, a prominent civil rights attorney, Cecile learned at a young age that change happens only because people make it happen.

This conviction saw her through years of organizing women earning minimum wage; contributing to her mother's campaigns for governor; starting her own organization, the Texas Freedom Network, to defend public education and religious liberties in her home state; working as deputy chief of staff for Democratic Majority Leader Nancy Pelosi; forming America Votes to help progressive organizations work together more effectively; serving as president of Planned Parenthood for more than a decade; and fighting for women's rights and full equality every day since then.

With grit, wisdom, and humor, Cecile shares her story and the lessons she has learned along the way—lessons from a life of fighting injustice that will inspire readers to stand up and do the same.

Topics & Questions
for Discussion

1. When Cecile was in school, she was taken to the principal's office for wearing an armband in protest of the Vietnam War, an act she sees as one of the first instances of her standing up to authority and making trouble. Looking back, was there a time you stood up to authority or went against the status quo when you were younger? What did these little (or big) acts of resistance teach you at the time? How do you feel looking back at them now?

2. How did living during a time when women were expected to stay at home and take care of the children affect Cecile's mother, Ann Richards? How did seeing her mother go from housewife to governor influence Cecile?

3. Cecile writes, "If there's one common thread that runs throughout my life, it's strong, kick-ass women." What did these women teach her about fighting for her beliefs and being willing to go against the majority? Who are some of the strong women in your life? Who have you looked up to (in your own life or in the public eye) and how have they inspired you?

4. Even a full generation after her mother broke into the "boys' club" of Texas politics, Cecile is candid about the fact that she faced gender discrimination. What are some instances when Cecile calls out discrimination against women and the double standard that

women have to deal with on a daily basis? What have you experienced, and how have you addressed it?

5. When Cecile discovered she was pregnant with her first daughter, Lily, she worried about how she was going to handle raising kids and the demanding work of being an organizer. How was raising her children while working on campaigns a challenge for Cecile? How was it rewarding? What are the challenges in your life that make it more daunting to go after your goals? Do you think anything has changed for women in your lifetime—for you, or for your daughters?

6. Cecile writes about how important her support system has been in her life, from her family at a young age to her colleagues at Planned Parenthood and beyond. At what points in her life has she called on her support network and how have they helped her over the years? Who is in your support system? How have they stood by you when you were in a difficult situation or came to your aid when you needed them? Whether you are an activist already or are looking to get more involved, what strengths and skills do you know these people would bring to the table if you asked for help?

7. When her mother decided to run for governor, Cecile dropped everything to return to Texas and work on her campaign. Research shows how much women's family obligations can stall or derail a career. Have you had this experience? What would it take to change this for women?

8. Campaign life as Cecile describes is exhilarating and introduces you to a whole new world of people who share your values. Have you taken part in campaign efforts in the past (phone banks, canvassing, rallies, etc.)? How can you get more involved in the campaigns of candidates you believe in in the next local, state, or federal election?

9. When Ann was unseated as governor by George W. Bush in 1994, Cecile talks about how everyone who had worked on the campaign and had worked for her mother faced such a crushing "emotional loss." What lessons did Cecile take away from that defeat? How did it push her to do more in the future? What is a time in your life when you lost or failed? What lessons did that experience teach you?

10. While working for Democratic Majority Leader Nancy Pelosi, Cecile saw the most powerful woman in Congress stand up to men in leadership, including in her own party. What difference do you think it makes to have women in political office? Do women lead differently? How do you think our government would be different if women made up half of Congress?

11. With both the Texas Freedom Network and America Votes, Cecile realized that when she saw a problem that needed solving, she could be the one to solve it. What organization would you start if you could do anything and weren't afraid to fail?

12. Cecile tells the story of how she almost didn't go to the interview for the job of president of Planned Parenthood because she didn't feel qualified. Even when she was offered the position, she dealt with fear and self-doubt about her ability to do the job. What pushed her over that hurdle and prompted her to accept the position? When have you been in a situation where you have doubted yourself initially but were ultimately able to take that leap? What advice would you give to other people who may need a push to do the same?

13. One of the major innovations that happened during Cecile's time as president of Planned Parenthood was to connect the chapters of the organization all around the country via the internet, creating a central website with more than 72 million visits a year. How did the internet help advance Planned Parenthood's mission? How have the internet and the use of social media changed how organizations

like Planned Parenthood operate on a greater scale? How have they changed the landscape of activism in general?

14. In her defense of Planned Parenthood against the Republican-led House Oversight and Government Reform Committee hearing, Cecile notes that the Republican side of the hearing was practically all white men and the Democratic side was a "diverse mix of gender, race, and ethnicity, more like our country in the twenty-first century." Why is representation of all races and genders in government so important? What factors in our society exist that keep diverse representation out of the top reaches of politics? What can we do to promote women and people of color to run for office to create more equitable, accurate representation? Who in your life do you know who may be suitable to run for public office (on a local or national level)? How can you encourage them to take action?

15. Cecile speaks fondly of the crowd who showed up in support of Senator Wendy Davis's filibuster in Texas and the success of the Women's March on Washington. How do these demonstrations of solidarity empower the people fighting for equality? When is a time you've been part of a show of support like this? How has that experience affected you? How can demonstrations like these be deployed most effectively?

16. If you already have some experience as an organizer or have been civically engaged in the past, what experiences or advice would you share with someone who's just starting to get involved?

Enhance Your Book Club

1. Find out about your local Planned Parenthood. What kind of services does it provide? What kind of events does it host? What can you do to support its work?

2. Learn about the different organizations that help people run for public office, such as EMILY's List, Ready to Run, Run for Something, Higher Heights, Voto Latino, and so on. Share this information via word of mouth with people in your community or share on social media and tag people who you think would benefit from it. Find out when the next local, state, and federal elections in your area are taking place and stay updated on the candidates and their positions on issues important to you.

3. Choose a particular issue you're passionate about right now (gun reform, immigration, reproductive health, LGBTQ rights, racial justice, climate change, etc.) and do some research about organizations in your area that are working on that issue. If you're not yet involved, how can you join one of those organizations? If you're already involved, how can you get more involved? If you're already passionate about one issue, have you tried stepping outside of your comfort zone and attending a meeting of an organization working on something else? Are there chapters or organizing groups you can join or internships or jobs you can apply for? Is there an area that you think is lacking that could be addressed by starting a new organization?